STRATFORD-UPON-AVON STUDIES 12

General Editors

MALCOLM BRADBURY
& DAVID PALMER

Already published in this series:

* *Under the general editorship of John Russell Brown and Bernard Harris*

STRATFORD-UPON-AVON STUDIES 12

CONTEMPORARY CRITICISM

EDWARD ARNOLD

First published 1970 by
Edward Arnold (Publishers) Ltd
41 Maddox Street, London W1

Cloth edition SBN: 7131 5557 4
Paper edition SBN: 7131 5558 2

c

Printed in Great Britain by
Butler & Tanner Ltd, Frome and London

Contents

Preface

OUR aim in collecting together the essays in this volume is a double one: to look at the state and function of criticism at the present time, and to offer an exploration of the various methods of critical procedure that are now prevalent. To that end we have drawn together some of the leading contemporary English and American critics (and they in turn have drawn into the discussion the important European critics) who might give the reader—whether he be the specialized student or the general reader—some sense of the lively issues in the current ferment of literary criticism on both sides of the Atlantic. But its purpose goes further, for the volume also aspires to be an argument and a questioning—about where criticism has come to, where it is leading, and what kinds of growth and difficulty lie before it. For criticism in the modern world has reached a point of considerable sophistication. Perhaps many will feel—like the American critic who complained a few years back that American criticism had become 'subtle to the point of secrecy'—that this sophistication, these days not only American, is not all for the best. There is, after all, an old ideal that criticism should be socially judicious—which is to say that it should be part of the public activity of a society, maintaining a general climate of discrimination, and helping the general reader to read better and to find his way through the best of literature with more profit and illumination. It has to be confessed that in many ways criticism today has passed beyond being the intelligent debate of society about its literature. Having acquired, in the academy, the privilege of a specialist audience, it has tended to grow more arcane and difficult, reaching its highest point of development not in the magazines but, as Graham Hough observes, in the headily advanced atmosphere of the graduate school. That sort of development might well have led to one of those ages of criticism—there have been some in the past, for instance with the coming of Romanticism to Europe—when the growth of critical theory and philosophy stirred all sorts of new energies in the creative arts. But even that hardly seems the case now; the professionalism of criticism today is a good deal more academic than literary; the common writer as well as the common reader often seem to lie outside its purlieus.

To some extent, though, the sense of increased difficulty derives from the fact that criticism has been transformed by new tendencies and approaches, so that the scene is much more confusing and less well defined than it was a few years ago. Some reasons for this ferment are discussed in these essays; but undoubtedly one feature of it is a growing concern with critical theory. The very procedures and the very nature of criticism have come under increasing analysis. At the same time, large new areas of approach have been drawn into its dialogues and discussion, not exactly dislodging that concern with practical reading and study of text which marked much New Critical practice, but shifting emphasis and direction. Whether this is to the good or bad is at issue: in different ways various essays here—especially Malcolm Bradbury's, Graham Hough's and W. K. Wimsatt's at the beginning of the volume and Ian Gregor's salutary piece at the end—raise the problem. Nonetheless, as Graham Hough points out, we live in a time of intellectual ferment when many of our received ideas about civilization, culture and literature are in question, and that is bound to make criticism engrossed with itself. This has led to an increasing tendency towards literary theory—to speculation about its own means and tactics, and speculation about the nature and meaning of literature. It is indeed possible for it to become *too* self-engrossed, so that criticism's own methods become criticism's paramount concern, and the literature it exists to discuss comes to seem secondary or distant. The fact remains that some speculation about the nature of criticism is inevitable; it has always existed, and each age tends to have to undertake the task again. Still, most of the critics in this volume would probably take it as axiomatic that no criticism is relevant or interesting which does not bear in mind the constant moving back and forth between text and the body of hypotheses that the practised critic can bring to it, just as they would recognize that sensibility and responsiveness are quite as significant as theory for adequate critical reading. But since criticism thrives by comparison, by extension of reference, by the capacity for elucidation, a degree of broad speculation is an inevitable part of its task.

The purpose of this book is to provide an up-to-date exploration of the current dialogue. The reader will find that certain essential themes recur from essay to essay, and some of them, certainly, are the themes that seem most at issue wherever one looks in criticism today. For instance, it was an old piety of the New Criticism that to understand the nature of a literary work one had to understand that its character was that of a *verbal* creation. However much it might have resembled life, it was a construct in words, a fiction, controlled and managed through linguistic and rhetorical features. But where New Criticism tended to be interested in the consequences of that awareness in terms of the inner structure of works of literature, emphasizing 'tension', 'irony' and 'paradox' as the essential constituents of literary works, and stressing the conscious treatment of the materials involved in the creative process, recent criticism has started to press further. It has, for instance, gone increasingly into language study, looking at the structural and social nature of language itself. Several of the essays that follow—notably Graham Hough's, W. K. Wimsatt's, and the lively, challenging piece by Roger Fowler—pursue various dimensions of the way criticism can go, perhaps *has* logically to go, in view of that insight. In one direction, this can take us into a new kind of formalism—and here the essays by John Fletcher and Allan Rodway raise some of the possibilities—where we seek to comprehend the nature of literary structures as typologies, recurrent structures to be illuminated by classification and comparison. In another direction, it can take us towards relating both the individual experience in individual works and the more general 'types' of literature to the orders and meanings of society, so inviting us to comprehend the 'cultural' existence of literature: this is the topic on which Richard Hoggart writes.

In the view of the editors, these lines of enquiry do suggest some of the most lively issues in criticism today. It is perhaps worth adding that they do seriously impinge on the question of what meaning and purpose we assume literature to have in a time of considerable social change; and in this sense they relate to many of the general intellectual urgencies of the day. The problems of the relationship between the 'fictive' and the world of society and history obviously engross many writers now, as they do many critics; and perhaps this volume might help to suggest why they do.

Our contributors, incidentally, include several who are associated with particular approaches to literature. We have sought to be eclectic and have invited them to explore the lineage and character of such particular approaches and to express their own convictions. So, in the following pages, we may see a variety of approaches, some of which may be viewed as complementary to others, some which may be viewed as exclusive. W. K. Wimsatt considers the approach through the text, Allan Rodway that through literary typologies like novel and poem, lyric and epic, John Fletcher that through broader forms of comparison derived from taking an international view, and Norman Holland, Richard Hoggart and Roger Fowler approaches illuminated by insights derived from psychology, cultural and language studies. We can record these in a plural way, as providing a composite view of the literary text; or in a competitive way, as offering different and contending approaches. Our editorial aim is not to suggest one or the other view, but rather to hope that the essays, taken together, will suggest the variety of opinion active today in the discussion of literature, as well as demonstrating some of the difficulties and uncertainties besetting the modern critic.

MALCOLM BRADBURY

February 1970 DAVID PALMER

Bibliographical Note

IN references to books throughout the volume the place of publication is London unless otherwise stated.

Acknowledgments

THE editors and publisher gratefully acknowledge permission given by the following to reprint copyright works: Routledge & Kegan Paul Ltd. and A. A. Knopf Inc. for an extract from *Literary Criticism: A Short History* by W. K. Wimsatt and Cleanth Brooks; Routledge & Kegan Paul Ltd. and Humanities Press Inc. for an extract from 'Autumn' in *Speculations: Essays on Humanism and the Philosophy of Art* by T. E. Hulme, edited by Herbert Read; Methuen & Co. Ltd. and Simon & Schuster Inc. for an extract from *A Single Man* by Christopher Isherwood; Jonathan Cape Ltd., Holt, Rinehart and Winston Inc., the Estate of Robert Frost and the editor for 'Mending Wall' and an extract from 'For Once Then Something' in *The Poetry of Robert Frost* edited by Edward Connery Lathem, copyright © Holt, Rinehart and Winston Inc. 1969; City Lights Books for 'The Day Lady Died' from *Lunch Poems* by Frank O'Hara, copyright © Frank O'Hara 1964; Ernst Eulenburg Ltd. for an extract from Haydn; *String Quartet in D* Op. 64 No. 5 (The Lark), Eulenburg Miniature Score No. 55; and MacGibbon & Kee Ltd. and Harcourt, Brace, Jovanovich Inc. for 'pity this busy monster, manunkind' from *Complete Poems* by E. E. Cummings.

Note

This list is concerned with general works on or overall surveys of criticism—histories of critical thought; comparative or synthetic studies of modern criticism; works which raise essential problems of critical approach, method or theory; and useful anthologies of critical essays. Critical works of a more specific kind are referred to in the *Notes* to later articles in this volume (and in the text of this and other essays).

Histories of Criticism. The best and most convenient one-volume study is W. K. Wimsatt and Cleanth Brooks, *Literary Criticism: A Short History* (New York, 1957); the introduction contains a very useful bibliographical listing of other histories. There are important larger works—J. W. H. Atkins's *English Literary Criticism* (3 volumes, Cambridge and London, 1943–51) and René Wellek's excellent *A History of Modern Criticism: 1750–1950* (4 volumes, New Haven and London, 1955–66). The most useful historical anthology is Walter Jackson Bate, *Criticism: The Major Texts* (New York, 1952); its admirable editorial commentary has been published separately as Walter Jackson Bate, *Prefaces to Criticism* (New York, 1959). M. H. Abrams's *The Mirror and the Lamp: Romantic Theory and the Critical Tradition* (New York, 1953) is an excellent account of the transition from neoclassic to Romantic criticism. George Watson's *The Literary Critics* (1962) is a good brief survey of English criticism.

Modern Criticism: Comparative Studies. The three most useful surveys are Austin Warren and René Wellek, *The Theory of Literature* (New York and London, 1949); David Daiches, *Critical Approaches to Literature* (New York and London, 1956), and Stanley Edgar Hyman, *The Armed Vision* (New York, 1948). Also see W. L. Guerin, E. G. Labor, L. Morgan and J. Willingham, *A Handbook of Critical Approaches to Literature* (New York, 1966). Various modern critics have sought to offer an overall critical perspective: notable works are T. S. Eliot, *The Use of Poetry and the Use of Criticism* (Cambridge, Mass. and London, 1953); Northrop Frye, *Anatomy of Criticism* (Princeton, 1957); I. A. Richards, *Principles of Literary Criticism* (1924); Kenneth Burke, *The Philosophy of Literary Form* (1941; revised edition, New York, 1957); R. S. Crane, *The Languages of Criticism and the Structure of Poetry* (Toronto, 1953); John Crowe Ransom, *The World's Body* (New York, 1938), and W. K. Wimsatt, *The Verbal Icon* (Lexington, Kentucky, 1954).

Modern Criticism: General Collections of Essays. Among the best of these are: *Critiques and Essays in Criticism: 1920–1948* edited by Robert Wooster Stallman (New York, 1949); *Literary Opinion in America* edited by Morton D. Zabel (New York, 1951); *Criticism: The Foundations of Modern Literary Judgment* edited by Mark Schorer *et al.* (New York, 1948); *The Critical Performance* edited by Stanley Edgar Hyman (New York, 1956), and *The Modern Critical Spectrum* edited by Gerald and Nancy Goldberg (New York, 1962).

More particular tendencies are represented in *The Importance of Scrutiny* edited by Eric Bentley (New York, 1948); *Critics and Criticism: Ancient and Modern*

Introduction: The State of Criticism Today

MALCOLM BRADBURY

I

IN the last few years, the activity of literary criticism, the general character of its dialogue and debate, has changed a good deal. The change has taken place, in different ways, in England, in the United States, and in Europe; and one striking feature of it is, indeed, the growing degree of interpenetration of the different national traditions. Now criticism has, of course, been one of the growth-industries of the twentieth century. For this critical boom there may be any amount of reasons—a rising intellectual population, an uncertainty about the received traditions in literature, an intense ferment within the literary arts themselves. We could take this critical expansion as a signal that literature has a more striking and significant place amongst us than it had in the past—though, equally, we can take the proliferation of interpretation as a sign that for many readers it now has a *less* important one. Whatever the significance (and the latter is more likely than the former), *something* has happened since the early years of the century, when Henry James was pleading for a criticism along other than infantile lines, when Ford Madox Ford was complaining of the total absence of the critical attitude, and when it was possible for a professor of English, Walter Raleigh, to say, in 1906, 'I begin to hate criticism. Nothing can come of it.'

'Time is ripe for the forging of a weapon of criticism, and for the emphatic assertion of literary standards,' wrote Harold Monro in the first number of his lively editorship of the *Poetry Review* in January 1912; and elsewhere in the same issue Arthur K. Sabin complained that criticism had achieved 'no consistent method by which the true artist

edited by R. S. Crane (Chicago, 1952); also, more recently, in *The Critical Moment*, introduction by Stephen Spender (1968), and *The Disciplines of Criticism: Essays in Literary Theory, Interpretation and History* edited by Peter Demetz *et al.* (New Haven, 1968).

can be distinguished from the false with any reliability' and that 'no standard of taste has yet proved sufficiently comprehensive to assay correctly the merit of a new poet and relegate him, as the critics still futilely attempt to do, to a fitting rank and station among his peers.' But over these years criticism was growing busy again, as a necessary aspect of the literary revolution that was transforming aesthetics, poetics and taste and establishing the existence of a remarkable new literary generation, one that still dominates the literature of our century. *The Egoist* began to print not only criticism but *discussion* of criticism by Eliot and Pound; *The Athenaeum*, in its final burst of glory under John Middleton Murry, reverted to its nineteenth-century practice and committed itself to a high level of serious reviewing, printing a succession of important articles and book reviews on literature by writers like Eliot, Murry, Katherine Mansfield, Virginia Woolf and Aldous Huxley. By the nineteen twenties a number of reviews with a considerable literary-critical content emerged (*The Criterion* and *The Calendar of Modern Letters* in England; the revived *Dial* and the *Hound and Horn* in the United States, for example), and gradually a new type of periodical devoted entirely to criticism—for instance, *Scrutiny*, beginning in 1932—started to emerge. Today any devotee of bookshops will know that there is probably more new criticism appearing than new creative writing; and criticism has become a discipline, like sociology or biology, the skills and techniques of which are in perpetual transmission through the classrooms of schools and universities.

T. S. Eliot once remarked, in *The Use of Poetry and the Use of Criticism*, that 'the development of criticism is a symptom of the development, or change, of poetry; and the development of poetry is itself a symptom of social change. The important moment for the appearance of criticism seems to be the time when poetry ceases to be the expression of the mind of a whole people.' The implication here is that criticism acquires a special importance when the arts need to be explained and mediated, rather than being taken 'directly' by the public; and that criticism is also closely related to the coming of a new selfconsciousness or an aesthetic revisionism in the arts. And in fact modern criticism *is* closely related, in its origins and spirit, to the literary ferments of the beginning of the century, and the kind of self-conscious analytic environment in which they were made; just as its persistence is—though perhaps a little less closely—related to the climate of aesthetic uncertainty and plurality that has affected all of subsequent modern writing. Indeed, the really important figures in the early stages of modern criticism are, precisely, the new writers themselves—Pound, Eliot, Lawrence, and Henry James. And to their eyes a central function of criticism was to create the enabling environment for those arts, to produce the taste by which they might be understood or, indeed, actually created. To Ezra Pound, for example, criticism had a specific use in stimulating and also changing the poetic environment, and it was hence a short-term and conditioned activity: criticism, he said, 'shd. consume itself and disappear.' It has not, of course: far from it. By the nineteen twenties the new poetics and the new aesthetics were becoming matters of general lore and systematic intellectual enquiry. There was a great coming of the critics, and over this and the next decade emerged a literary critical generation almost as powerful as the literary generation just prior, producing their classic texts in their turn—I. A. Richards's *Principles of Literary Criticism* (1924) and *Practical Criticism* (1929); William Empson's *Seven Types of Ambiguity* (1930); Kenneth Burke's *Counter-Statement* (1931); F. R. Leavis's *New Bearings in English Poetry* (1932); Allen Tate's *Reactionary Essays* (1936); Yvor Winters's *Primitivism and Decadence* (1937); and John Crowe Ransom's *The World's Body* (1938), for example. Critics like these were, on the one hand, responsible for a vast new attentiveness to works of literature as something to be read, closely, intensively, responsively, and studiously (Cleanth Brooks's and Robert Penn Warren's contribution, *Understanding Poetry* (1938), perhaps the most influential book of all, was specifically a *classroom* text), and for a new, applied practicality in criticism. On the other hand, they were also responsible for creating, implicitly or explicitly, a body of critical assumptions about the nature of literary language and literary energy which was in fact fairly precisely derived from the modernist or neosymbolist movement in literature at the beginning of the century; the intellectual threads reach back to Eliot, Pound, James and others—and beyond them to *their* sources in T. E. Hulme, Bergson, Remy de Gourmont and French symbolist aesthetics. In the former activity, they undoubtedly democratized criticism, which became an inalienable right of all men; it was not good taste but attentive effort that lay behind critical reading and responsiveness. In the latter, they reached into a line of complex aesthetic theory that encouraged certain sorts of evaluative preferences (for instance, for complex, witty, ironic poetry) and a certain theory of the nature of literary language, which was markedly distinguished from all other language by its internal, neosymbolist, self-sustaining coherence. And overall they made criticism both an educational activity *and* a dedication, a commitment to distinct and discrete literary values, even to a literary *assessment* of the culture as a whole.

The result of this situation was a period of remarkably intensive critical activity and enquiry, running along two main lines. One of these was the elucidation of literary texts themselves, which were subjected, in classrooms and in print, to singularly intensive analysis, to the profoundest scouring and searching out, so that no word, set down on paper with whatever anguish or gay abandon, went unanalysed, no symbol went unturned. The other was an intensive analysis of criticism itself, a questioning of its methods and procedures, a rationalization of all readerly responses. Though it became fairly obvious early on that there was no sense in which the methods of literary criticism could be in any final way scientific ones, producing precise and agreed-upon results, the idea that criticism could become vastly more exact, and produce certain irrefutable hypotheses about the nature or structure of a text or more broadly about the nature and structure of literature itself, tended to develop. There were certain features common to all literary language; and literature was essentially a structure *in* language, not mirroring life but creating it through the controls of technique. If literature did not quite exist in a timeless vacuum, then it was assumed, usually, to exist in a discrete verbal world. And though that world made reference to life, the prime requirement on the artist, the prime perfection of his art, was his aesthetic control, his craft or his technique. In that respect this criticism—the broad label for it is the 'New Criticism'—was formalistic. But at the same time it was humanistic and generous, in that it regarded the individual competence of the writer, his designing and controlling hand, his achievement finally as the exemplary artist, as the true moral centre of literary art, and as a power in society. (I stress this aspect because part of the current change in criticism is, I think, an inclination to turn away from technique and to be interested in the broader fundings of myths and themes which are 'social', impersonal, unsigned.)[1] It was felt that there could be a

[1] A particular instance of my point here would be the work of French 'structuralist' critics like Roland Barthes, or certain forms of mythocentric criticism in America. However, one might note than the tendency has obviously struck in creative writing as well—in the happening, in poetry and jazz, and so on. Here art is conceived of as a manifestation much more than as a creation;

'common pursuit of true judgment', to draw on Eliot's classic phrases that there were certain hypotheses about a particular literary text, or about the nature of literature generally, which could acquire a kind of proven status; that force and power in literature could be demonstrated; that not only in elucidation but in valuation a certain core of essential points of worth, a certain number of 'touchstones', could be established. (It seems evident that many critics have now come to feel that many of the apparent statements of 'fact' on which agreement seemed to have been reached were really concealed statements of value; this is perfectly true, though not invalidating, since after all it is presumably essential that critics *should* assume that literature does, by being literature, embody for themselves and others a certain body of essential values.) In short, then, the New Criticism contained a search for precision which was also a search for an essential body of standards in literature that came from its inherent nature *as* literature. It pursued an idea of relevance and exactness, seeking to contain its discussion and dialogue within something like an agreed framework, by concentrating on the single text and then on purely literary standards. In trying to define the appropriate aspects of its activity, it increasingly pointed to one primary object of critical attention—not the critic's own appreciative sensibility; not the writer's biography or psychological background; not his intellectual, social or historical context; not the creative process or the readerly response; but the one central, ascertainable object that critics could discuss in common and constantly refer to: the text, the 'words on the page'. Here was the irreducible literary minimum; here was that which let us regard criticism as a debate focussed round a common centre and moving towards a single meaning; here was that which might encapsulate both elucidation and evaluation, those twin properties long linked with critical activity; here was that which enabled us to think of literary criticism as educational, since by illuminating a text we could illuminate our own response to life and value, could acquire sympathy, responsiveness, and regard.

Today, of course, the New Criticism is not new, and it is with the change beyond it that I am here concerned. Nonetheless, I suppose that many critics, perhaps most, today would hold still that the New Criticism had a convincing logic behind it, and perhaps even that it

---

it is, as I have argued in another place, rather a 'culture of politics' than a 'politics of culture'.

has been the central mode of twentieth-century criticism. It properly shifted us away from, on the one hand, those responses to literature which assume that literature holds the mirror up to nature, that there is direct equivalence between the thing written and the life in the world it imitates; anyone who reads at all seriously in modern literature knows about the fictiveness of all our fictions. It has shifted us, on the other, away from those responses that devote the main part of critical sympathy to particular charismatic personalities (John Keats, Jane Austen, Henry James) whose lure lies in their very lives rather than in their written achievement. In passing beyond certain forms of generalized appreciation, and in transforming the once common view that literary study could take the form only of historical, textual or philological scholarship, the New Criticism has pressed us towards an understanding of the internal, holistic momentum of a work of literature, and directed us to the one secure object of literary study we have (this poem, this novel, this play), with a logic that we cannot evade.[2] It has been a rich criticism, especially with texts having the concrete internal intensity, the tension and paradox, the high linguistic pressure that it saw as essential characteristics of literature. (Its best objects of study were the lyric poem and the short story.) And, as I have said, in its concern with technique—what Mark Schorer called 'technique as

[2] What I am describing here is of course the so-called 'ontological' approach to literature. Its assumptions are that the poem or fiction can be judged from within itself; that adequate reading will reveal the constituents necessary for understanding and interpreting the work because it is self-supporting and self-extant, unified because of its coherence as language; and that the only potential directions of reference outside the text are really (a) to life, by judging the poem as a distillation of experience, (b) to other poems, by judging it comparatively and (c) to an acquired literary-historical sense derived from the progression of forms and language. But in fact this 'intrinsic' or 'ontological' approach is one which various New Critics have formulated in different, and more or less 'purist', ways. For one important version, see John Crowe Ransom, 'Poetry: A Note on Ontology' (1934), reprinted in R. W. Stallman, *Critiques and Essays in Criticism: 1920–1948* (New York, 1949). A further elaboration of this view, pointing to the logical dangers of going beyond the text for information extraneous to satisfactory analysis, is to be found in W. K. Wimsatt and Monroe Beardsley, 'The Intentional Fallacy' and 'The Affective Fallacy', both in W. K. Wimsatt, *The Verbal Icon* (Lexington, Kentucky, 1954). It should be added that they do not deny the uses, but only the *incautious* or illogical uses, of such information. An up-to-date discussion of the ontological view of criticism and indeed of its potential breadth is to be found in W. K. Wimsatt's essay in this collection.

discovery'—it illuminated from the powers of modern art the art of the past. It also had one important further dimension related to that: it valued the literary intelligence as a power in society as in art. It saw the literary intelligence as a distinctive and value-laden one, capable of intervening significantly in social and cultural affairs from the standpoint of its own distinctively literary commitment. And equally it tended to assume that, just as the writer was a central humanistic intelligence, so was the trained critic; sharing in literature's distinctive way of knowing and evaluating, he had something essential to say not only about literature but about life itself.

The New Criticism had its period of greatest intellectual energy in the nineteen thirties, and its greatest period of acceptance shortly after the war.[3] But one result of its long presence amongst us has been that it has tended to schismatize and pluralize its theology, as well as to produce spectacular apostasies. Today, if we are still in the climate of New Criticism, we are in the climate of the Revised New Criticism; and we may well be moving out of it altogether. There are signs that many of its convictions—about the primacy of the text and the power of individual technique within it; about the capacity of literature to exist autotelically, as a self-sustaining and a-historical luminous symbol; about the force of literature as a social power, a resonant centre of *substantiated* and lived-through values—are in question, in an era that is uneasy about any man's entitlement to evade history or to claim singular authority for his prowess. Ours is a Tocquevilleian age in which the writer must be the ordinary man, and in which the individual signature on anything is in doubt; we are tempted to believe that literature must be written by societies or particular stages in the historical process, rather than by persons; and we are tempted to doubt

[3] I have already suggested the names of some of the critics we associate with the 'New' Criticism—in England F. R. Leavis, William Empson, I. A. Richards; in the United States Cleanth Brooks, Allen Tate, Robert Penn Warren, John Crowe Ransom and perhaps R. B. Blackmur, Yvor Winters and W. K. Wimsatt. It was Ransom who used the phrase as the title of his book *The New Criticism* in 1941; but of course it is a very loose label, and most of those listed would be unhappy about the attribution. In fact to go back to its dialogues— as one can, for instance, in Stallman's *Critiques and Essays in Criticism*—is to realize how large and varied a debate the phrase must cover. My point is that the varied enquiry had certain common emphases and biases—in its sophistication of practice and theory; in the high integrity and competence of its exponents; and in its general cultural influence (which reached to writers, the condition of letters generally, and education).

the conviction of any species of creativity, or any discipline, that it should not be confronted on terms other than those it prescribes itself. We tend to see literature less as a force for value in society, and more as a phenomenon of it. Moreover not only do we live in an age of different values; we also live, apparently, in an age of *fewer* values, significantly held in common. As a result, literary criticism seems to have become a good deal less sure about the evaluative activity that has always been considered a part of its function, and has tended recently to proliferate description and interpretation rather than judgment. Finally, one legacy of the New Criticism was some profound uncertainty among writers and critics about the ways in which the relationship between a fiction and 'reality' could be accredited. As I have suggested, literary criticism came to a considerable extent from modernism, and carried many of modernism's paradoxes—about the relation between a symbol or a fiction and a thing, about the relation between a crisis in the word and a crisis in the world, about the very mode of subsistence of literature itself in a climate when its credit seemed not to be high. It tended to be an aspect of a situation in which a specialized writer (the 'serious artist', in Pound's phrase, which often came to mean the modernistically oblique artist) was expounded by a specialist interpreter (the critic-teacher) to a specialized audience with a classical, minority assent about serious literary values. And while it tended to uphold the idea of the critical faculty as an humane force, a positive value in the society, it increasingly tended to find, as Lionel Trilling has pointed out,[4] that the artists with which it dealt were not themselves humanistic. For all these reasons, something of that classical ideal of critical consensus—the ideal of 'the common pursuit of true judgment'—seems to have evaporated in recent critical activity. Indeed the new pluralism can in some ways be seen as a weakening of the morale of literary criticism itself, and to contain a certain loss of certainty about literature as a source of values.

II

In recent years, criticism has tended both to extend the insights of the New Criticism, and to extend beyond them. For New Criticism especially represented three things: it marked the movement of

[4] Lionel Trilling, 'On the Teaching of Modern Literature', in *Beyond Culture* (1966).

criticism into the academy and out of the context of general thought; it established criticism as a serious form of educative study, based not on scholarship but the intensive reading of major texts; and it encouraged critical democratization by making appreciation and competence dependent not on the 'possession' of taste but on effective training. Its early days in the academy were days of battle, involving an assault on the scholarly view of the nature of literary study. Today, literary criticism has become *the* method of literary study—its primary methodology or 'discipline', the selfconscious tactic of the subject. Now critics and criticism are not only safely lodged in departments of English or schools of literature; they are the carriers of the method of those schools, and predominate over those who would call themselves literary scholars or literary historians.[5] Despite what Raleigh said, a great deal *can* come of criticism, including academic promotion. By the end of the war Malcolm Cowley, reporting on the American literary situation, was commenting that many of the new literary energies were to be found not so much in creative writing as in criticism—indeed, he said, a good deal of the new writing had the air of being written to illustrate the best prevailing critical principles, and was being produced by authors themselves academic teachers and critics.[6] Cowley saw this situation as an almost unprecedented cultural evolution; a new era of classicism in which the old desire for the literary academy has been institutionalized on campus. Certainly the large-scale appropriation of criticism by the academy is a novel modern development. It marks a change in the social location and function of critical activity. In the past, criticism has normally occurred in an environment reasonably close to that of literary creation. Often the great critics (Ben Jonson, Dryden, Samuel Johnson, Coleridge, Matthew Arnold, Henry James, Eliot, Pound) were themselves men of letters: selfconsciously creative writers, or intellectuals of literary perspective and commitment. Much criticism was activity preparatory to creation; or it was concerned with creating the taste by which writing might be understood; or it was part of a literary-cultural interpretation of society.

[5] This struggle, and the sense of the idea of the critic in literary study as an intruder, has been thoroughly reported on—for instance, in the work of F. R. Leavis in England, and in that of Yvor Winters in the United States (see for instance the title essay in Winters's *The Function of Criticism*, 1962).

[6] 'The New Age of the Rhetoricians' in *The Literary Situation* (New York, 1954).

Writer and critic tended to cohere round a shared view of culture and value, administering often the standards of creation and at the same time those of a social-literary intelligence.[7] As I have said, modern criticism started in a similar location, but it did not stay there. To begin with it was largely writers (so Ransom, Tate, Schorer, Warren in the United States were all considerable writers) who carried it into the academy; and today one senses a large divergence of function between most modern writers and most modern critics—a schizophrenia of the cultural community in which the critic has outstripped the creator in professional confidence. This produces the paradox that, when many critics are claiming that conditions of literary production are declining and that the age of the book is over, they hardly seem to share the sense of literary concern.[8] They hardly need to: the audience for *criticism* is assured; critics but not writers can gain academic tenure; a vast body of texts for study exists; and in a climate of university expansion with large enrolments for literary study, they are in, as we say, a growth-area.

In short, this is a time in which we now have a large critical salariat, for whom the methods of literary criticism are the received methods of their (more or less new) profession *and* the token of their professionalization. It was inevitable that this would lead to a proliferation of methodology, exegesis and abstruse distinctions; that it would encourage the notion that reading was a highly professional activity, not lightly to be undertaken by amateurs;[9] and that literary creation was

[7] Even Matthew Arnold, who held that criticism had a profound educational function, still assumed a close link between criticism and creation—it was a fecundation of the national and international mainstream of thought, of propagating the best that is known and thought, of creating the stream of fresh ideas on which literature depended. But today criticism's self-justification often (though not always) seems to lie in its capacity to refine and to make abstruse its own methods and techniques, rather than to contribute to general ideas.

[8] For an interesting instance, see *Innovations* edited by Bernard Bergonzi (1968), a collection of essays on the contemporary avant-garde by leading critics, in which they are to be found speaking of the end of the book and of Graeco-Roman civilization with near-equanimity.

[9] One can illustrate from the confusion that occurs when those who read meet, at parties or elsewhere, those who *really* read. A good example was the Old Bailey trial for obscenity of *Lady Chatterley's Lover*, when the judge, surveying the assemblage of professional readers called for the defence, who had patently read the text in an unfamiliar way, remarked: 'As we all know, in these days the world seems to be full of experts.' (At the same time, it might

not something always prior to, but simply an enabling feature of, the existence of criticism. These are almost inevitable attributes of the bureaucratization of a subject. So, where many of the New Critics felt they spoke in a personal way for the need for literature and for writers, many modern critics see themselves not as engaging in a secondary activity dependent on a primary one, but rather working in a situation of intensive study in which writers themselves are a kind of walking intentionalist fallacy, a dangerous biographical intrusion into the critical environment, which is prime. Criticism stops being a part of the enabling environment of creation; it becomes the method of what we call a discipline, competing on equal terms with all the other disciplines in the academic map of learning; and one of its perpetual objects of study is, precisely, criticism itself. In many respects this is an advance and a fulfilment, and indeed John Crowe Ransom expressed the hope for something like this in the nineteen thirties:

> Rather than occasional criticism by amateurs, I should think the whole enterprise might be seriously taken in hand by professionals. Perhaps I use a distasteful figure, but I have the idea that what we need is Criticism, Inc., or Criticism, Ltd.[10]

That managerial revolution has in fact occurred, more or less. From it Ransom saw two different kinds of advantage. One was a movement towards an adequate 'poetics' of literature, derived from a critical concern with the objective reading of a text in the light of its technical practice, and leading towards a broad generic and aesthetic sense of the character of literary language and structure. The other associated movement was towards critical impersonality, the suppression of individual cranks and tares, and an objective interest in literary experience as words on the page. And what lies behind both assumptions is that criticism is unlike creative writing in that it can actually progress— advance in method and accuracy, improve on the criticism of the past, outdate the old lore in the subject, make new and more precise syntheses. In short, criticism might become a developing discipline analogous to science.

As far as literature itself is concerned, we would not normally want

---

be proposed that—in the light of his refusal to listen to evidence about the author's intention, and his achievement in other works—the Judge was himself a crypto-New Critic.)

[10] 'Criticism, Inc.', in *The World's Body* (New York, 1938).

to take that analogy very far. We speak of the 'development' of literature, and for instance recognize in much modern writing a remarkable
and sophisticated preoccupation with technique, built in part on the
refinement of the resources of the past of literature as a body of inherit-
able practices. We can indeed see traditions grow, sequences form,
practices reach higher points of elaboration. But of course we do not
assume that a new work outdates an old one, even if, as Eliot has told
us, the existing order of works is altered by each new one that comes
along. Criticism certainly is in a slightly different position, since it is
not primarily a creative activity but a form of *post facto* analysis and
evaluation. It is in these terms that we can think that it gets better.
As Robert Wooster Stallman has put it:

> Our age is indeed an age of criticism. The structure of critical ideas
> and practical criticism that British critics—Leavis, Turnell, Empson,
> Read—and American critics—Ransom, Tate, Brooks, Warren,
> Blackmur, Winters—have contributed upon the foundations of
> Eliot and Richards constitute an achievement in literary criticism
> which has not been equalled in any period of our literary history.[11]

So modern criticism has grown more apt, accurate, appropriate and
analytical than ever before. I have no doubt that most modern students
of literature do believe this to be the case, and within limits they are
right to. We normally assume the tasks of criticism to be two: interpretation and judgment, or in Eliot's phrases the elucidation of works
of art and the correction of taste. In the former activity of elucidation,
at least, we can see a certain process of refinement taking place. At the
'practical' level of reading of text, we have seen a vast extension of
exegesis, a discarding of certain obviously false or weak readings or
surmises; at the broader level of theory, or concern with poetics, we
can see a marked refinement of terminology. As critical techniques
become more complex, so our responsiveness should. In fact, though,
the model on which such an idea of progress depends is a model of
consensus, so that everyone is talking in a common way about a
common thing; and only to a point is that model applicable to criticism.
There is no absolute sense in which the criticism of, say, Dr. Johnson or
Samuel Coleridge becomes out of date, if only because criticism does
depend on specific qualities of personal responsiveness. We can scarcely
propose an absolute advance in method, though we can propose a kind

[11] 'The New Critics', in *Critiques and Essays in Criticism*, p. 506.

of refinement of it. But even this refinement is itself historically located, so that aesthetic or critical universals that appear to acquire broad adherence can seem potentially explosive: neoclassicism proposed a universal of generic typologies based on 'general truths that will always be the same', the Romantic universal lay in a mixture of the divine inspiration of the poet and his alliance with historical evolution, the Symbolist universal in the resonant internality of words themselves. For New Criticism it was the text itself that was postulated as an empirical experience independent of the persons experiencing—an ideal text to which all critics, provided they purge themselves of quirks of personality, misfortunes of upbringing, environmental, social and political preferences, might share in as a common fund. But of course men not only experience differently but express their experience differently; and diversity was inevitable. So the difficulty of acquiring a level of judgment sufficiently 'literary' to be communal and independent of external referent struck most critics. Hence Eliot found himself proposing for his common pursuit an ideal of critical orthodoxy close to the Christian ethic. More successfully, Dr. Leavis, by postulating a minority 'contemporary sensibility' committed to literary standards and urgencies, focussed around 'values essential for profound and intelligent living', evoked a remarkable possibility—which has, though, suffered in the long term from the fact that for many contemporaries, writers and readers, moral and aesthetic experience appear in no way to coincide. In short, it is impossible in criticism to draw ready lines between statements of 'fact' and statements of value, while critical usefulness is not entirely a consequence of the 'principles' or methods used.

Today the hope for consensus seems to have acquired new forms. If one definition of science is that it is a language people speak to one another when they have no other values in common, then the direction of the new consensus seems to be towards science: current endeavour seems to be less concerned with an idea of common judgment than a common pursuit of theoretical agreements. If we cannot agree about what is good, or what constitutes humane or literary quality, can we not agree that literary language has such a nature, or that these techniques function as types in literary structure, or that these developments in linguistics, sociology, anthropology or psychology illuminate literary phenomena? But the potential danger with this approach is that criticism tends to seek its community and authority not from its commitment to literature at all, but from its capacity to integrate and assimilate disciplines by nature more scientific. The result is that critical analysis then tends to lose its points of reference in literary texts and to lose its own distinctive standards of relevance, simply conducting a spectacular dialogue around literature in which any purely literary points of reference are bonuses. And in the long run this bias towards eclectic speculation tends to overlook the fact that criticism is aways and necessarily a *post facto* activity—one not only dependent on the existence of creative work, but having its standards of relevance determined by it, both in its general sense of what literature is (a tradition of works that *must* be seen as having things in common, but also as changing and open-ended) and in its particular sense of individual works demanding specific responses to their nature.

In moving towards Criticism, Inc., or Criticism, Ltd., then, criticism has faced a number of remarkable dangers and many of them it has by no means solved. Part of its development has been, as I have suggested, towards an increase in speculative theory: but theory can be of two kinds. It can be theory derived from literature—I would take it that the right word here is 'poetics'—and from the accumulated and ever-changing practice of writers, so that a sophistication of typology, an increasing accuracy of internal analysis, a greater understanding of complexity of language and structure, ensues. Or it can be theory created about literature and applied to it, theory perhaps devised in the first instance for another purpose (the study of language, say, or of society, or of cultural myths) and then, because it has certain points of appropriateness to literature, brought to it. Of these two kinds of theory, I would think the first to be a good deal more important than, though not exclusive of, the second. (To take one significant crux at the present time: it seems necessary to say to those who remind us that literature is intrinsically language that they are right, but it is *in the first instance* intrinsically literature, for there are other written forms which are also intrinsically language and are *not* literature.) The danger of theory moving towards scholasticism is therefore considerable; and we can see in the multiplication of exegesis (minor articles in minor journals about minor symbols and their minor function in a minor work by a minor writer) and overplus of method applied to a minimum of text the conventional consequences of this movement. But more important is the tendency of criticism, in pursuing its aspirations, to acquire the form of a primary as opposed to a secondary mode of discourse—so that instead of being capable of creating its theory out of texts, and doing so in a form flexible enough to respond to change in the creative sphere (literature, one always need to remind critics, is not over yet), it moves insensibly from description to prescription.

One particularly striking form of this latter tendency is the inclination of contemporary criticism to move away from matters of value. As a result of this, there is an increasing tendency in criticism to take works of literature as phenomena, as objects or events. This reification can take a variety of forms, so that the words on the page are simply to be regarded as linguistic, symbolic, sociological or socio-cultural moments according to what critic one is reading; but the consequences are the same. The freedom of the writer is assumed to be conditioned; either he becomes a chance manifestation of community, or the carrier of some necessary historical crisis. As Graham Hough argues in his essay in this book, this approach is partly a consequence of the knowledge that literature cannot be regarded as an historical constant; it is indeed deeply conditioned by the social order in which it occurs, and the kinds of structures and orders available to it. One of the attractions of French structuralism—to which many of the critics in this volume refer—is that it affords a particularly complex form of historicism which synchronizes internal analysis of text and the general analysis of the total culture. But it means that criticism, from the stuff of its growing theory, becomes capable of creating expectations which the writers of the time may well not be able to satisfy. Only those kinds of work which fit in with some standard derived partly from values or methods external to literature become objects of critical concern. The way in which descriptive typologies can become prescriptive ones can be seen at work in some of the contemporary arguments about the 'crisis' of modern literature. For example, we are told that in certain forms of bourgeois capitalist society there is an inevitable alienation of language, so that modernism, a separation of the fictive from the real, and 'absurdity' become logically necessary conditions for writers or for literature. There are of course various kinds of this imposition, and it is less dangerous when applied to the so-to-speak 'completed' writing of the past than to the writing of the present. But its tendency to deny to writers an appropriate freedom of will and invention, and to explain writing according to large-scale systems of causality, is in the long run anti-literary and reductive.[12] In many ways, of course, this represents

[12] The most striking example of this form of historicism occurs in Roland Barthes (*Writing Degree Zero*, 1967), who discerns a linguistic 'fall' in the

a valuable opening out of criticism into general intellectual discussion; and in any case I would not at all want to deny the advantages of theory in criticism, nor to argue against the view that modern criticism has in certain respects progressed. Certainly one of the ways it has progressed *is* through this very plurality of dialogue and the desire, conveyed in this volume, to see literature in as many lights as possible. My point is simply that in the end what must draw together the many approaches in criticism to literature are standards of relevance derived *from* literature. Finally, I think, the only effective kind of critical theory is one that is empirically descriptive rather than prescriptive; one which tolerates the variety of literature's variation and innovation and is accordingly *post facto*.

III

It may be objected that what I have said here better fits the state of critical affairs in the United States or France than in England, the classic source of 'empirical' critical approaches. Criticism in the United States has after all shown a marked predisposition towards theory, as a comparison between 'New Critical' activity in both countries in the nineteen thirties will show. In France and Europe, of course, criticism has frequently been a branch of philosophy or sociology. The English tradition has been both markedly empirical and markedly culturalist (by which I mean concerned with literature from a standpoint *within* its cultural commitment and situation rather than by external surveillance); and in many respects that empirical tradition still survives today. David Daiches has made the point—in his book *Critical Approaches to Literature* (1956)—that, while the distinction between critical theory and critical practice is an artificial one, it is often profitable to draw upon it; and he points out that some critical traditions and some periods have been much more concerned with the one rather than the other. If, in fact, all practice has theory implied in it, the fact remains

---

mid-nineteenth century; the more positive aspects of his insights are discussed by Graham Hough. More attractive, to my mind, is Frank Kermode who, in *The Sense of an Ending* (1967), recognizes the recurrence of certain forms of modern myths, structure and languages but grants the writer the freedom of clerkly scepticism in relation to them, in terms rather larger than Barthes's 'écriture'.

that the British tradition has frequently made a virtue, if not a methodological necessity, out of its empiricism. (In criticism, empiricism is
of course a somewhat delicate if not dubious term; but I use it here
to mean a concern with giving a personal and detailed response to a
given text or writer, as opposed to the abstract substantiation of an
aesthetic or a poetics.) It has tended to lay its stress on the importance of
entering sympathetically into a work, and on the imaginative power of
literature to lead us towards experience and insight, and hence towards
an assessment of life itself. Where, then, modern English criticism *has*
been theoretical, it has theorized less about the nature of literary language, or formal structure in literature, or literary aesthetics. It has,
rather, tended to stand closer to literature and to theoretize about
society—to ask questions about the relationship of the arts to the
general culture while taking literature as a source of the values and the
emphases that are brought to those questions. A convenient instance of
the emphasis comes out in a famous debate between F. R. Leavis and
the American critic René Wellek in the nineteen thirties, when Wellek,
after giving due praise to Leavis's *Revaluation*, commented:

> . . . I could wish you had stated your assumptions more explicitly
> and defended them systematically. I do not doubt the value of these
> assumptions and, as a matter of fact, I share them with you for the
> most part, but I would have misgivings in pronouncing them with-
> out elaborating a specific defence or a theory in their defence. Allow
> me to sketch your ideal of poetry, your 'norm' with which you
> measure every poet: your poetry must be in serious relation to
> actuality, it must have a firm grasp of the actual, of the object, it
> must be in relation to life, it must not be cut off from direct vulgar
> living. . . .

Leavis's reply was that a work of literature does not invite us to think
about and judge, but to feel into or become. Poetry is immediate, and
demands an immediacy and a sympathy of response, a felt response
allowing no real space for 'ideals' and 'norms'. And, though he recognizes there are theoretical implications to this position (there is, he
says, 'a chance that I may in this way have advanced theory, even if I
haven't done the theorizing'), he clearly feels that theory must represent a less immediate level of response than the one at the critical
centre.[13]

[13] Hence, then, criticism is a distinct activity, separate from philosophy or
morals or any other discipline, as Leavis indicates in the same response:

Now though Leavis's is only one response, I suppose we would regard it as one with a marked and a conscious relation to the English critical tradition. Behind it lie two features of that tradition—a strongly *personal* character, and a sense of association with a communal debate. That his kind of critical thinking has an important place in English critical thinking can be seen, for example, in two special issues of *The Times Literary Supplement* a few years back, in which critics from various countries gave their views on the function of criticism and literary study. What is so striking about the results—collected in book-form as *The Critical Moment* (1965)—is the very marked divergence between the views of the English and those of the American and French contributors, and also the relative agreement among the English writers about the *a*-theoretical nature of criticism. So Richard Hoggart argues that literature is 'the most creaturely' and hence in a sense the most impure of the arts, but, by virtue of its particularizing qualities, it has the ability to give the *whole* sense of an experience; L. C. Knights argues that literature must be first 'intuitively apprehended and so it may bring our lives to consciousness'; John Wain argues that it exists to tell us the truth, and requires of us a yielding to that truth; George Steiner argues that it assails and occupies the strong places of our consciousness, even though it may mislead us and has not always saved us; and Graham Hough speaks of the danger to criticism of too formalistic and over-professional a view of the critical act. For most of these critics, then, the stress fell on particular texts, and on particular, full responses to those texts, and then on the way those responses are educative in the sense that they 'extend our imaginative grasp of much in human experience.' The emphasis is broadly away from theory of literature as such—even though there may of course be

---

'The critic—the reader of poetry—is indeed concerned with evaluation, but to figure him as measuring with a norm which he brings up to the object and applies from the outside is to misrepresent the process. The critic's aim is, first, to realize as sensitively and completely as possible this or that which claims his attention; and a certain valuing is implicit in the realizing. As he matures in experience of the new thing he asks, explicitly and implicitly, "Where does this come from? How does it stand in relation to . . .? How relatively important does it seem?" And the organization into which it settles as a constituent in becoming "placed" is an organization of similarly "placed" things, things that have found their bearings with regard to one another, and not a theoretical system determined by abstract considerations.' (F. R. Leavis, 'Literary Criticism and Philosophy', in *The Common Pursuit*, 1952.)

in this approach all sorts of implicit theories about culture or education as well as about literature itself. In short, there lies in these views a common humanism; and if one can generalize a view from the range of different positions taken, we can see that it would contain assumptions about the importance of the autonomy of single texts, and their distinctive distillation not only of language but of human values; about the way in which the body of works of art acquires a classical status and function as a court of humane appeal; about the intense interpenetration then of the literary and the 'life' elements in them; and about the kind of responsive sympathy that might be expected of the adequate reader. We can call this sort of approach 'empirical' or 'practical', however, because, by putting emphasis on the individual, the mimetic and representational features of literary works, and emphasizing the distinctiveness of the critical response needed in each case, it does not acquire the feel of a theory. But against such views, most of the American and European critics contributing to the same volume seem arrayed; and they set forth very different ones. They argue for more theory, or they act as if a great deal of it were in existence; they demand more complex descriptive strategies which specifically involve setting any given work at a greater distance in order to see both what constitutes and conditions it. René Wellek, like others in the volume, points out that what constitutes it is language: literature must be seen as the 'world changed into language'—which means that it has its own distinct procedures derived from the character of discourse, and hence it is as discourse and not as life that we must approach it. In similar terms most of the European contributions stress the need for studying literature through poetics and increasingly these poetics mean semantics. Some of the contributors in fact show specific irritation with the English approach, either because it is too old-fashioned, too didactic or too humane. Emilio Cecchi appeals to a larger sense of relationship with the critical traditions of the past, with their philosophical grandeur. Umberto Eco argues the case for studying literature as one aspect of the process of signification or making meaning in society, and so he rejects the idea of art as being an independent absolute while urging that, because values exist in literature only as an aspect of their structure, we must study it formally. Roland Barthes, in somewhat similar terms, argues that it is up to criticism to recognize its character as a metalanguage, or a secondary semantic system created for the analysis of a primary semantic system, which is literature itself.

Criticism is therefore the application of logic to literature, and should depend on prevailing logical resources, which, says Barthes, mean today the four-fold philosophies of existentialism, Marxism, psychoanalysis and structuralism.

Whether or not *The Critical Moment* was an entirely fair reflection of the state of English criticism in 1965, it undoubtedly reflected many of its features. It seems unlikely that a similar collection made today would show the same emphases. Over the last few years, the climate of English criticism has, I have said, changed a good deal; and one aspect of the change has been a growing dialogue between English critics and American and French ones. There has, indeed, been a considerable penetration into its activities of the Revised New Criticism in its various forms—from critics like W. K. Wimsatt, Northrop Frye, Wayne Booth, R. S. Crane, Leslie Fiedler and Marshall McLuhan in the United States, and like Eco and Barthes in Europe. As we have seen, this undoubtedly represents a kind of professionalization of English criticism of a sort it has not had in the past, for good or bad, and has involved a sharping speculation in the critical forum, along with a certain loss of some of those virtues of involvement and response, of polemical engagement with literary values, of immediacy, which provided part of the urgency of some earlier critical activity. A number of books have come out lately—for instance, Donald Davie's *Articulate Energy* (1955), Winifred Nowottny's *The Language Poets Use* (1962) David Lodge's *Language of Fiction* (1966), William Righter's *Logic and Criticism* (1963), John Casey's *The Language of Criticism* (1966), Graham Hough's *The Dream and the Task* (1963) and *An Essay in Criticism* (1966), and Frank Kermode's *The Sense of an Ending* (1967)—which, though quite various in emphasis and method, do show a drift in the direction of theoretical enquiry and a concern with large typologies of literature. The range and the methodology advanced by these books or implied by them is wide indeed, though the recurrence of the word 'language' in their titles suggests one recurrent theme. But two things are apparent. The first is that in various ways they not only assume but pass beyond the assumption, stronger in the American New Critics than the English ones and especially associated with later figures like W. K. Wimsatt, that a work of literary art is primarily and inescapably a verbal artefact. The second is that there has been a sharp inclination to diverge from the long-term concern in English literary discussion with the humanistic and humane aspects of literature as a moral medium, a 'storehouse of recorded values', in I. A. Richards's phrase. In short, there has been an increase in critical neutrality and objectivity, an obsession with procedural and methodological logic, a desire for a more inclusive but also a more descriptive poetics.[14] On the one hand, we can see a conscious effort towards much more conscious and objective methods, to more theory, towards the refining of principles and methods. On the other hand, however, we can also see an effort towards a different *kind* of theory, in some ways much more inclusive than what had gone before, attempting to offer general methods, but also involving new emphases and primacies. For we should not suppose that when criticism 'refines' its methods it thereby does what it has done before in better and more precise ways; its theoretical nature and its precision involve new emphases and new aesthetic assumptions.

To a considerable extent, these emphases and assumptions can be linked with what is going on in other countries at the moment, and in particular with the prevailing concern about relating formalistic descriptive theory with broad intellectual speculation about the nature of literature in society. English criticism has over the last few years acquired two important features of this sort of speculation: first, a strong stress on the semantic or linguistic nature of literature, its character as discourse; and secondly, in some quarters at least, a concern with the relation between linguistic structures and other orders of expression and consciousness in a society. It might well be thought that these interests are contradictory; indeed, W. K. Wimsatt's essay in this volume indicates some of the ways in which they might be held so to be. However, it is not hard to see how such links can come about.

[14] So in an article, 'The Critical Moment 1964', in *Critical Quarterly* VI (Autumn 1964), David Lodge was to be found pleading for a much less empirical approach in English criticism, and appealing to the American example. He made the point that it was no longer realistic to assume that criticism was an offshoot of the prevailing developments in creation, or that it was written for the common reader; it was now a university activity, indissolubly wedded to teaching and research. 'This means', he said, 'that [criticism] will progress in future, not by a series of violent revolutions and exciting transformations, but slowly, by constantly putting its own house in order. Principles and methods will be re-examined and refined. . . . This process requires above all a capacity for keen theoretical thinking about literature and criticism.' Three years later, in another review article in the same journal ('Current Critical Theory', *Critical Quarterly* IX, Spring 1967), discussing some of the books I have mentioned, he was remarking that the state of affairs he had been arguing for in the earlier essay now seemed to have come into existence.

For the tendency in New Criticism was to reach towards an impasse in which it became virtually impossible to talk effectively about the mimetic or social dimension of literature at all. A work of literature was a whole object for contemplation, existing sollipsistically within itself. The exemplary case was the lyric poem, which could be apprehended as a visible whole, so that you could hold the parts together as a discussable unit, reading backwards and forwards through the text. But modern criticism has tended to move its emphasis away from lyric poems or short stories towards novel and drama, both of which tended to be, not ignored, but certainly under-emphasized in the prewar period. In doing this, modern criticism has tended to moderate some of its formalism, while still holding onto the neosymbolist assumptions of New Criticism. Works still may be considered as verbal constructs, language-complexes; but the language they use is not discrete only to them. So, for instance, Roger Fowler and Peter Mercer note in a survey of recent critical debate in England that, while criticism still insists on the importance of studying the language of literature, it has tended to assume that

> there is no aprioristic reason why any single element of poetic language should, if isolated, be uniquely significant; that is, there is no need to set up one feature, say 'paradox', as the defining characteristic of poetic structure.[15]

One likely result of this shifting emphasis is that stress on the formal features of a work, on the control of technique, tends to be diminished. The semantic or linguistic nature of literature, its character as discourse, can still be emphasized, but its structure and form can come to be taken as aspects of the communal or social structure of language as a species of ordering and perceiving. Hence the tendency in a good deal of recent criticism to stress not the separate internal energy of literary language but its relation to *all* language, to explore not the conscious control of the artist but the substrata of literary language—its communal unconscious, so to speak. So literature tends to become included as part of the broader structures of consciousness and expression in society. It is not

[15] Roger Fowler and Peter Mercer, 'Criticism and the Language of Literature: Some Traditions and Trends in Great Britain', *Style* III (Winter 1969), pp. 45–72. As they note in their article, in assimilating such views English critics of the nineteen sixties are 'no longer in a specifically British tradition' of criticism. (Further implications of this point are drawn out in Fowler's contribution to the present volume.)

so much an art of (as New Criticism tended to assume) creative techniques and distinctive literary values; it is rather a distillation of broader myths and typologies, values and perceptual systems, on which the artist imposes his modicum of personal signature.[16]

Not all criticism is moving in this latter direction, but its temptations are obvious. By taking the emphasis off the controlled and created aspects of literary technique, it tends to lead us out of the old dilemma about whether literature is primarily 'form' or primarily 'content'; it is simply a particular, refined instance of the social nature of language as a means of ordering and expressing consciousness and ideology in society. This enables us to think of literary study as part of a general science of man—so that we can regard literature not simply as a body of individual creative instances but as part of larger blocks of expression. In a time of increased uncertainty about literary or any values, it also enables us to see all forms of writing, 'serious' or otherwise, as in some sense linked. On the other hand, since it tends towards taking written texts as phenomena, determined by forces beyond the conscious control of the artist, it readily leads us away from directly literary questions towards various forms of historicist *a priorism*.[17] Many of its questions are determined not by an interest in responding empirically to particular texts, nor even by broad responses to writing generally, but by the desire to locate literature as an aspect of some larger entity. In many respects my own sympathies are with this tendency,[18] but

[16] I am thinking here of such assumptions as those in Frank Kermode's *The Sense of an Ending*, which brilliantly argues that the structures of novels and the 'typologies' by which we perceive historical and chronological sequence are closely linked. Kermode, though, is noteworthy in his stress on the distinctive contribution of the individual writer: his 'clerkly scepticism'.

[17] By 'historicism', I mean the desire to 'unmask' ideas or forms of consciousness by showing their external determinants. Men may think themselves free individuals, but they are 'really' the subjects of the roles they perform. (The most familiar versions of historicism are those which urge that consciousness is a superstructure determined by some fundamental 'reality' underlying the historical process, for instance the economic substructure. But equally historicism may take the form of the assumption that the writer is committed by the resources of language prevailing at a particular time, so that certain styles are 'right' in certain contexts; modernism is historically necessary in a late bourgeois world. Similar exercises are possible if the *a priori* assumptions are drawn from psychology; see Norman Holland's comments on this point in his essay in this volume.)

[18] As I indicate in 'Literature and Sociology', *Essays and Studies 1970*, edited by A. R. Humphreys (1970).

B

where it becomes dangerous is when it becomes 'axiomatic' that a poetics of literature should be derived in the first instance from outside literature: from theories of expression or structure, from theories about language, or from notional models of society. And this in turn raises certain questions about the nature of literary 'poetics' to which I should like finally to turn.

IV

All criticism, whether empirical or not, contains a poetics—which is to say a mode of analysis based on assumptions about the relevant object of attention in criticism, and the relevant procedures or modes of talking that can be brought to bear upon it. We do not, as critics, read each work of literature totally anew; we come to it with certain assumptions and expectations derived from our prior experience of literature. These may be formulated as principles of an axiomatic kind, or they may be less positive assumptions, either because we believe that criticism should be a sympathetic exercise in reading or because we have formulated our principles in such a way that fixed expectations are unlikely. Nonetheless, once we start to talk as critics, we have to have a language of discussion and a sense of relevance, and this will normally be derived by our comparative experience of literature as it exists to date. We need a language of relevance which gives us the means both for appreciating and for assessing the competence and success of the particular literary experience we confront. Now in criticism there are four main objects to which attention can be drawn —the writer, the writing, the 'subject' of the writing, and the reader. On the whole the tendency of modern criticism has been, as we have seen, to focus on the second of these things: the stable text, the one thing we possess in common and to which we can return again and again for verification. Our modern poetics, then, is usually a language for the discussion of text, and involves our means of separating out parts from the whole in order to speak of them. This means that when we use terms like 'plot', 'character', or 'description', which sound innocuous enough, we are using a critical language which has its own presumptions. They are that a work of literature is 'mimetic' or imitates life, contains life-elements within itself with which the writer has engaged; that its design and structure can be derived from and tested against familiar human experience both in given instances and as a significant structure ('plot'). If, though, we speak rather of the primary features of a work as 'point of view', 'narrative strategy', 'irony', 'paradox', or 'ambiguity', we are much more likely to assume that the main medium through which a writer works is not his observation of experience but the technical resources over which he has creative control; he does not so much represent and evoke life as create a fictional sense of it through his power to manage words and structures. And if we speak of the primary features as 'linguistic registers', or 'archetypes', or 'mythic themes', or 'symbols', then we raise other possibilities and other implications—for instance, that the language of literature is not so much a matter of the individual competence and control of this writer but a particular and distilled form of all language. As it happens, criticism in this century has tended to move through these various types of description, and roughly in the order in which I have mentioned them; the New Criticism was a reaction against the emphases of the first type of criticism, and the present changes in criticism seem to take the form of an expansion of the New Critical assumption that language and technique are the essential aspects of critical discussion into new areas. As it also happens, these different poetics bear some relation to types of writing prevailing at the time when they were or are most current; the first terminology, applied to the novel, obviously better fits nineteenth-century fiction; the second Jamesian and post-Jamesian modernist writing; the third applies best to a kind of synthetic fusion of the two, a new kind of fictional historicism, that has emerged since the war. And as it further happens, each seems to reflect assumptions about the role of the writer in society: in the first case, a role in which he is an involved perceiver; in the second, in which he is a selfconscious bearer of distinctive craft; in the third, in which he is socially exposed, as a kind of democrat, to the fundings of his culture, is the expression, active or passive, of the prevailing languages and myths of his time, is a version of *homo sociologicus*. And, as we have seen, these distinctions also have something to do with the kind of engagement we have with writers: in the first case, they are higher versions of men like ourselves: in the second, they are men of a distinctive creative wisdom; in the third, they are men who are the equals of ourselves, subject as we are to historical limitations and causalities.

In short, the various approaches involve various levels of emphasis, and various degrees of closeness to or distance from the writer and his work. And we might therefore assume that the ideal state of affairs in criticism is a kind of pluralistic one in which questions of all these orders can be raised to get a 'total' view. But of course the problem with such pluralism is that the poetics do not always prove consistent one with another; they tend in fact to be mutually inconsistent. Empirically, of course, we can regard them as the tools of criticism, to be used in an enabling way to help us with particular problems on particular occasions, so supporting and illuminating our sense that all literature is variously interesting. But there is a tendency to distrust this very order of empiricism, since there is also a tendency to require of the critic not so much that he be impressionistically right but logic-ally consistent. This, to a point, is natural enough; it seems entirely right and proper that we should require critics to say something, and that what they say should be adequate within itself and subject to our own verification. In fact, though, what tends to become apparent is that no critic can speak to any other critic, though all may speak to readers of criticism; the common pursuit becomes a contentious battle-ground.[19] If the answer to this is to bring criticism to the point where all its axioms are totally logical, however, then the area of possible debate and analysis becomes startlingly narrowed. Alternatively it becomes remarkably broad, as criticism seeks by various means to gain the support of science, or sociology, or politics, or anthropology, or linguistics to acquire a base *for* verification. Today there are signs that both of these things are happening. On the one hand, then, criticism seems to have capitalized on its resources to deal with those problems of a literary text which derive from linguistic recurrences, syntactical features, tones and registers; and, on the other, to deal with large-range problems about literature's relationship to cultural typologies and myths. What it seems to have lost is its capacity to deal with those middle-range problems which used to be the essential preserve of criticism, and which, in the long run, seem to have to do with its primary competence and its very nature. Here the problems I mean are those of analysing, describing and evaluating those features of struc-ture, design and organization that are the essential constituents of any recognition of the complexity both of aesthetic and of experience which gives us our sense of the texture and quality of major art.

This too requires a poetics, a language for discussion and evaluation.

[19] For a superb analysis of this state of affairs see R. S. Crane, *The Languages of Criticism and the Structure of Poetry* (Toronto and Oxford, 1953).

But it means a poetics derived in the first instance from literature itself, rather than from linguistic or cultural theory. It means a poetics that is empirical, in the sense that it is responsive, in a *post facto* way, to the character of any given work to which critical attention is taken— responsive to its particular organization, dispositions and structure, its feel, its way of persuasion. It also means a poetics that is eclectic, capable of responding to works already in existence, deriving from many environments and many different aesthetics, and also to works yet to be written. It must in short be a criticism without a predetermined set of hypotheses; yet a criticism capable of providing the means of making hypotheses in sympathetic relation to the works that it is reading. For it is precisely with the conscious, created, persuasive elements of a literary text, those features of making and shaping that give it its essential existence and its essential independence, that the test of an adequately *literary* criticism lies. 'The axioms and postulates of criticism . . .,' says Northrop Frye in his *Anatomy of Criticism* (Princeton, 1957), 'have to grow out of the art it deals with. The first thing the literary critic has to do is to read literature, to make an inductive study of his own field and let his critical principles shape themselves solely out of his knowledge of that field.' That is not necessarily the final principle of criticism, as Northrop Frye's own work itself shows; but it is, I think, the right *first* principle, and an inescapable one. The present problem for criticism seems to be to reach towards the means of maintaining that traditional enough premise, in such a way that criticism can support its claim to be a genuinely worthwhile mode of knowledge while still recognizing literature's place in the social and historical life of mankind.

Note

References

The traditional statements for the humanist nature of critical study occur in Matthew Arnold, *Culture and Anarchy* (1869) and 'The Function of Criticism at the Present Time' in *Essays in Criticism: First Series* (1865); also in T. S. Eliot, 'The Function of Criticism' in *Selected Essays* (1932: revised edition 1951); in F. R. Leavis, *The Common Pursuit* (1952) and *Education and the University* (1970); and in Lionel Trilling, *Beyond Culture* (1965). With I. A. Richards's two studies, *Principles of Literary Criticism* (1924) and *Practical Criticism* (1929), these books could be taken as reflecting a central view of the educational and social function of criticism until lately.

In my discussion of new approaches in criticism, the main works referred to are as follows. In section I, Roland Barthes, *Le degré zéro de l'écriture* (Paris, 1963), translated as *Writing Degree Zero* (1967). In section III, I refer to Erich Auerbach's *Mimesis: The Representation of Reality in Western Literature* (New York, 1957); my reference is to pp. 485–7 of the Anchor Books edition. In section IV, I refer generally to Sartre's critical work, as in *Literary and Philosophical Essays* (1955); but especially to 'Qu'est ce que la littérature?' in *Situations II* (Paris, 1948), translated as *What Is Literature?* (1950), and the essays on Merleau-Ponty and Camus in *Situations IV* (Paris, 1964). References in section VI are to Arnold Hauser's 4-volume *The Social History of Art* (New York, 1951; new edition, London, 1963) and to the following works by Georg Lukacs: *Die Theorie des Romans* (Berlin, 1920; reprinted Neuwied-am-Rhein, 1963; translated into French, *La théorie du roman*, Paris, 1963, with a valuable appendix by Lucien Goldmann on Lukacs' early work); *Studies in European Realism* (English translation, 1948); *The Historical Novel* (English translation, 1962). Lucien Goldmann's work on Pascal and Racine is in *Le dieu caché* (Paris, 1955), translated as *The Hidden God* (1964); his *Pour une sociologie du roman* (Paris, 1964) should also be mentioned. Max Raphael's *The Demands of Art* (1968) is an English translation from unpublished German manuscripts. (For work of similar perspective, see *Note* to W. K. Wimsatt's essay.)

II

Criticism as a Humanist Discipline

GRAHAM HOUGH

I

To the two familiar concepts of language and style modern French critics have added a third—*écriture*, or 'writing'. The term is sometimes used neutrally, but in the work of Roland Barthes it has a special significance:

> Language and style are blind forces; writing is an act of historical solidarity. Language and style are objects; writing is a function: it is the relationship between creation and society, it is the literary language transformed by its social destination, it is form considered as a human intention and so linked to the great crises of history.

'Language' here has a Saussurean sense—the public, conventional aspect of language, the system described in dictionaries and grammars, the code that stands outside and above the individual user, unalterable by individual volition. Style as Barthes employs it means personal style at its most intimate, something almost biological, a mode of expression rooted in the psycho-physical constitution of the individual. And 'writing'? It is, as he defines it elsewhere, 'the language of a linguistic community, that is, of a group of persons who all interpret in the same way all linguistic statements.' For the writer language is simply given; style is rooted in his individual being; but a mode of writing is arrived at by an act of choice. Not indeed a completely free choice. The writer chooses the social area within which he situates his work, but he chooses under the pressure of history and tradition. He cannot behave as though the whole gamut of possible modes is open to him in a non-temporal fashion. Much that once existed is out of reach; much that is available is contaminated with undesired associations. But a choice must be made, and when it is made it is a commitment to one aspect or another of the society of the time.

Barthes' argument, brief as it is, sketches the outline of a criticism that could be both literary in the strict sense—concerned with the literary use of language—and in a broader sense a humanistic study—concerned with human intention, with the choice of ends and means under the social and historical pressures in which men actually live. *Le degré zéro de l'écriture*, the brilliant essay of which it forms a part, also gives some summary illustrations of this criticism in action. It is to my mind the most impressive of Barthes' writings, some of which are certainly open to the objections that have so abundantly been brought against them. I cite it here not because it has any special pre-eminence in current critical theory, but because it is a striking example of a way of thinking about literature that has no analogue in English criticism. In England when we think of literary criticism as expanding into a humanist critique of culture in general we think of something that began with Matthew Arnold and has been going on with steadily decreasing momentum ever since.

II

'There is not a creed which is not shaken, not an accredited dogma which is not shown to be questionable, not a received tradition which does not threaten to dissolve. . . . More and more mankind will discover that we have to turn to poetry to interpret life for us, to console us, to sustain us.

So Arnold wrote in 1884; and forty years later I. A. Richards echoed his words:

It is very probable that the Hindenburg Line to which the defence of our traditions retired as a result of the onslaughts of the last century will be blown up in the near future. If this should happen a mental chaos such as man has never experienced may be expected. We shall then be thrown back, as Matthew Arnold foresaw, upon poetry. It is capable of saving us; it is a perfectly possible means of overcoming chaos.

Poetry (to be interpreted probably in this context as imaginative literature in general) becomes the humanist scripture, an open multiform scripture to supersede the closed authoritative sacred text. This premise, sometimes unspoken, sometimes expressed in language shorn of its theological overtones, has been fundamental to nearly all later English criticism of the more comprehensive kind. It lies behind the early work of Richards and the endeavours of *Scrutiny*. All that large body of critical and pedagogical writing that sees literature as the central humanist study depends upon it. Salvation lies in 'sincerity' or 'maturity' or 'awareness', and by searching the secular scripture that literature has become the way of salvation is to be found.

Serious and in many ways sympathetic as this kind of criticism is, it rests on a fallacy, or rather on two fallacies. The first is the belief that a coherent formation can be derived from the vast heterogeneous body of literature, regardless of our own historical situation or that of the work we study. It is an idea left over from the days of a defined cultural tradition, a classical and Christian tradition defined by forces outside the literary field. In those days men received from literature what their civilization had already agreed to allow into it; contradictions and dissentient voices were simply ignored. This is no longer a possibility in the imaginary museum in which we live. There is little that our civilization is agreed upon; a literary canon that includes Genet and the Marquis de Sade is ill adapted to the education of the guardians; literary canons are selected almost arbitrarily, and what professes to be the authority of literature is really the authority of whoever has drawn up the syllabus. The dangers of employing literature as a *paideia* in our present circumstances are that it will either expand to utter formlessness or that it will be cut down by some more or less well-meaning system-maker to what is supposed to be our need.

The second fallacy is that this way of thinking hypostatizes poetry or literature, sets it above and over against the world of historical experience. Society is corrupt, and literature is the repository of the compensating idea. But we have no right to this assumption. Literature is a product of society and history, not an authority outside them. True, it also helps to shape history; but if we are to use literature as a means of understanding our condition we can only do so by seeing it as what it is, a product of the continual to and fro of human and social action, in which ideas, beliefs and aesthetic constructions arise from general human activity, and in their turn fall back into the melting-pot to contribute to the shaping of new activities in the future. Poetry is not a supra-historical reservoir of consolations and values to be drawn upon at will; it is a symbolic form, probably the richest and most fertile of all the symbolic forms, in which men mostly very different from ourselves have interpreted their various worlds. Poetry is not a pantheon of timeless truths, to be encapsulated in Arnoldian touchstones. It has indeed a history and a logic of its own, independent or partly independent of the logic of social development. But that is only valid within the closed aesthetic sphere. So far as poetry tells us anything it tells us something that is historically conditioned; and it tells it to us in our historical condition; and this relation is constantly shifting and changing its shape.

It is of course essential to Richards's position that poetry does *not* tell us timeless truths; indeed that it does not *tell* us anything. But for him and those who follow him poetry seems to achieve another hypostasis—not as informant but as shaper of our minds. It does not tell us anything, but it possesses a more mysterious power—that of harmonizing our impulses, adjusting our attitudes, balancing our appetencies. Poetry has its own special kind of integrity, which depends not on its relation to any outward state of affairs, but on its internal harmonizing of discordant impulses. The outward projection of this process, never very clearly described, seems to be that in reading poetry we internalize its harmonizing activity, and so achieve a beneficent state of psychic equilibrium. The demonstration of this mode of functioning was left in Richards's early criticism to a future science of psychology that so far has not appeared. To see the action of poetry in this way corresponds to seeing the scriptures not as a source of history or doctrine, but as a source of spiritual illumination of a non-cognitive kind. It is evidently close to Arnold's interpretation both of literature and scripture. The crude empirical evidence, scattered and uncertain as it is, does not seem to offer this view any very strong support. Common observation does not suggest, however much we may wish it to do so, that those with a purely literary formation have achieved a higher degree of equilibrium or spiritual insight than those nourished on other studies.

III

If literature is to be a scripture, criticism is presumably its theology. The parallel is fairly close. The Bible is a collection of ancient writings of extremely various kinds—myth, history, poetry both sacred and secular, preaching, meditation. It includes extremely various views of man's destiny and conduct. Imagine it being read by one entirely ignorant of the vast labour of interpretation that has gone on around it. In such a case it could not appear as a totality. No general sense could be extracted from it, and such paths as came to be discerned through its heterogeneity would be partial, uncertain and broken. It is centuries of exegesis, Jewish and Christian, that have traced in it the pattern of Israel, chosen, lapsed, captive, wandering and redeemed; and within that an analogous pattern for the individual human soul. The later parts of the scriptures have been composed in the light of earlier explanations. It is Christian interpretation that has inserted the life-story of the individual redeemer into the messianic hopes of the ancient Jewish world. It is theological authority that has decided the relative status of canonical and apocryphal books. And in a similar way it is criticism in the widest possible sense that has traced a path through the vast diverse jungle of surviving literature. If the educated man thinking of the literature of our civilization is aware of an intelligible pattern proceeding from Homer to the Greek tragedians, to Virgil, to the Christian literature of the Middle Ages, to the Renaissance, to the Enlightenment, to the revolutionary and Romantic age, to whatever it is we live in now—this possibility is the result of centuries of unconsciously collaborative critical work. If Northrop Frye is able to see the whole expanse spread out as it were in a simultaneous spatial design, he is enabled to do so by innumerable preceding critical labours. It is virtually impossible to separate what is actually 'in' the Biblical text from what has been read into it by the hopes and needs of successive generations. And so it is with literature. Our understanding of the literature of the past is a critical construction. In popular literary thinking creation and criticism are often opposed; but for culture as a whole they are inseparable factors in a single symbolic structure. The Arnoldian concept of criticism as something more than mere literary judgment, as 'a disinterested endeavour to learn and propagate the best that has been known and thought in the world' is a recognition of this as the true state of affairs. Arnold's proposal in 'The Study of Poetry' to read poetry as a kind of scripture, his proposal in *Literature and Dogma* to read scripture as a kind of poetry, implies a proposal to regard criticism as a kind of theology. Leo Spitzer has said it in so many words, 'Yes, we humanists are theologians.' And as long as it was possible to regard western civilization as a continuing unity this was a possible way of thinking.

I believe however that it is necessary now more than ever to realize the difficulties of this position. Arnold writes 'There is not a creed which is not shaken, not an accredited dogma which is not shown to be questionable, not a received tradition which does not threaten to dissolve'; but it is hard to suppose that he really means it. The whole tenor of his later writing, even the tenor of the passage from which these words come, is to suggest that by a simple adjustment of perspective, a refocussing of the binoculars, literature instead of dogma, this blurring and confusion can be overcome, and the eternal verities, or all that really matters of them, will once more stand out in their former clarity. I cannot help contrasting with Arnold's easy acknowledgment of disorder the profound sense of cultural dissolution in the closing pages of Auerbach's *Mimesis*. Auerbach has been tracing a path through the whole expanse of Western literature, from Homer to Proust, Joyce and Virginia Woolf. It is a temporal sequence that he examines, a series of literary methods, historically considered. And when he finally arrives at the method of our century what he principally distinguishes in it is 'a symptom of confusion and helplessness . . . a mirror of the decline of our world'. In the prose fiction of our time with its multiple reflection of consciousness he finds 'a hatred of culture and civilization, brought about by means of the subtlest stylistic devices which culture and civilization have developed, and often a radical and fanatical urge to destroy.' These are the words of a man no longer young, writing towards the end of a war that had destroyed the Europe that he knew, and his own kind of life. The feeling with which they are written arises from a personal situation; but the fact to which they point is surely a fact. The Hellenic-Roman-Christian civilization which cultivated Europeans of Auerbach's generation had felt that they possessed, had grown up to regard as a great continuing totality, has really ceased to exist. The view of literary and cultural tradition presented in Eliot's early criticism is a factitious, almost posthumous attempt to think it into continued existence. But no one thinks like that now. And soon nobody will know enough even to think of thinking it.

Or rather, they will not know enough of what traditional literary culture formerly considered essential. They will know many other things; indeed they already do. Any man in late middle age must have noticed how his juniors, no more intelligent than himself and by received standards less well informed, possess without effort whole ranges of experience that he can only grasp with difficulty and labour. The Hegelian vision of history as the continuous unfolding of Mind is in one sense a simple fact. Consciousness is here and now expanding with extraordinary rapidity, in a hundred different ways. Formal culture in the traditional sense is manifestly in decline, but something that is certainly a culture in the anthropological sense is in a state of runaway growth, both in distribution and in depth. It is not however a literary culture, and it is not open to the influence of criticism, in either the restricted or the Arnoldian sense, as the older culture was.

Literature is inclined to assume an ecumenical position that it no longer really holds. It is a commonplace (even Marshall McLuhan has noticed it) that the literary sphere has contracted in our day. For a time it seemed otherwise. With the decline in the authority of religion it seemed that the Arnoldian prophecy had come true, and that literature was become the prime source of social and personal values. But this was not the beginning of a new cultural orientation; it was the swan-song of high-bourgeois civilization. Even in the last few years the position of literature has been changing. As simple entertainment it has many new rivals. The drama—the serious drama more than the trivial—is receding from literature towards a form where gesture, action and inarticulate half-utterance takes the place of self-subsistent dialogue. Many good modern plays are barely intelligible except in performance. The great international modern art-form, the cinema, depends so little on its literary content that it survives without much loss in dubbed versions or with translated subtitles. In education much that used to be mediated by literature is now absorbed into programmes of a non-literary kind. Sociology offers to provide what used to be mediated by the novel. Open shelves are replaced by data-retrieval machinery. The visual arts, once discussed by critics who were essentially men of letters, in essentially literary terms, are now discussed in terms of topology and cybernetics. It is idle to suppose that this is a passing phase and that the old literary programme will come in again to occupy its old station. The whole technical and productive organization of the modern world is moving in the other direction.

In this new cultural situation criticism can no longer expect to have the scope and authority that it once claimed. Arnold's conception of a largely literary culture, refining and fertilizing the life of its time, may survive as a pious formula, but it only commands the allegiance of those past middle age. It has little to do with the pressure of the world as it is. It is easy to relapse into an Arnoldian attitude and see this development as a substitution of 'machinery' for the life of the spirit. But this will not really do. Culture has always depended on the productive and social machinery of its age. Until fairly recently that machinery was largely controlled by verbal and linguistic processes—processes, that is to say, which have some obvious affinity with literature and an obvious connection with literary culture. That is no longer the case. Think, for example, of the manifest decline in the importance of forensic oratory. The change has been extraordinarily rapid, and the effects on the literary outlook are profound, if as yet not fully realized. Men still living (it would be easy to name them) who in the prime of their lives saw themselves as forerunners of a new literary outlook are by now the priests of an almost abandoned cult. The forms and rituals survive but their content has been eroded. Old controversies drag on and some new ones have arisen out of them; minor actions are still won or lost; but the campaign is no longer important. The real action has moved elsewhere.

IV

Meanwhile, the study of literature in the academic sense flourishes as never before. Literary faculties in the universities are crowded, and many applicants described as well qualified have to be turned away. Graduate schools are full of Ph.D. candidates. In libraries the dykes can hardly hold against the flood of literary publications. A young man has only to gather together his undergraduate essays and someone will almost certainly be found to publish them as volume of criticism. This is the culmination of a process that has been going on since the thirties. The literary and critical movement that began after the first world war made an unusually rapid advance into the academic system. It is an honourable feature of Eliot's early criticism that it made its way without coterie backing, without institutional support, simply in the ordinary traffic of the higher literary journalism; but it soon found its way into the university programme. The methods inaugurated by Richards's *Practical Criticism* and the doctrines of *Scrutiny* both belonged to it from the start. 'Criticism' was opposed to 'history' as an educational method, and within a few years a large new public was created, both in England and America, for critical writing. Many of the objectives of the new criticism were attained. A re-orientation of English literary history took place, accommodating the most active and original writing of the early twentieth century and revealing buried areas of the past.

This movement fortuitously coincided with educational and social change. First a decline in classical teaching and a consequent assumption of the main weight of education in the humanities by English literature. That in itself meant a democratization of literary culture, and it was the natural concomitant of far-reaching changes in the English class system. The economic and social developments showed up particularly clearly in education—an expansion of the secondary school population and a change in its class composition after 1942, and a later expansion and change in the universities. The continued influence of Leavis and *Scrutiny* on educational practice was in part a consequence of these class movements. *Scrutiny* was always inveterately hostile to elegant belles-lettres and an aristocratic literary establishment. An important part of its programme was to claim for the lower bougeoisie the whole heritage of culture that had formerly been thought of as an upper-bourgeois preserve. Lionel Trilling has expressed surprise[1] that so small a class conflict should have generated so much emotion in Leavis's mind. It is not surprising at all. In England the most sensitive of all the lines of class division for more than half a century has been the one drawn immediately below the upper middle class. The years between the wars saw the passing of the time when this class could claim any real superiority of taste, culture or knowledge. To break an obsolete barrier and to throw literary discourse open to wider social forces was one of *Scrutiny*'s most genuine achievements.

So far this summary chronicle sounds like a success story. A thoughtful and strenuous criticism had widened its audience and altered the direction of literary thinking in several decisive ways. More people were thinking seriously about literature than ever before, and literary ideas seemed likely to acquire some extension over the general intellectual field. But there was a price to be paid. The influence that criticism had acquired was transmitted almost entirely through scholastic channels. The popular literary journals moved still in the old circle; they retained the ethos and the personnel of an earlier time. Most of the new kind of criticism was produced in the universities; it was consumed almost entirely in universities and schools. From being a freelance movement against an existing cultural establishment it passed as early as the mid-thirties into being an institution, an institution with a predominantly pedagogical cast. This is the point to change the tense to the present, for the situation has remained the same ever since. The predominantly educational ambience is a new situation for criticism.

[1] *A Gathering of Fugitives* (1957), p. 106.

Instead of addressing a diversified adult public, immersed in the business of the world, its culture a part of the world, criticism finds itself with a captive audience of students and teachers, concerned with literature only within an institutional frame. Its work is formed by the current scholastic programme, its scope defined by the canalized habits of a special group, engaged in a special activity. The readers of criticism live within parentheses, its writers address a parenthetic world. A criticism that addresses the larger world outside has already become a rarity.

This is nobody's choice. In present conditions general periodical criticism is required to be so hurried and so short-winded that those with more serious literary ambitions are driven into the institutional fold. Institutional criticism divides into two branches; we could call them the graduate and the undergraduate divisions. The graduate criticism springs from research. Its claim is to be a contribution to knowledge. But as it is usually concerned with a subject on which there is plenty of accessible knowledge already, there is a difficulty. New *information* is not generally in question. In the first place, there probably is none; and if there were, the result of its application would be 'scholarship' not 'criticism'. So the pressing need is to find a new line of approach—to apply to a particular topic a piece of critical machinery that has not been applied to it before; or to enlist the aid of some non-literary discipline-psychology, sociology or linguistics. Sometimes the result is a genuine illumination, but more often the project did not start from the asking of a real question and its fulfilment has no meaning outside the institutional setting. Another book on Milton or Wordsworth that shuffles the cards in a partly new and possibly interesting fashion finds its way into the bibliographies. But it would never have been written, would never be read, if there were not a prefabricated public institutionally devoted to the consumption of books on Milton and Wordsworth. The undergraduate branch of criticism has a different origin. It arises from the opportunities of the teaching programme. No one has written a decent general book on *X* for some years, or the old standard work is out of print. *X* is an author who figures in the normal literary syllabus. So a new book is written—with interest, with hope, with mild ambition, but effectively with a student audience in mind. It would ill become me to complain of this genre, for I am a contributor to it; but to call it criticism—is it not perhaps the grand name without the grand thing?

A singular instance of the gearing of criticism to the pedagogic machine occurs in Leavis's recent American lectures.[2] He is maintaining that Yeats wrote only a few great poems—asserting a judgment rather than presenting the arguments on which it is founded. If one is not going to argue perhaps one had better appeal to some existing body of opinion; and this Dr. Leavis does. But the only consensus called to witness for his reading of Yeats is the following: 'I have discussed him this past academic year with keen and well-read undergraduates at my new university . . .' Keen undergraduates at the University of York! What a strange court of appeal for a judgment on one of the greatest European poets of the last hundred years. And 'well-read' too. I am sure that the keen undergraduates of the University of York have all the reading proper to their age and station. But could reading of no more than four or five years' standing, could any degree of well-readness possible to a twenty-year-old, make much contribution to such a judgment? This is a bizarre example of the readiness to cut down the literary intelligence to classroom proportions, but it is not wholly unfair to the assumptions with which much criticism now is carried on.

Dr. Leavis's undergraduates were keen and well-read. Not all are of this happy breed. It is for the others, I suppose, that the ignoble procession of Reader's Guides and 'case-books' is turned out, this detritus of criticism that seems to exist for the purpose of preventing anybody from reading anything for himself, A well-known series[3] (which in fact, fortunately, includes some distinguished items) announces 'It has become increasingly clear in recent years that what both the advanced sixth-former and the university student need most by way of help in their literary studies are close critical analyses and evaluations of individual works.' It has become increasingly clear to me in recent years that this is exactly what they do not need, or should not be allowed to have; and that such things should be written only because their authors feel they have something important to say, not in response to supposed educational needs. But I am afraid of my own temerity in saying in print what is usually kept to the unguarded privacy of conversation, and I turn with relief to a less sensitive area.

Thirty-five years ago among the intelligent young there was a passionate engagement with literature. Today I believe there is a change. It is not at all a dishonourable change, but it is a serious one from the point of view of literary study. The great attraction of the

[2] F. R. Leavis and Q. D. Leavis, *Lectures in America* (1969), p. 60.
[3] *Studies in English Literature*, Arnold.

schools of English literature in the universities is no longer primarily literary. It is that they are so flexible, so accommodating, especially in some of their newer forms. An able and wayward mind can make almost what it will of them. What passes for philosophy in England today is so dismally constricted; most English sociology is of such a flatly positivist cast; history is so closely geared to a specialist and technical scholarship that the interests which those studies at other times and in other places might have been expected to fulfil are more easily satisfied, after a fashion, within the loose confines of the English school. The real interests of many of the most intelligent young people in literary faculties today are philosophical, or sociological, or in the broadest sense political; yet they feel in some undefined way that these can be better satisfied within one or other of the varieties of a school of literature. I can hear the professors of these other disciplines saying, Yes, they prefer an amateur literary dabbling to the rigours of the real thing. This has a measure of truth, but isn't the whole truth. Is it not the case that what these students are feeling for is a more authentic and capacious criticism, one that will retain the imaginative freedom of literature, yet still be the vehicle of an intention? The literature of the past is what it always was; the business of criticism is to insert it into the living fabric of the present. I doubt whether the young feel that this is happening now.

Of course they are unfair to us—they always will be; and it is a sad thing that thoughtful and devoted teachers, men who had with justice felt themselves to be leaders and reformers, should be delivering a message that is steadily less regarded. But the elegiac mood will not help us. Yesterday's literary revolutions mean nothing to our juniors, and if they feel that the end-product, which is all they see, is an inert mixture of scholarship, factitious ingenuity and pedestrian moralizing —well, they may be wrong but they still feel it. I suspect that behind a confused unrest there are two real needs. One is for a clearer methodology, a method capable of giving a genuine sense of direction to intellectual development. The other is for a far closer engagement with social reality, with the history that still surrounds us, not with the history that exists over against us as an accomplished past. I may be projecting my own intentions on others, for these seem to me the real needs of criticism today quite apart from an internal unease in the academic system. One can think of several wrong ways of satisfying them; a right way will be hard to find; and it will not be found simply by redesigning a syllabus. If our literary thought could exist more vigorously outside the academies the problem of what goes on inside them would largely solve itself. Culture is not generated in undergraduate seminars; the vitality of undergraduate seminars depends on a vigorous cultural life existing in a larger world.

V

We had better give up the idea that criticism will ever be the conductor of the cultural orchestra, as Arnold and Leavis hoped. But it will still have its work to do. Even in a non-literary civilization men will still want to take stock of their past and see how it lives in the present; and it is through literature that we make our most direct contact with the past. They will still want, not only to read the literature of their own day, but to reflect on it, to compare it with their own experience and that of others. They will still use the literature of their own country and their own language to form their sense of cultural identity. If we ask how the great criticism of the past fulfilled these functions there is one answer that is clear. The great critical documents in our language are also political acts—or call all political action in question. Johnson, Arnold, Wordsworth, Yeats—they work to reinforce an existing culture, or to change its direction, or to establish a new and different culture. Their field is the field of letters and they employ its proper skills; but their work is also part of an ideology, and it is from this that it draws its strength. Our recent criticism, with all its variety of accomplishments, has lacked this source of strength. It is only part of an institution, or part of nothing at all. If the sphere of criticism is to be more restricted than it was in earlier expectations, it is the more essential that it shall not work in isolation, that it shall be part of a general enterprise of intelligence and imagination. It has been so in France, in our own day; but not in England.

Looking back over the Sartre period in France, now I suppose ended, it is not hard to see both intellectual and moral absurdities. The obstinate abstraction from immediate realities, the habit of living on the moral capital of the Resistance, the obsession with defining a shade of difference from the Communist Party while claiming credit for being on its side—these are not much to be admired. The reverse McCarthyism which leads Sartre to announce his undying belief that all anti-communists are dogs is merely detestable. And it is not a matter for self-congratulation to discover with agonies of disillusionment facts about the USSR that only a wilful self-blinding can have failed to make obvious before. Yet I can only write these words with reluctance, because the passion and intelligence released by Sartre's often perverse commitments is so great, and so much to be envied by a country that has had nothing like it. It is not an example that Arnold would have enjoyed, but it would be hard to find a better example of his desideratum that the critical power should 'make an intellectual situation of which the creative power can profitably avail itself.' One must always allow for mediocrity, of which we have a great deal; and for the sudden efflorescence of startlingly varied powers, which is an uncovenanted mercy. But even if in England we had had a writer of Sartre's range and fertility—in philosophy, in drama, in the novel, in criticism, in polemic—a career such as his would hardly have been a possibility. In this country where ideologies are so faint, controversy so fitful and soon exhausted, the intellectual debates in which Sartre has expended himself would have died from want of opposition.

The great political controversies in *Les Temps Modernes* have a special focus that is far from what we ordinarily call criticism; but they sometimes result in criticism, of an energy and grandeur that reveal possibilities long forgotten by us. I think of the moving record of friendship and parting with Merleau-Ponty, the bitter and deeply felt 'Réponse à Albert Camus':

> L'équilibre que vous réalisiez ne pouvait se produire qu'une seule fois, pour un seul moment, en un seul homme: vous aviez eu cette chance que la lutte commune contre les Allemands symbolisât à vos yeux et aux nôtres l'union de tous les hommes contre les fatalités inhumaines. En choisissant l'injustice, l'Allemand s'était rangé de lui-meme parmi les forces aveugles de la Nature et vous avez pu, dans *La Peste*, faire tenir son rôle par des microbes, sans que nul ne s'avisât de la mystification. Bref, vous avez été, pendant quelques années, ce que l'on pourrait appeler le symbole et la preuve de la solidarité des classes. C'est aussi ce que paraissait être la Résistance et c'est ce que vous manifestiez dans vos premières œuvres: 'Les hommes retrouvent leur solidarité pour entrer en lutte contre leur destin revoltant.'

We have had our struggles too in the last thirty years, but we have not had any critical writing like this. (There are, now I recall it, some imitations; but of such repellent spuriousness that one goes back with

relief to Thematic Patterns in the Later Eighteenth Century Sonnet.)
The normal outcome of an intellectual dissension in England is a few
testy letters in the weekly papers.

What are the questions, serious questions, with which criticism ought
to be occupying itself, here and now? One I have mentioned in passing;
it is the question of our cultural identity. It is in danger of being lost,
and no one likes to mention it. England has not had to worry about
this before. It was the centre of a world-wide linguistic community,
and the other participants had no massively independent cultural
character of their own. Now it is no longer the cultural centre. English
literature is only a part of a body of writing in the English language, coming from several societies, the major one being the USA.
They share a language, yet each of these societies has its own character
and its own vision to present. Many pressures, most of them commercial, make it much the easiest course for us to submerge ourselves in the
much larger American mass. Do we want this to happen? Do we see
it as our destiny? Is it possible to see it otherwise? Can we retain our
intellectual independence, when political independence has been lost,
or sold, or betrayed? These are real questions and, unlike most real
questions, ones on which men of letters can have something to say.
I can respect a genuine English-speaking internationalism which
chooses to see the fate of our literature and our thought as part of the
culture of a single linguistic community, including America, Canada,
Australia and all the scattered users of the language. I can respect it,
though I do not accede to it. What no one can respect is what we
actually get: the literary pages of the Sunday papers filled each week
with reviews of American pornography; the appearance in London of
anthologies of modern English poetry filled entirely with the work of
campus poets-in-residence; the flaccid acceptance of all the dreary
baggage of the academic American-literature industry and its inflated
valuations; the automatic mid-Atlantic gabble that obscures all real
differences, all judgments, all clarity of view. Much of this springs from
economic causes over which criticism has no control; but the literary
results are something with which criticism is directly concerned, on
which it could have a direct influence if it cared to open its mouth.

If we were to consider our present cultural identity seriously we should
almost certainly be led again to question our past, to discover how
much of it still lives in us, how much of it we are prepared to stand on.
This was done, we are often told, forty years or more ago, in the work

of Eliot, Pound and their successors. Do we need to dig up the roots again so soon? It was done indeed, in a way; and the results are still evident. But it has always seemed to me that the revision and re-assessment of our literary history brought about by 'the men of 1914' was a more limited affair than is supposed. It was undertaken for the special needs of two innovating poets, both as it happens Americans, one with a cranky relation to English society, the other with none at all. Their interest was in a special area of poetry, very little in other kinds of literature. It is to the credit of the English literary mind that it responded so quickly to Pound's and Eliot's hatred of the stuffy and the sham, to their sharp sense of unfamiliar poetical excellences; and heaven knows at that time it was in no state to do the re-assessment for itself. But this *was* half a century ago; the spiritual disorder after the first world war was only a rehearsal for the far graver disorder of recent years. Cultural discontinuities now become so deep that we must soon either lose most of our past (to archaeology and the museum basement), or sift and take possession of it anew, in a much more fundamental way than that of the last generation. This will not be done by men past middle age formed on traditional literary habits; and speaking as one of them I cannot imagine what the outcome is likely to be. But I would rather see a purposeful spring-cleaning than a mere letting-go.

VI

I spoke in passing of the want of a methodology for criticism, and I can hardly do more here than sketch an elliptical abstract of what was in my mind. I have suggested that in present conditions criticism can no longer see its role as that of a privileged busybody, using literature as a base from which to pronounce on all other departments of life. Sartre may seem to be a contrary example; but his real base (as with most continental critics) is in philosophy—in a great international philosophical movement to which he has made powerful and original contributions. For a variety of reasons a phenomenon of this kind is not likely to occur with us. But I cannot think that criticism can continue to live on descriptive techniques and personal responses alone. On this basis it will soon meet the impasse which Wittgenstein describes as 'running out of problems'. The most promising role for criticism today is that of one humanist discipline among others, widely available to readers who care to take the trouble, but with a method and a purpose of its own sufficiently powerful to give it an authority beyond the mere individual *ipse dixit*. Criticism now needs at least to know its sphere of operation, and the kind of operation that is possible within it. Surrounded on all sides by new varieties of the human sciences, none of them manifestly irrelevant, it is apt to clutch desperately at whatever fragments of anthropology, psychology, sociology and linguistics happen to come within reach. Since literature deals with everything, this is the fate of critics, and they must make what they can of it. But they could with advantage decide what other kinds of knowledge are closest to their interests and are most likely to attach them to the main currents of thought in their time.

One choice is obvious. Critics deal with language, with structures of thought and feeling that only exist so far as they are embodied in language. It is bound to go on to areas where it has no special privilege: that is its hazardous borderland. But its own territory is the literary language. The concern with language is inescapable.

> Hardly are those words out
> When a vast image out of Spiritus Mundi
> Troubles my sight

—for is there not a science of linguistics, huge, intricate and ever-growing, eager to extend its empire over every contiguous discipline? It has been claimed that linguistics should provide the model on which all adjacent studies are to be based; and it is willing, only too willing, to come to the aid of criticism. Some of our best friends are linguists; and it would be mistaken to reject this offer out of hand. But criticism would be wise to accept it only on conditions, and with strict reserve. I wish to maintain at the same time that the primary concern of criticism is with language, and that only a minor part of scientific linguistics is relevant to that concern. The concern of criticism with language is both narrower and wider than that of linguistics. Linguistics is an interconnected, systematic study; the illuminations it can bring to criticism are fragmentary and partial. Chomsky is reported recently to have ended a lecture on transformational grammar by saying 'I now come to the question that is trembling on all your lips: What has this to do with literature? I can reassure you: nothing whatever.' I am willing to accept his authority. Semantics in some of its departments is of critical interest. Jakobson's distinction between metaphor and metonymy and his projection of it into larger areas of discourse is of obvious literary importance. But *la langue* in general, the system of language, is not an object of investigation for criticism; it is a datum. It is the linguistics of *la parole*, individual utterance under the pressure of needs, wishes, hopes, that criticism is mainly concerned with; and this forms only a small part of the modern science. But it is also true to say that the interest of criticism in language is wider than that of linguistics. Most of the work of criticism begins with the more complex and elaborately structured elements of language, elements above the level of the sentence that linguistics does not deal with. Criticism is concerned mainly with the structure of large, continuous bodies of discourse. Even such things as 'characters', 'plots', 'descriptions' are structures of language, and criticism should be capable of dealing with them as such; but linguistics has nothing to say about them. There is real need for an enquiry into the literary applications of linguistics; but it will not be met by saddling the student of literature with a weight of science that has entirely different objects from his own.

Criticism has undoubtedly suffered from linguistic ignorance. The new criticism of the twenties and after professed a closer engagement with the workings of language than the old-fashioned belles-lettres. But if we observe the development of the movement we cannot help seeing how fragmentary and capricious its dealings with language have been. This has been damaging in several ways. It has led to confusion of terminology and concepts, to perpetual fresh starts, without any building up of a consistent scheme of knowledge. It has led to the proliferation of innumerable methodological contraptions, many of them of an ingenious charm, but obviously home-made, run up for the occasion without reference to any coherent and generally valid order. Above all it has led to the scandal of amateurism and indirection that still hangs around literary criticism in the judgment of philosophers, historians and natural scientists. I think this scandal ought to be dispelled: not as a matter of public relations or out of a desire for scientific respectability, and certainly not out of a belief that criticism is or ought to be a science. But it ought to be a more cooperative and progressive activity than it is; and it will have to become so if it is to hold a place in the general intellectual economy. It is a present necessity for criticism to define its concern with language and to find means for actualizing it. To do this it will no doubt need to borrow concepts and methods from linguistics. But it had better do the borrowing itself, in the full knowledge of its own needs, rather than take over wholesale an intricate apparatus designed for other purposes.

Criticism so conceived—as a study of literary language—both pays its tribute to the autonomy of literature and defines an area where it can speak with special knowledge. But the autonomy of literature is relative; and there is another requirement that seems to impose itself. Criticism should be able to give some intelligible account of the relation of literature to the social order. There is a methodology for this, and so far as I know there is only one. To think on this subject at all requires some application of Marxism—a proposition that will not be obvious to anyone acquainted only with English Marxist criticism. That indeed puts little strain on the theoretic powers, and brings correspondingly little illumination. Its confusions and inadequacies have been well analysed by Raymond Williams.[4] The situation is different elsewhere. I am not thinking so much of a book like Arnold Hauser's *Social History of Art*, which for all its massive erudition merely attempts to make a simple one-way correspondence between particular social conditions and the literature that comes out of them. It is to Lukacs's studies of the novel, where insight into historical causality is used to illustrate the inner structure of the work itself, that we go for something deeper than socio-economic determinism. To Lukacs, and to Goldmann's work on Pascal and Racine, extravagant but also profound. And to Sartre's criticism, penetrated with Marxist ideas employed in new and highly original ways. Marxist interpretation of the arts has been vulgarized to aridity and platitude; it has been adopted from political attachment and evaded from political disapprobation; but it is inescapably part of twentieth-century literary equipment. It is not of course unfamiliar in England, but it has never been absorbed into the general literary consciousness as, say, psychoanalysis has been, probably because there is in England a powerful Socialism of a distinctively non-Marxist kind. It is notable that Raymond Williams, our principal social critic of literature, though a long-term revolutionary, is not a Marxist and writes from a wholly different moral point of view. But the revolutionary implications of Marxism are not in question; it is a question of using Marxist theory as, say, Karl Mannheim does in the sociologx of knowledge—without commitment to the doctrine in its

---

[4] *Culture and Society* (1958), part III, chapter 5.

totality. The chief Marxist critics do in fact make this total commitment; but the value of their work for the interpretation of literature is
independent of it. One would be ill-equipped to write on the language
of symbolism without a knowledge of *The Interpretation of Dreams*. But
this does not entail an acceptance of Freud's view on the aetiology of
the neuroses.

Orthodox Marxist criticism, of which I suppose Lukacs's work on
the novel is the most impressive example, suffers from one great
deficiency. It passes too quickly to the larger narrative and historical
structures and does not take the fact of language sufficiently into account. In Lukacs's chapter on Scott, for example, we find a profound
analysis of the narrative structure of the novels as a revelation of historical forces, but no real acknowledgment that this has been achieved
only in a structure of language. He talks helplessly about 'colourful and
varied richness'. The major form and meaning of the novels is revealed
as it is nowhere else—but from a distance. The relation of the elementary facts of writing to the totality is never brought about. To perceive
and explain this relation is indeed a task of extreme difficulty. The most
heroic attempt I have met to see art as an intelligible product of social
forces while still doing full and minute justice to its actual creative
procedure is Max Raphael's uncompleted study *The Demands of Art*.
His theme is painting; we have nothing like it for literature. Auerbach's
Mimesis might suggest the methods that might be used. But it is a huge
enterprise that criticism has hardly yet engaged with. If criticism looks
like running out of problems here is one that is almost untouched.

I began by quoting Barthes, and it was for a reason. Those few
sentences of his are an indication that writing is both a spontaneous
individual expression and a willed social commitment made under
defined historical conditions. Barthes has called himself a para-Marxist,
and his attitude here is far from the socio-economic determinism that
is commonly associated with Marxist criticism. Fundamentally *Le
degré zéro de l'écriture* brings us against the paradox that lies at the
centre of Marx's interpretation of culture. It is that Marx can say,
between the covers of the same book, that all cultural superstructures,
of which art is one, are determined by the material basis; and yet 'that
certain periods of highest development of art stand in no direct relationship with the general development of society, nor with the
material basis.'[5] A brisk positivism could decide that these opposed

[5] Karl Marx, *A Contribution to the Critique of Political Economy* (1904).

sentences simply cancel each other out, and that to say both of them is to say nothing at all. On the contrary, it is to state the fundamental problem which criticism now has to solve.

Note

The ontological or 'internal' approach to literary art and the counter approaches converge from the whole literary horizon. My exposition will be best served if some of my references occur in footnotes. Some of the essays collected in my *Verbal Icon* (Lexington, Kentucky, 1954) touch earlier phases of holistic or internal 'contextualist' criticism in modern English studies. Here I list a few recent works which survey recent developments and some which have contributed most directly to the shape of the argument I here attempt. Section I: Murray Krieger, *The Tragic Vision: Variations on a Theme in Literary Interpretation* (New York, 1960) and *A Window to Criticism: Shakespeare's 'Sonnets' and Modern Poetics* (Princeton, 1964) survey essential difficulties for this criticism. Ingo Seidler, 'The Iconolatric Fallacy: On the Limitations of the Internal Method of Criticism', *Journal of Aesthetics and Art Criticism* XXVI (Fall 1967), pp. 9–15, shows some recent parallels between two largely independent national areas of debate, the American and German; Edgar Lohner, 'The Intrinsic Method', in *The Disciplines of Criticism: Essays in Literary Theory, Interpretation, and History* edited by Peter Demetz *et al.* (New Haven, 1968), expands the perspective to take in Russian and Czech formalism and even French *explication* since 1902. Lee T. Lemon, *The Partial Critics* (New York, 1965), chapters V and VI, surveys the same difficulties as Murray Krieger. And see Graham Hough, *An Essay on Criticism* (1966), especially chapters III and XXII, on formalism and the 'metaphor' of 'organic form'.

In section III, expounding current notions of 'context' as external, the boundless milieu of the literary work, I refer to the symposium on literary criticism held at Yale in 1965. Six articles from it are in *Modern Language Notes* LXXXI(5) (December 1966): see especially Geoffrey Hartman, 'Beyond Formalism' and J. Hillis Miller, 'The Antitheses of Criticism: Reflections on the Yale Colloquium'. I go on to refer to J. Hillis Miller's 'The Geneva School', *Critical Quarterly* VIII (Winter 1966), pp. 305–21; see also A. E. Dyson's editorial welcome in this issue; Miller's book *The Disappearance of God: Five Nineteenth Century Writers* (Cambridge, Mass., 1963); and Sarah N. Lawall, *Critics of Consciousness: The Existential Structure of Literature* (Cambridge, Mass., 1968), with chapters on six Geneva critics and one on J. Hillis Miller.

For my reference in section IV to developments in post-Bloomfieldian linguistics, see, e.g., Archibald A. Hill, 'Linguistics since Bloomfield', *Quarterly Journal of Speech* XLI (October 1955), pp. 253–60; 'An Analysis of *The Windhover*: An Experiment in Structural Method', *Publications of the Modern Language Association* LXX (December 1955), pp. 968–78; and ' "Pippa's Song": Two Attempts at Structural Reading' in *Readings in Applied English Linguistics* edited by Harold B. Allen (New York, 1958). At the end of this section I discuss

III

Battering the Object:
The Ontological Approach

W. K. WIMSATT

To what base uses we may return, Horatio! Why may not
imagination trace the noble dust of Alexander till 'a find it stopping a bunghole?

'Twere to consider too curiously, to consider so. (*Hamlet* V. i)

THE QUESTION about the correct, or most plausible, object of literary
study blurs today into the question whether such a question can be
correctly asked. The best short statement of this modern problem that
I know appears near the end of Murray Krieger's book *The Tragic
Vision*. From a richly elegiac thirteen pages lamenting the demise of
American 'formalist' criticism, I select a few eloquent enough sentences.

structuralism; see *Structuralism*, *Yale French Studies* 36-7 (October 1966), on
structuralism in anthropology, psychoanalysis, linguistics and literary criticism,
with valuable annotated bibliographies—and especially the essays by André
Martinet, 'Structure and Language'; Geoffrey Hartman, 'Structuralism: The
Anglo-American Adventure'; and Michael Riffaterre, 'Describing Poetic
Structures: Two Approaches to Baudelaire's *Les Chats*'. Also see Roman
Jakobson and Claude Lévi-Strauss, 'Les Chats de Charles Baudelaire', *L'Homme*
II (1962), pp. 5-21; Jakobson's 'Two Aspects of Language and Two Types of
Aphasic Disturbance', *Fundamentals of Language* ('S-Gravenhage, 1956), pp. 64-
72 (reprinted as 'The Cardinal Dichotomy in Language' in *Language: An
Enquiry into its Meaning and Function* edited by Ruth Nanda Anshen, New York,
1957); and his 'Closing Statement: Linguistics and Poetics', in *Style in Language*
edited by Thomas Sebeok (New York, 1960), the proceedings of a conference
held at Indiana University in 1958. In the collection *The Disciplines of Criticism*,
cited above, see F. W. Bateson, 'Linguistics and Literary Criticism' and
W. K. Wimsatt, 'Genesis: A Fallacy Revisited'. The contextual relations of the
'intensional' poetic object are discussed in terms of English philosophy of
language by John Casey, *The Language of Criticism* (1966), especially pp. 1,
12, 27-8, 100 and 162.

Organicism and inviolability of context being matters of kind and not of degree, poetry must be seen as a form of discourse in some sense nonreferential even as it must be in some sense referential to be a form of discourse at all.

This dilemma seems to me to represent the crucial point, if not the dead end, reached by modern criticism.

Future theorists who will want to preserve the gains of . . . these critics and who will not want to see them washed away into the common stream of Platonic theory will have to find a way to keep poetry's contextual system closed; to have the common materials which enter poetry—conventions of word meaning, of propositional relations, and of literary forms—so transmuted in the creative act with its organic demands that they come out utterly unique.[1]

These passages stress the problem of distinguishing the poem as a separable and knowable object amid the welter of our complex experience both real and verbal, rather than the complementary or closely dependent problem with which Krieger in this book—arguing 'Manichaean' versus 'Platonic' choices—is mainly concerned, that of the truth and value of the conceptual patterns necessarily implicated in the structure of the knowable object. The former problem, that of knowledge of the object (or in loftier language, epistemology), is what I am here directly concerned with.

The development of this little knot of ideas has been no less slow, roundabout, and gradual than that of most ideas. But for our present purpose, I believe only four critical moments need be distinguished. The first two of these are separated from each other by about a century. The third and fourth, following hard upon the second, are occurring simultaneously today. It is on these that I will mainly dwell.

I

The modern idea of the art work as a separately existent and in some sense autonomous or autotelic entity is closely tied to the idea of a vital organic form. A squirrel running in a tree and the rooted tree are more respectable and convincing *things* than a chunk of crumbling clay or even a hard piece of rock broken off a mountain side. That much is Aristotelian. But the modern status and emphasis of the idea

[1] Krieger, *The Tragic Vision*, pp. 236–7.

was achieved only in the era of Romantic art and nature theory. The full image of organic form in poetry had its seedbed and first growth in the tropical rain-forest of eighteenth-century *naturphilosophie* and early scientific accounts and drawings of living forms, the biological world of Kant, Goethe, Schelling, Coleridge and Keats. Organicism was a literary content, a very material subject matter (as in Erasmus Darwin's *Botanical Garden*), for several decades before it became the rarefied metaphysics of a theory of aesthetic knowledge and form. Coleridge, with an eye intent both on living nature and on Shakespeare, specified five characteristics of biological form and hence implicitly, and in part explicitly, of the art work. He said in effect that works of art, like living organisms, were wholes (not assemblages of parts—'The parts are nothing'). Art works grew like living plants, assimilating diverse elements into their own substance. They were shaped from within, not by external pressures or moulds. The parts were inter-dependent ('interinanimating').[2] This has remained a classic and much respected account. Certain locally brilliant parts of poems (couplets or soliloquies) the modeller's clay, the sculptor's stone and chisel, the noise of the typewriter or the smell of cooking, the moulds of bronze statues (even like those of sugar cookies and aspic jellies), the inter-dependence of two children on a seesaw—notions such as these may stir, if we let them, some questions about that metaphoric complex. But it will be scarcely on these grounds that we care to prolong the discussion.[3]

II

The practical position elaborated by the American New Critics in essays of the late nineteen thirties and the forties had been earlier

[2] The evidence in Coleridge's *On Poesy or Art*, Shakespeare Lectures, *Table Talk*, *Philosophical Lectures*, and *Treatise on Method* has recently been reassembled by Philip C. Ritterbush, *The Art of Organic Forms* (City of Washington: Smithsonian Institution Press, 1968), pp. 19-21. In his book-length introduction to this catalogue of an exhibition of modern pictures and sculptures (Odilon Redon, *c.* 1905—Catharine Homan, 1968), Ritterbush argues, interestingly, that the universal of organic form is nowadays being realized by both science and art at the submicroscopic level.

[3] See the issue discussed in the idiom of general aesthetics by Richard Peltz, 'Ontology and the Work of Art', *Journal of Aesthetics and Art Criticism* XXIV (Summer 1966), pp. 487-99; and, in response to Peltz, Patrick A. E. Hutchings, 'Works of Art and the Ontology of Analogy', *Philosophical Studies* XVI (1967), pp. 82-103.

asserted with great dramatic force and a tenacious strategy by I. A. Richards in the first part of his *Practical Criticism* (1929), a sort of machine or trap constructed out of experiments he had undertaken at Cambridge—upon poems with students, and upon students with poems. It was an implication, though scarcely a demonstration, of Richards's book that a good poem could be distinguished from a bad one by resolute examination of its internal relations, joined from outside only by a 'sincere' response of the reader's whole personality. The thirteen anonymous, untitled and undated poems selected for display (along with choice betrayals, 'protocols', by his students, and a limited number of sly intimations by Richards himself) may begin to assume, if one revisits them in the context of today's debates, somewhat the appearance of a collection of small mammals, birds and insects, with perhaps a fossil, a stick or a stone thrown in for good measure, each exposed under a vacuum jar, with instructions to pupils from a presiding scientist: 'Examine thoroughly and determine which are alive.' Yet they did not look that way to an interested young generation of academics in the nineteen thirties. Perhaps they do not altogether look that way now. Not many, I imagine, of the most resolute external–contextual critics today would maintain that under the artificially purified conditions of Richards's experiment they would honestly be unable to discern any difference in point, tone, poetic entity (and poetic value) between the first stanza of Richards's Poem IV,

> There was rapture of spring in the morning
> When we told our love in the wood.
> For you were the spring in my heart, dear lad,
> And I vowed that my life was good.

and the first four lines of his Poem III,

> At the round earth's imagined corners blow
> Your trumpets, angels, and arise, arise
> From death you numberless infinities
> Of souls, and to your scattered bodies go.

III

Given the extreme vulnerability of father figures, the instructions of Freud, and the consequent awareness that has prevailed in the academic world of our time, it was not to be expected that the stance of the

American New Critics, even at its most convincing, could turn into anything like a stasis, or that their ideas could enjoy anything like so long a reign as those of the preceding entrenchment of historicism. The explosion of the academic population in the post-war period and the consequently appalling escalation of publishing efforts have worked towards the same revolutionary result. New persons, new professional generations, need new platforms. Pound's injunction to the poet has been found equally cogent advice for the ambitious critic. Positive programmes have to be ushered in by protests too, which may be the louder and more easily defined part of the doctrine. Critics under fifty years of age today are very likely, on one occasion or another, to have voiced their distress at the wave of Alexandrian pedantries, the merely mechanical applications of 'Anglo-Saxon formalism', that have followed on the vogue of the New Critical theory. It would appear that exegesis is 'our Whore of Babylon, sitting robed in Academic black on the great dragon of Criticism, and dispensing a repetitive and soporific balm from her pedantic cup.'[4]

In a report on a symposium of young scholars held at Yale University a few years ago, we encounter the complacent announcement that 'native formalism' and its chief antagonist of but yesterday, the archetypal system of Northrop Frye, no longer 'figure centrally' in wise deliberations. There is hostility to neither. But their lessons can be taken for granted. The next inspirations will come from Europe. The director of the symposium was a member of the Yale French department. Most of the participants were 'European trained' or at least were teachers in departments of romance language or comparative literature. The commentator whom I have been quoting was J. Hillis Miller, Professor of English at the Johns Hopkins University. We have Hillis Miller's report in another place, at about the same moment, on what has come to be known as the 'Geneva School'[5] of French criticism, whose heritage runs back immediately through the *Nouvelle Revue*

----

[4] *Modern Language Notes* LXXXI, p. 556.

[5] J. Hillis Miller, 'The Geneva School', *Critical Quarterly* VIII (Winter 1966), pp. 305–21. The critics of the Geneva orientation are: Marcel Raymond (b. 1897), Albert Béguin (1901–1957), Georges Poulet (b. 1902), Jean Rousset (b. 1910), Jean Starobinski (b. 1920), Jean-Pierre Richard (b. 1922). Poulet and Starobinski have held posts at the Johns Hopkins University, 1952–1957, 1954–1956. See another account by Laurent Le Sage, 'The New French Literary Critics', *The American Society Legion of Honor Magazine* XXXVII (1966), pp. 75–86.

C

Française and certain nineteenth-century English figures to Romanticism—and is ultimately, I should think, Longinian. 'Consciousness of consciousness', the critic's consciousness of the author's consciousness, in an identical transparency—this makes or is criticism. It is union of subject with another subject, spiritual activity—almost angelic. The *work* of literature as objectified by Aristotelian conceptualism is only an opaque obstacle. Nothing less than a whole consciousness, diffused through a whole canon of expressions, both the complete and the fragmentary, the deliberate and the accidental, will assuage that yearning for communion. At the same time (and paradoxically, in spite of a necessary self-effacement on the part of the critic in the presence of his author), criticism is the pursuit of the critic's own spiritual adventure (as in days gone by, with some differences, for Anatole France and for Oscar Wilde). It is a secondary artistic act, a genre of creative literature, faithful to the native Swiss tradition of meditation, reverie, confession, in the manner of Rousseau, Sénancour, Constant, Amiel, Ramuz.

In a volume of studies in nineteenth-century English literature, *The Disappearance of God*, Hillis Miller had already put example before the precepts delivered apropos of the Yale Symposium of 1965. In a preface to a paperback edition (1965) of this work he elaborated:

> . . . it appears possible that European ways of doing criticism . . . may present themselves to Americans as alternatives to the creation of another indigenous criticism . . . assimilating the advances of European criticism in the past twenty years, but reshaping them to our peculiarly American experience of literature and its powers.

'If literature is a form of consciousness,' his original hardback preface had expounded, 'the task of the critic is to identify himself with the subjectivity expressed in the words, to relive that life from the inside, and to constitute it anew in his criticism.' A concluding long chapter of *The Disappearance of God*, on Gerard Manley Hopkins, is perhaps the book's most ample illustration of the Genevan method transplanted to the literary experience of the USA. Poems, devotions, undergraduate notes, journals, letters, essays, 'late' and 'early', are pulverized and reassembled in a mainly *a*-chronological dialectic. We inspect the reconstruction of a mind—one specially isolated in acute consciousness of the 'taste' of itself, yet restlessly yearning through the manifold inscapes and instresses, the metaphors, the rhyming and chiming, of a

diversely dappled world of words and poetry, towards the harmony
of a sense of immanence of God in nature and the human soul. The
emphasis is recurrently and emphatically on the manifold. The helter-
skelter, the staccato and dappling of the Hopkins experience, the stip-
pling of the fragmentary record, make him an ideal example for this
kind of exposition by shredding or atomization. A fine mist of the
mind of Hopkins is generated. A critic of some old-fashioned biographical school (from whose clutches modern American critical discourse, by the way, was liberated by no other than the New Critics)
might well complain that here we are given very little shape or line
of a life, or even of any mental career, very little contour, episode,
approach or climax. This sort of shape by shapelessness no doubt bears
some relation of counterpart to the orthodox Genevan inattention to
the author's own achieved poetic shapes. 'Glory be to God for dappled
things . . . Praise him.' This one exquisite curtal-sonnet *Pied Beauty* is
examined with considerable loving care, for the critic looks on it as a
kind of synopsis or emblem of the Hopkins rhyming consciousness. It
seems equally a good emblem, in its asserted meaning, if not in its
cunning form, of the critical method being demonstrated.

Murray Krieger is another American professor who of recent years
has been watching the Geneva critics very closely and sympathetically
—though with a good deal of artful capacity to resist them. Two of his
most recent lectures, addressed to a Johns Hopkins University Humanities Seminar in the spring of 1968,[6] dilate on that notion of the poem
as a conceptual obstruction arising between the critic and the pure
consciousness of the author. The dissolution of such a mediate entity,
all too successfully promoted by critics of the Genevan inclination, is a
very narrowly averted outcome towards which Krieger's own dialectic
has often led him in spite of himself. He points in passing to the extreme impatience of the American Ihab Hassan, who in his flight from
the poetic object nearly but not quite asserts the nihilism of silence.
(Here too might have come a distinguished voice of silence from
Cambridge, England, that of George Steiner, and here also that of
Susan Sontag, New York dissenter from *Interpretation*.) At heart

---

[6] *Mediation, Language, and Vision—and the Reading of Literature*, Lectures I
and II, at the Johns Hopkins University, May 1968, typescript. I am profoundly
indebted to Professor Krieger for his kindness in letting me read these lectures
before publication—in *Interpretation: Theory and Practice*, edited by Charles S.
Singleton (Baltimore, 1969).

Krieger does not want this destruction. And now again, as in his *Window to Criticism* (1964), he invokes the last-minute miraculous analogy of a closed poetic room of 'mutually reflecting mirrors' opening (presto!) so many windows back to outside reality. Or he has a newer formula: The poem is both 'discourse' and 'thing' and as such 'is motion and is in motion. Yet it is motion in stillness, the stillness that is at once still moving and forever still.'[7] Thou still unravished bride of quietness! The extreme anti-mediators of the Geneva School, chief among them Georges Poulet, have dwelt much on the theme of 'time', that Bergsonian interior dimension in which consciousness, the human dynamism, has its true being and movement—in contrast to those coldly spatialized objective mediations into which Platonists and New Critics, formalists all, would harden poems.

The more narrow the escape from the flux of time, as Murray Krieger sees it, the better. One can earn one's right to the poem as entity only by first confronting and accepting its literal non-entity. Those who are not brave enough to run that risk and whose skill is hence never really tested make up the numerous and diverse ranks of the critics who nowadays more than ever indulge in over-mediation or materialization of the poetic object. The point seems well taken. We can repeat the distinction along national and cultural lines. Here, in this garden of the definable mediate categories, though Krieger politely refrains from urging it, are to be located the present very flourishing crop of American home-grown disguises of the poetic object. The debate of the late nineteen fifties in America between the old New Critical assertors of the poem and the new archetypists and mythopoeists and their demi-allies the demonic visionaries (a kind of Pyrrhic victory for the latter, in that they gained much ground but were consumed in their own heat) has been followed among younger critics by a phase of frenzied bolting and grabbing for the most tangible and durable equipment in sight on the historical shelf. In this new era one book urges the revolutionary argument that the long-overlooked and only correct key to the reading of Chaucer lies in medieval rhetoric, and another finds the same key in a so-far unsuspected deep

[7] Krieger develops this idea at greater length in his essay 'The Ecphrastic Principle and the Still Movement of Poetry; or *Laokoön* Revisited', in *The Poet as Critic* edited by Frederick P. W. McDowell (Evanston, Illinois, 1967), pp. 3–25; reprinted in Krieger's *The Play and Place of Criticism* (Baltimore, 1967), pp. 105–28.

affinity of Chaucer for the geometry of medieval architecture.[8] Another book, written in a vein of super-annotation which the author's mentor the Hopkins Professor Earl Wasserman has had much to do with developing, demonstrates that Pope's Horatian poems ought to be read, image by image, not only in the perspective of Horatian satire and epistle but in that of Renaissance commentary on Horace— *Horace moralisé*.[9] 'There is no rational and methodological concept, no attempted translucent universal,' I have ventured in another essay, 'which is not capable of being transformed, and very quickly, into an opaque historical gimmick.' Let me add now that there is no opaque gimmick or dead piece of critical history which is not capable of a galvanic revival when rediscovered by a seminar in search of vehicles, and perhaps by scholars too intent on the future to have been vividly aware of a former demise. One will think now especially of the recent programmes for literary 'genre' (shades of Brunetière, Babbitt, Croce!), which spring up like chestnut saplings round the venerable blighted grey trunk of the Chicago School of Neo-Aristotelianism. Genre, which was once a classical norm for censures and exclusions, which has always been a needed part of the literary historian's descriptive vocabulary, and which under New Critical auspices has recently been usefully invoked as a part of a poet's language or frame of reference enabling his own expressive departures, is now rediscovered in German handbooks and becomes a part of liberal historical perspective and critical method and as such a norm for explanations, inclusions, and critical tolerance. Samuel Johnson's *History of Rasselas* has characters who speak throughout like philosophical puppets and pompous pedants, and yet it is a successful tale and—as most of us would say— justly celebrated. How does Johnson bring off this stylistic feat? The answer is to be found in the fact that *Rasselas* is not a novel but an apologue. An apologue had its own rules, and these provided for and led to the expectation of abstractive and moralistic language.[10] A group

[8] Respectively, Robert O. Payne, *The Key of Remembrance, A Study of Chaucer's Poetics* (New Haven, 1963); and Robert M. Jordan, *Chaucer and the Shape of Creation, The Aesthetic Possibilities of Inorganic Structure* (Cambridge, Mass., 1967).

[9] Thomas E. Maresca, *Pope's Horatian Poems* (Columbus, Ohio, 1966). See G. S. Rousseau's trenchant review of this book, *Philological Quarterly* XLVII (July 1968), pp. 407–9.

[10] Sheldon Sacks, *Fiction and the Shape of Belief: A Study of Henry Fielding with Glances at Swift, Johnson and Richardson* (Berkeley and Los Angeles, 1964),

of young scholars centring at the Chicago Circle branch of the University of Illinois have recently begun the publication of a journal entitled *Genre*. They have sponsored a forum on genre at the 1967 Modern Language Association meeting in Chicago; and they have published (No. 3, July 1968) a symposium on a new treatise on hermeneutics, *Validity in Interpretation* (1967), by Professor E. D. Hirsch, of the University of Virginia. In a long chapter of this book Donald Hirsch spirals around the term 'genre' a series of momentary concepts, excluding the fixed broad definitions of the traditional literary genres and moving towards a plane *just* above and all but identical with the unique meaning of each work—or perhaps in fact identical with that and tautological. Hirsch thinks he can keep the 'genre' apart from each work but close enough so that he can operate a rule that correct interpretation depends on knowing the genre. I doubt that he can. I think that in all broader (and usual) senses of the term 'genre' we discover the genre of a work by being able to read it, and not vice versa. I cite this instance of Hirsch's reasoning because it seems to me to be, like Krieger's, one of the more subtle and valiant (though I think mistaken) current attempts to lay hands on, without destroying, the poem's delicate mediate status between poet and reader. Under bushes in the garden behind an old house near my office lies a small slab of stone bearing the inscription:

LOTTERY

NOV. 25, 1889.

LOVING

FELLOW-CREATURE

About midway of my interpretation of this document (starting from the bottom) I conjecture the genre in the broad sense; this helps with the rest of the interpretation; and this in turn leads to near certainty about the genre in a broad sense and to a highly plausible conjecture about a more narrow sense. If a dog was acquired in a lottery and named for that reason, it might well be that the date of the birth was not known.

---

especially pp. 49–60. René Wellek, 'Genre Theory, the Lyric, and "Erlebnis",' *Festschrift für Richard Alewyn* (Köln, 1967), pp. 392–412, reviews two modern German revivals of genre methodology—Emile Staiger, *Grundbegriff der Poetik* (1946) and Käte Hamburger, *Logik der Dichtung* (1957).

IV

The third moment in our modern history of the poem as entity, that of reaction and rejection which we have just seen, has been simultaneous with a fourth, a phase of the last fifteen or twenty years which emerges with a continuing activity of the old New Criticism (as in Cleanth Brooks's manorial *William Faulkner: the Yoknapatawpha Country*, 1963) and which has been strengthened by developments in post-Bloomfieldian American linguistics and more recently by arrivals from a second tradition of continental criticism, identifiable most readily, if so far somewhat vaguely, under the name of 'structuralism'. The contemporary Parisian vogue or energy called 'structuralism' is a manifold: 'structuralism' is anthropological, it is psychological, it is linguistic, it is (in perhaps its least developed extension) critico-literary. Literary structuralism descends along fairly obvious lines from the Russian formalism of the world war I era (expounded for the English-speaking world by Victor Erlich in 1955),[11] and from the immediately post-war Prague Linguistic Circle.[12] Today it is increasingly enveloped and merged with general linguistics. Neither the Slavic background and authority nor the marked literary bent of the most eminent of contemporary linguists, Roman Jakobson, are to be seen as accidents. 'Formalism' having been converted into a bad thing by Marxist censures, the term 'structuralism' has evolved into the acceptable European equivalent. Even some critics of Genevan or Baltimorean orientation incline towards some kind of 'structure' (or 'structuralism'). They look on these as better terms than 'form' (or 'formalism'), because 'structure' can be reconciled with temporal experience and hence with the essentially romantic subjectivism and dynamism of the human consciousness, whereas 'form', as we have seen, is spatial and external conceptualization.[13] For Murray Krieger, even 'structuralism' is too much like New Critical formalism and is hence an enemy, one of the 'over-mediators'.[14]

[11] Victor Erlich, *Russian Formalism: History-Doctrine* ('S-Gravenhage, 1955). And see Tzvetan Todorov, *Théorie de la littérature; Textes des Formalistes russes reunis, présentés et traduits* (Paris, 1955)—with a *Préface, Vers une Science de L'Art Poétique*, by Roman Jakobson.

[12] Paul L. Garvin, *A Prague School Reader on Esthetics, Literary Structure, and Style* (Washington D.C., 1955) (an anthology of translations from the Czech).

[13] See Hillis Miller in *Modern Language Notes* LXXXI, 562, 569-70.

[14] Lecture I at Hopkins, 1968. (See note 6 above.) Krieger's idiom often

At this point I interject a few homespun observations—about objects of study, their contexts, and their status.

We know that literary study sometimes focusses (1) on an age or an aspect of an age, an audience or a genre (baroque, pastoral, bourgeois, tragic, paradoxical), or (2) on an author considered etiologically as the explanation of his works, or (3) on the author just as a sufficiently interesting personal object in himself (as in most literary biography), or (4) on the author as a pure translucent consciousness revealed in the canon of his works (as in the Geneva-Hopkins criticism), or (5) on the literary work itself (what we are driving towards), or (6) on some sort of parts or passages of literary works (the figures and tropes of classical rhetoric, the elemental symbols of Bachelard, the album-reading for spiritual motifs by Croce). It is no doubt never feasible or desirable to legislate anybody's preference among such objects. It may be possible, however, to observe some differences of status among them. The author Shakespeare or the author Proust, I find myself compelled to assume, is a better entity than any biography of him or any aspect of his biography, a better entity than either the age he lived in, the genre of any one of his works, or any one of his works itself—better *a fortiori* than the collection of his works. For authors, like the rest of us, are capable of absent-mindedness, of emotional off-balance, even of obtuseness, of inferior moments, of being young and callow, of growing old and weary, garrulous, repetitious. It is their extra-ordinary capacity for transcending these usual human limitations at certain intense moments of their living and working—i.e., in their individual and separate works—which makes them great authors. These remarks are intended to converge by analogy upon the question what kind of entity is enjoyed by the literary masterpiece. 'Imperial Caesar, dead and turn'd to clay, Might stop a hole to keep the wind away.' But our critics who are most scrupulously worried about the kind of status they can grant a poem (without making it something 'objective', 'spatial', merely mediatory), are never, so far as I have read, much worried about the Caesar or the Napoleon problem. We run now into an area where it is very easy to be charged with merely

---

seems to accuse poetry and criticism of an identical sin, or to imply that poetry in the end *is* whatever criticism finds itself forced to make of poetry. Structur-alism is an 'over-mediator' in the sense that it would make poetry an over-mediator.

indulging in metaphors. Yet I have noticed that the very person who objects most earnestly to spatial metaphors for the poetic entity (the urn or the icon) is likely enough to reach for the metaphor when his own crisis arrives. These critics write at moments with the air of a person finding things where they are not lost, pouncing triumphantly upon or insistently explaining difficulties that have always been evident and which have actually been the source of tension and interest in the metaphors that the theorists have contrived to circumvent them. Murray Krieger, for instance, is one who certainly demands of the theories of others a degree of literalism which he himself is far from being able to achieve in those 'magical' mirror-and-window or time-and-space moments of his own dialectic.[15] That Genevan and Bergsonian theme of conscious duration is one of the most receptive to metaphor and most demanding of it—boundless metaphoric quicksilver of the external world drawn into the vortex of the spirit's self-awareness. 'Lips that meet', 'an abyss that fills up to the brim', 'the beat of a wing', 'a firebrand', a 'sheet of water', a 'shadow', the 'chase', the 'catch', the 'folds' and 'windings' of our nature, 'the agility of the soul', 'the suppleness of thought'—what image can be imagined that could not be summoned into the utterly valid spectrum of metaphors which express the time consciousness for Pascal in only three pages of a study by Georges Poulet?[16] As an English writer once said in a much simpler classical context: 'Time is, of all modes of existence, most obsequious to the imagination.'

A poem is an utterance which bids for, or at least often receives, attention for its excellence. That is to say, it is contemplated and can be

[15] Cf. my review of Krieger's *A Window to Criticism* (1964) in *Modern Philology* LXIV (August 1966), pp. 71–4. One does not begrudge Krieger his time-and-space manipulations, so long as they are not taken too literally and triumphantly as a magic solution of any critical problem. An important service recently performed by Professor Marshall McLuhan and his associates (despite certain obscurities and oversweep in the theory, as I see it) has been their manifold (electronic) recapture of the ancient truth that not every kind of 'space' and 'environment' is visual. My own preference is to urge that some kinds of order and concept are neither visual nor spatial. The current simple dichotomy between temporal dynamics and spatial rigidity is a complacent vulgar error. See Marshall McLuhan and Harley Parker, *Through the Vanishing Point; Space in Poetry and Painting* (New York, 1968), especially pp. 238–67.

[16] *Studies in Human Time*, translated by Elliott Coleman (Baltimore, 1956), pp. 84–6. Cf. my review in *The New Scholasticism* XXXII (October 1958), pp. 523–36.

criticized and judged; it is hypostatized as an object, and metaphorically as a spatial object. We can ask what kind of rights the poem has
to be considered an object, or what kind of protection it has for its
limits and structure. And I would urge, at least, that we ought not to
talk as if the poem had to meet some kind of impossible angelic or
metaphysical standard of absolute entity—or else be considered as
nothing at all. It would seem silly to expect of the poem a kind of
hardness and self-sufficiency which the best entity we know directly—
its author the human person—himself does not have. I am thinking of
context, of course—not internal, or verbal, in Krieger's main sense, but
the external envelopment, both verbal and real, which under the drive
of our historical studies has in modern times tended to pull the poem
apart or absorb it atomically into the boundless. We might slide off
here into an emphasis on the ecology[17] or mutually modifying relation
of organism and environment—and this would suit very well in a discussion of the creative force of vision in poetry or the continually
renewing reciprocity between poems and tradition, as in the formula
of Eliot. But I am saying something easier than that Eliot's *Waste Land*
alters either the modern landscape or that of Homer. One part of
mutual modification is selection. True, there is a sense in which the
whole of the environment (that is to say, the universe) must tolerate
the organism. We read that if the earth's magnetic field ever dwindles
towards a reversal of direction, as no doubt it can, certain harmful solar
electrons and protons will get through and may well cause mutations
in the human species. Yet as I hike through the primeval forest, it is
the needle on my wrist that responds directly to the magnetic field,
and not my own bones, though these, luckily for me, are pulled by
the earth's gravity. A man's momentary states of mind, his moods,
his conversations may be even closer to the analogy we seek. Our
moments protect themselves—sometimes against very urgent outer
forces or against establishments of very long standing. It is possible to
be driving a car on a familiar but somewhat monotonously featured
road, and at a given moment not to know whether or not we have
yet come to a given village. Professor *A*, about sixty years old, is walking across the campus on a Saturday morning and encounters Professor
B, about sixty-eight years old, recently retired, on his way to some

[17] *Cf.* Harry Berger, Jr., 'The Ecology of the Mind', *The Review of Metaphysics* XVII (September 1963), pp. 109-34.

hours of fruitful work in the library. Professor *A*,' smiling ruefully: 'I am on my way to the oral examinations.' Professor *B*, cheerfully: 'I am sorry for you.' The context which explains this flicker of an exchange is the fact that for about fifteen years past these two professors have often sat together on tedious oral boards on Saturday mornings. A further context, we may be surprised to learn, is that much earlier, about thirty years earlier, Professor *B* had sat on the oral board of *A*, then himself a candidate for the Ph.D. But that earlier incident, sunk to a level of stratification where it could now be revivified only by a pointed conversational effort, is not present to the mind of either professor on this Saturday morning. It would utterly spoil their joke. Let us recall one small curious moment of the eighteenth century—that when Mrs. Malaprop gets off her expression 'as headstrong as an allegory on the banks of Nile'. There is something which Mrs. Malaprop does not know, but which the audience of London ladies and gentleman do have to know in order to get the laugh. Not allegories, but alligators, close their incisive jaws on the banks of rivers. But wait. There is something else that perhaps none of those Londoners knows—though it could be learned approximately in Johnson's *Dictionary* or in chapter XXXIX of *Rasselas*. As critics no doubt we ought to tell them or their present-day surrogates, our students. Alligators (short, broad snout, dark colour) are found in Florida or China. The kind of large saurian found on the banks of the Nile is the crocodile (long, sharp snout, greyish or greenish colour). Doesn't this enlargement of context have some bearing on Sheridan's joke on Mrs. Malaprop? Emphatically not. We had better not ever mention it again.

'Where,' asks Hillis Miller, 'does the context of a poem stop?' Where indeed? Where does it begin? What paths through the ambient does it take? At what immediate or at what remote reaches of the stratification of the abstractive sheathing of environment does the context resonate? The internal structure of the poem plays a strong role in all this. There was a student once who wrote a paper saying that a couplet by Alexander Pope, '. . . no Prelate's Lawn with Hair-shirt lined, Is half so incoherent as my Mind' (*Epistle* I. i. 165–6) ought to be read in the light of a couplet in another poem by Pope: 'Whose ample Lawns are not asham'd to feed The milky heifer and deserving steed' (*Moral Essays* IV. 185–6). Since I believe in the force of puns and all sorts of other verbal resemblances in poetry, I do not know quite how to formulate the rule of context by which I confidently reject that connection.[18] But I seek first ineluctable confrontations, only later, if at all, rules. The result of the boundless and atomically even absorption of poem in context which Hillis Miller conceives is best conveyed in his own sentences. The poem's 'relations to its surroundings radiate outward like concentric circles from a stone dropped in water. These circles multiply indefinitely until the scholar must give up in despair the attempt to make a complete inventory of them. . . . as he proceeds in his endless quest, the poem . . . gradually fades into the multitude of its associations. . . . Instead of being a self-sufficient entity, it is only a symptom of ideas or images current in the culture which generated it.'[19]

The study of language in the classical Western tradition—vocabulary, grammar, rhetoric—has all along of course been structural. There was literally nothing else it could be. The reason why contemporary linguistic studies deserve in some special sense to be called 'structural'

[18] A structural linguist might say that the range of meanings associated with *lawn* (grass) is not 'actualized' in the passage containing *lawn* (cloth).

'All very true, no doubt,' says I. A. Richards about a student remark on a word in Marvell's *Garden*, 'but not anything that the semantic texture of the language will allow the two lines to mean or that the rest of the poem will invite us to understand here. Surely a teacher-to-be should have a better sense than this of what is and is not admissible in an interpretation. What can have been happening to cause this alarming condition, this reckless disregard of all the means by which language defends itself?' ('Poetic Process and Literary Analysis', in *Style in Language*, edited by Thomas A. Sebeok, New York, 1960, p. 23.)

The so-called poetry of 'inclusion' expounded by the early Richards has never, of course, included more than a few snatches of all there is (the universe).

[19] In a note to his article, Hillis Miller refers to a then forthcoming, now published, essay of his which celebrates the doctrine of absorptionism at greater length ('Literature and Religion', in *Relations of Literary Study: Essays on Interdisciplinary Contributions* edited by James Thorpe, New York, 1967). I am not sure I understand how this ultimately unavoidable dispersion is consistent with Hillis Miller's avowed devotion to the 'novel and unique beauty' of each author to which we have already referred. If the poem fades, why doesn't the author too—in what his essay calls 'the gray dusk of historical and parahistorical generalizations'?

lies in the great advances they have made in the study of 'relations', in analysis and generalization, in the definition of linguistic entities smaller than words, and, perhaps most important of all for literary criticism, in the recognition of a wide range of implicative (iconic and diagrammatic) powers of language. This is formalism in the strictest sense. We arrive at a conception of language, not as a random or merely spontaneous accumulation of unconnected conventions, but as an emergent system of analogical and interlocking relations of expressiveness. This holds not only for the structural logic of given individual expressions,[20] but for patterns of whole languages lying in dictionary and grammar and considered as potentials for individual expressions.[21]

It is a little more than thirty years since I. A. Richards, adapting some features of Leonard Bloomfield's analysis of 'root-forming morphemes', propounded the extremely persuasive and significant rhetorical doctrine that hidden mimetic powers of words in a given language (the theme of Plato's *Cratylus*) reside neither in 'verbal magic' (favourite notion of belletristic criticism) nor in simple or direct onomatopoeic powers, but in networks of pervasive intimation—both syntactic (or present and actually heard) and paradigmatic (contextually implicit equivalents of words in a text).[22] This is a convenient juncture for the observation that the elusive word 'structure' as it is employed in the contemporary vogue is perhaps most elusive in that it is used (sometimes almost simultaneously) to refer to what we may describe broadly, with respect to any given object of attention, as both internal and external structure, the two conceived as mutually reflective—in language, 'syntactic' structure (along the line of contiguity in the utterance) and 'paradigmatic' structure (in the dimension of the enveloping

[20] For instance, the parallels (*parisosis, homoioteleuton*) observed by classical rhetoric and even nowadays a muted resource of some expository writing.

[21] Such specially morphemic or mutually mimetic word families, for instance, as *sister, brother, father, mother*, or such expressive patterns as phonemic crescendo in comparative and superlative degrees of adjectives—*big, bigger, biggest; altus, altior, altissimus*. See Roman Jakobson, 'Quest for the Essence of Language', *Diogenes* LI (1965), pp. 21–37.

[22] In the same year as Richard's *Philosophy of Rhetoric*, 1936, appeared also perhaps the earliest of the American textbooks in the new mode, Brooks, Purser and Warren's *Approach to Literature*, first published by the Louisiana State University Press, now by Appleton-Century-Crofts, and in its fourth revision.

linguistic context).[23] There is a slender but important difference between truism and the Saussurian observation that making sentences
consists in a simultaneous act of selecting words (from ranges of
similar or 'equivalent'—and at the same time more or less antithetic—
alternatives) and of combining these in associative and causal sequences
or contiguities. Roman Jakobson in a suggestive essay of 1956, 'Two
Aspects of Language and Two Types of Aphasic Disturbance', shows
how these two essential language aspects are related not only to the
classic figures of metaphor (similarity) and metonymy (contiguity) but
to two kinds of *aphasia* or pathological splits in speech performance—
elliptical racing along contiguous sequences and manifold clutter of
loose equivalences. At a conference on 'style in language' held at
Indiana University in 1958, Jakobson in his 'Closing Statement: Linguistics and Poetics' ventured this bold compression: '*The poetic function projects the principle of equivalence from the axis of selection into the
axis of combination.* Equivalence is promoted to the constitutive device
of the sequence.' The pronouncement seems specially relevant to the

[23] *Hal had his hat.* A syntactic rule of the language forbids us to say *Hal
hat his had.* But this rule can be applied in this instance only in virtue of the
phonemic structure of the English language, in which the voiceless dental *t* is
significantly distinguished from the voiced *d*.

Such systems as Cambridge anthropology and Frye's archetypes are larger
instances of 'structuralism' for those who push the mythic *exo*-structure of
stories and their societal values. See Geoffrey Hartman's brilliant essay already
cited (see *Note*), 'Structuralism: The Anglo-American Venture' especially
pp. 151–2.

Internal structure too can, of course, be viewed in larger ways than the
verbal and lyric which I am about to use as a convenient exhibit. See, for instance, Malcolm Bradbury, 'Structure', *Novel: A Forum on Fiction* I (Fall 1967),
pp. 45–52; Tzvetan Todorov's already cited (see note 11 above) collection
Théorie de la Littérature; and such essays by Todorov himself as 'Les Catégories
du récit littéraire', *Communications* VIII (1966), pp. 125–51; 'Le Récit primitif'
and 'Les Hommes-récits', *Tel-Quel: Science/Littérature* 30, 31 (Été, Automne,
1967), pp. 47–55, 64–73.

Not critical 'truth', but internal coherence or validity of the *critical* structure
(corresponding to a similar value in literature) is the emphasis of Roland
Barthes, an editor of the influential structuralist organ *Communications*; see his
clear statement 'Criticism as Language', *Times Literary Supplement,* 27 September 1963, pp. 739–40. The structuralist critic reaches out for frames of reference
for his coherencies in various places—sociological, psychoanalytic, and anthropological. See Barthes, *Critique et vérité*, Paris, 1966, a brief polemic against
Raymond Picard of the Sorbonne, and the somewhat distracted hints concerning the Parisian scene in a *Times Literary Supplement* front article, 23 June 1966.

metrical aspect of poetry (a formality which no doubt enables much else),[24] and Jakobson proceeds to make the metrical application at some length. A person interested in the poem as an object involved in transactions with both a verbal and a real external context might observe that this account implies that poetry is a very highly concentrated compression of external structure into internal.[25] In the same masterly paper, during the course of an argument illustrating the pervasiveness of the poetic 'function' in many types of language use, Jakobson throws out the following analysis of a political slogan:

> 'I like Ike' /ay/layk/ayk/, succinctly structured, consists of three monosyllables and counts three diphthongs /ay/, each of them symmetrically followed by one consonantal phoneme, /. .l. .k. .k/. The make-up of the three words presents a variation: no consonantal phonemes in the first word, two around the diphthong in the second, and one final consonant in the third. . . . Both cola of the trisyllabic formula 'I like/Ike' rhyme with each other, and the second of the two rhyming words is fully included in the first one (echo rhymes), /layk/— /ayk/, a paronomastic image of a feeling which totally envelops its object. Both cola alliterate with each other, and the first of the two alliterating words is included in the second: /ay/—/ayk/, a paronomastic image of the loving subject enveloped by the beloved object.

That was a humorous capsule—perhaps the largest illustration of a linguistic analysis we can afford to transplant. But far from the largest available. Imagine a discourse of this tenor, in its whole range (from the consonantal phonemes *l* and *k* to the loving subject enveloped by the beloved object), amplified and subtilized fifty- or a hundred-fold in an essay of sixteen pages written by Jakobson in collaboration with

[24] In a native version of this situation which I once contrived ('Verbal Style: Logical and Counterlogical', *Publications of the Modern Language Association* LXV, March 1950, pp. 5–20), metrical 'parallel' was the artifice which enabled various kinds of verbal equivalence (alliterations, agnominations, near paronomasias) to appear on the axis of contiguity without the effect of accident and illogicality which often marks their appearance in prose.

[25] 'In poetry,' says Jakobson later in the same paper, 'not only the phonological sequence but in the same way any sequence of semantic units strives to build an equation. Similarity superimposed on contiguity imparts to poetry its thoroughgoing symbolic, multiplex, polysemantic essence which is beautifully suggested by Goethe's "Alles Vergängliche ist nur ein Gleichnis" (Anything transient is but a likeness). Said more technically, anything sequent is a simile. In poetry where similarity is superinduced upon contiguity, any metonymy is slightly metaphorical and any metaphor has a metonymical tint.'

the anthropologist Lévi-Strauss and devoted entirely to the structural exposition of a French sonnet.[26] Charles Baudelaire's *Les Chats* (*Les Fleurs du Mal* LXVI) asserts a fusion of romantic passion and visionary contemplation in the image of those ambivalent little household pets (*puissants et doux, orgueil de la maison*), mythologized through the superimposed image of sphinxes sunk in their endless desert dreams. The cat-sphinxes, as I understand it, are in a sense both enveloped by and in turn envelop and unify the two kinds of humans who love them. (*Les amoureux fervents et les savants austères/Aiment également . . . /Les chats. . . .*) 'I like Ike.' Imagine further this essay having such an impact as to provoke from an American professor of French, Michael Riffaterre, a counter essay of forty-three pages—or it may seem perhaps largely a complementary essay—rehearsing this sonnet again, almost phoneme by phoneme, in terms no less refined and elaborate—from the title ('The definite article and the plural lead us to expect a precise and concrete description: against such a back-drop, the spiritualization of the cats will be more arresting') to 'a global, summative apprehension' of a 'sequence of synonymous images, all of them variations on the symbolism of the cat as representative of the contemplative life.' Our aim has been to show how the different structures of the poem interact, say Jakobson and Lévi-Strauss, '. . . donnant ainsi au poème le caractère d'un object absolu.' To this Riffaterre assents emphatically.[27]

The combined and partly convergent efforts of the three structuralists do make an impressive case for the linguistic and ideational entity of the sonnet. It remains only to observe that the literary critic who welcomes this kind of argument may run some risk of finding it in the end somewhat too impressive. At the end of his own interpretation, Riffaterre believes that he has 'covered every aspect of the

[26] '*Les Chats* de Charles Baudelaire.' The article, except for an introductory note by Lévi-Strauss ('On s'étonnera peut-etre . . .'), has little of an anthropological slant and reads like a pure burst of fireworks from the linguistico-critical faculty of the Russian master.

[27] 'Describing Poetic Structures: Two Approaches to Baudelaire's *les Chats*.' Riffaterre writes a jealously assertive account of the screening powers of Baudelaire's text in its reception of the rest of French language and the canon of his poetry. He makes the keen observation that structure of symbols (an invariant pattern of variant materials) is more relevant than simple content. So Baudelaire's two poems titled *Le Chat* (*Fleurs* XXXIV and LI) seem less relevant to *Les Chats* than the prose poem *La Chambre double*, with its symbolism of furniture.

text'. And he has some abusive words for the literary scholar of the 'humanist stripe', who has 'always assumed that grammar failed because it was incomplete.' 'The linguist,' he says, 'sees all the data.' This is good modern structural linguistic doctrine, that linguistics can write a grammar for all the aspects of poetry, even for the metaphors. On the other hand, it would scarcely occur to any linguistic critic, I suspect, to say that even the combined relentless analyses of Jakobson–Lévi-Strauss and Riffaterre provide, for a person unacquainted with the text of Les Chats, sufficient instruction for writing out the text. So far as one could approximate this feat, the reason would be the numerous quotations from the text carried by the critique. The humanist literary critic, in reaching out to avail himself of the linguistic defence of the literary object, should, I believe, be in no great danger of succumbing to this tyranny of the exhaustive theoretical claim. The alternative, as some no doubt would urge, may appear to be a ticket with Poulet or Hillis Miller in their voyage into boundless consciousness. Having been very willing to avoid that journey and to notice, on the contrary, the structuralist testimony in favour of the poetic object, I report in conclusion my persisting, perhaps paradoxical, but I think not perverse, conviction that the critic who wishes to retain his humanism and his identity as a literary critic will have to persevere in his allegiance to the party of Coleridge and Croce. These philosophers knew that no rules either of language or of poetry will ever be formulated which speakers and poets, responding to the manifold of actual life with the abandon of catachresis and metaphor, will not rejoice in violating, and that the same logic applies for the critic in his exploration of the uncatalogued and uncataloguable past.[28] This should seem no more implausible to the critic than his intimate experience that he can recognize his own person and distinguish himself from Julius Caesar, while at the same time he is convinced that no science, either anatomical or psychological, has charted or is likely to chart his person exhaustively.

[28] F. W. Bateson, in 'Linguistics and Literary Criticism' in The Disciplines of Criticism, uses the insufficiency of the Saussurian circuit de la parole to urge similar arguments against the totalitarian linguistic claim [an interesting form of which appears in Roger Fowler's essay in this volume: cf. various debates between Bateson and Fowler in the pages of Essays in Criticism]. On this also see David Lodge, Language of Fiction (1966), pp. 49–69, discussing stylistics and linguistics, and Harry Levin, Why Literary Criticism Is Not an Exact Science (Cambridge, Mass., 1967).

Note

Generic criticism, or the approach through study of the 'kinds' of literature has long been fundamental to literary criticism; the classical precedent, of course, being Aristotle's *Poetics*. Though today it is often consciously (and usually disparagingly) associated only with neoclassicism, we still depend on it automatically for many crucial distinctions: among novels, poems, and plays; tragedy, comedy, and epic. However, examples of a conscious and formal 'poetics' approach are to be found in modern criticism. Northrop Frye's *Anatomy of Criticism* (Princeton, 1957) and R. S. Crane's edition of work by the Chicago Aristotelians, *Critics and Criticism* (Chicago, 1952) are two of the most eminently controversial among them.

The following study does not attempt to be controversial, but may well not escape that fate. What it does attempt is, firstly, to see how far the generic approach still can and still needs to be used, and secondly, to account for, and if possible to reconcile, those differing attitudes towards that approach which are indicated by the preliminary quotations from: Irvin Ehrenpreis, *The 'Types Approach' to Literature* (New York, 1945); René Wellek and Austin Warren, *Theory of Literature* (New York, 1945); William K. Wimsatt and Cleanth Brooks, *Literary Criticism: A Short History* (New York, 1957); and Northrop Frye, *Anatomy of Criticism* (Princeton, 1957). See also: Benedetto Croce, *Aesthetic* (1922); John Erskine, *The Kinds of Poetry* (New York, 1929); and J. L. Calderwood and M. R. Toliver, *Forms of Poetry* (New Jersey, 1968). Also see Allan Rodway and Brian Lee, 'Coming to Terms', *Essays in Criticism* (April 1964).

IV

Generic Criticism:
The Approach through Type, Mode and Kind

ALLAN RODWAY

Preparatory note

THE *kinds* of literature go under many aliases (genres, species, forms, types, modes). They have been defined, irrespective of alias, according to the literary works' setting, subject, time, theme, attitude, content, structure, origin, history, purpose, occasion, psychology (correspondence with faculties of the mind), or sociology (correspondence with aspects of society). And the history of genre-criticism is as long as it is complex. To attempt in a preparatory note to summarize the compendious labours of workers in this tangled field would be presumptuous, and also tedious. Even the following drastic selection of (contradictory) quotations may seem rather a surfeit than an appetizer. However, they are no more than the preliminary minimum the subject demands:

> Scholars are fairly well agreed today that there is no one definition of a kind of literature. (p. 5)

> Irene Behrens has shown that while epic, drama and lyric may have existed from antiquity, none of them has retained the same name for the same kind. (p. 6)

> Until the end of the eighteenth century the common view of genres was that they were established patterns to which authors conformed. The historical evolutionary view of the nineteenth century changed this. . . . independent of Herder, the notion of evolution in itself emphasizes genres; theories of literary evolution must by their very nature imply such classifications. (pp. 18–19)

> The genres to which Europeans and Americans are accustomed have no existence independent of their material and background.

They are not implicit in the nature either of literature or of the
human mind. (p. 50)

(Irvin Ehrenpreis, The 'Types Approach' to Literature)

Theory of genres is a principle of order; it classifies literature and
literary history not by time and place (period or national language)
but by specifically literary types of organization or structure. Any
critical and evaluative—as distinct from historical—study involves,
in some form, the appeal to such structures. (p. 235)

Anyone interested in genre theory must be careful not to confound
the distinctive differences between 'classical' and modern theory.
Classical theory is regulative and prescriptive. . . . Classical theory
not only believes that genre differs from genre but also that they
must be kept apart, not allowed to mix . . . there was a real aesthetic
principle . . . involved: it was the appeal to a rigid unity of tone,
a stylized purity and 'simplicity'. . . .
   Classical theory had, too, its social differentiation of genres. Epic
and tragedy dealt with the affairs of kings and nobles, comedy with
those of the middle class (the city, the bourgeoisie) and satire and
farce with the common people. (p. 244)

Modern theory is clearly descriptive. It doesn't limit the number of
possible kinds and doesn't prescribe rules to authors. It supposes that
traditional kinds may be 'mixed' and produce a new kind (like
tragicomedy). It sees that genres can be built up on the basis of
inclusiveness or 'richness' as well as that of 'purity'. (p. 245)

(René Wellek and Austin Warren, Theory of Literature)

The evolution of criticism has produced four, perhaps five genre
conceptions dominant enough in their eras to serve as focuses for the
poetic whole. Each of these (with perhaps one exception) seems to
have had its advantages, each has enabled a certain understanding
not only of one literary genre but of the whole poetic structure and
problem. Aristotle's view was dramatic . . . and this had the great
advantage of opening up the more broadly 'dramatic', the ethically
problematic and tensional aspect of poetry as a whole. . . . The next
basic view is that of Horace, conversational, epistolary, idiomatic,
ironic, satiric. . . . This view has the advantage of opening up the
linguistic, the idiomatic, the metaphoric, and in that sense again the
'dramatic' aspect of all poetry. Next is the high, the grand, the
ecstatic view of Longinus—which on the whole opens up more
dangers and confusions perhaps than effective advantage, and is not

a view according to literary 'species' (but just the opposite) unless we look on it as making a large contribution (via Boileau) to the new genre of the 'heroic' in the third quarter of the seventeenth century. . . . Meanwhile, in the same essays of Dryden which defend the heroic, a theory of courtly wit and ridicule is asserted, and by the time of Pope and Swift, this can be considered a second focussing of the Horatian conversational and satiric ideal. And in close liaison, appears the mocking genre of the anti-heroic or burlesque. . . . Lastly, the cycle of genres is completed in the era of the romantics with the now affectionately remembered lyric ideal and its attendant opinion that a long poem is a contradiction in terms. This had the advantage of exploiting a new view of 'expression', a view of subjectivity both as cognition and as feeling, and of metaphor as the small-scale model and touchstone of the whole poetic business. (pp. 750–1)

(William K. Wimsatt and Cleanth Brooks,
Literary Criticism: A Short History)

We discover that the critical theory of genres is stuck precisely where Aristotle left it. The very word 'genre' sticks out in an English sentence as the unpronounceable and alien thing it is. Most critical efforts to handle such generic terms as 'epic' and 'novel' are chiefly interesting as examples of the psychology of rumour. (p. 13)

The strong emotional repugnance felt by many critics towards any form of schematization in poetics is again the result of a failure to distinguish criticism as a body of knowledge from the great experience of literature, where every act is unique, and classification has no place. (p. 29)

(Northrop Frye, *Anatomy of Criticism*.)

I

Disagreement obviously abounds. Ehrenpreis argues that kinds can be classified, and have been classified, according to *any* sort of similarity. Wellek and Warren exclude classification by time and place. For them, too, an approach through kinds was necessary for any 'critical and evaluative—as distinct from historical—study'. By contrast, nineteenth-century evolutionary criticism of this sort was specifically useful in teasing out traditions and influences, and relating them to social change—that is to say, it was useful *precisely* in historical study. Where Ehrenpreis says 'genres . . . are not implicit in the nature either of literature or of the human mind,' Frye insists that they are archetypal in both. The long quotation from Wimsatt and Brooks indicates that kind-criticism may have given to the literature of different periods focal concepts as fruitful as 'gravity' or 'relativity' have been to physics. On the other hand, there seems to have been little theorizing on the usefulness of the idea of 'kind' or 'mode' itself to the universe of criticism—save in the cases of Croce (*Aesthetic*, London, 1922), who thought it nothing, and Frye, who thinks it everything. And, to come full circle, Frye's enthusiasm for modes leads him not to the 'critical and evaluative' standpoint of Wellek and Warren, but to an appreciation of their indispensability for anatomizing the universal body of literature *without* evaluation: 'criticism,' he says, 'has no business to react against things, but should show a steady advance towards undiscriminating catholicity.' He is concerned with what kinds of literature exist, but not with what is worth reading, and on what grounds. Further probing reveals only more differences of opinion or emphasis.

Gregory Smith very convincingly says that in Elizabethan criticism the practice of dividing literature into kinds was generally a method of justifying imaginative literature 'against the attacks of a vigorous Puritanism'. The defenders' aim was to show that poetry is useful and moral; therefore their definitions of kinds were necessarily in terms of content and effect. Turn, however, to detailed studies, and what do we find?—in Weinberg's *History of Literary Criticism in the Renaissance* (Chicago, 1961, II, 13, V. pp. 635–714), nearly a hundred large pages recording thousands of pages of inconclusive wrangling that covered most aspects of the topic, under the umbrella-theme of tradition versus change. And, just as we can have doubts about neoclassical practice, so there seems much to be said against the 'biological', evolutionary, kind-criticism of the nineteenth century. After all, a work is what it is, regardless of how it came to be so. Searching into its antecedents may be supposed to destroy responsiveness to what it uniquely has to offer. Moreover, the supposed antecedents may be merely coincidental analogues. In any case, biological analogy may well foster false history as well as superficial responsiveness, by inducing a belief—apparent in a very sophisticated form in Northrop Frye—that literature evolves from more simple forms, getting more varied and complex as it does so, but always retaining an archetypal, umbilical link with its origin:

propositions open to question about both their truth and value. On the other hand, a logical point like the following makes it impossible to believe that the analogy with biology is entirely mistaken: 'Works of art are not structureless, and their structures must like all structures be mutually comparable' (Sparshott, *The Structure of Aesthetics*, Toronto, 1963, p. 174).

Yet, if nothing is straightforward, it is nevertheless unduly polemical of Frye to assert that two thousand years of discussion have left 'the critical theory of genres stuck precisely where Aristotle left it.' Not only has the discussion led to the 'focussing' concepts already mentioned, and to a procedure for the social and historical study of literature, but it has also led to Frye's own brilliant and stimulating (if fundamentally metacritical) structure of speculation. It has gradually become evident, too, that the grammar of form is more stable, and therefore more useful for classification, than the lexis of content. Furthermore, the methods of both literature and criticism have been gradually sorted out and clarified. It has become clear, for instance, that two inclusive classes of kind-criticism exist. Distinguished not by what defining similarities they use but rather by an ultimate philosophic tendency to either universalism or nominalism, idealism or empiricism, they are the *prescriptive* (which urges writers to approximate to some pure Platonic kind) and the *descriptive* (which derives the kinds from existing works, and is likely not to censure the mixing of established kinds but to call the result a new kind or evolved form). It has become clear too that, though the descriptive class is now dominant, it is rather because of the post-Romantic nature of literature and the consequent multiplication of kinds in the last century, than because all the philosophic questions have been finally settled.

The 'descriptive' side has in fact had rather the better of the argument, but we can now see that this is irrelevant. Prescriptive kind-criticism clearly derives from, and is relevant to, the 'classical' mode of writing—that which prefers the 'reality' of unmixed feeling (on the grounds that there is something false about a feeling easily infiltrated or supplanted by another), and therefore tends to strict structural form. Since writers who look to authority and the help of given forms will continue to exist alongside those who prefer the perils of freedom, both classes of criticism will continue also. The prescriptive may have been generally discredited in academic circles, but every commercial reader, editor, producer or director who criticizes scripts is of this class, saying 'if you follow such and such rules, then on the basis of experience we can say you are likely to succeed in this kind.' A much maligned class of men, but usually helpful and right—for all but original geniuses. Descriptive kind-criticism is innately more useful for the academic pursuits of literary history and for refined discrimination amongst works that might mistakenly be thought similar (witness the vague generality of the popular use of 'novel' as against the academic distinction between 'novels' and 'romances', or the preferable 'report-novels' and 'romance-novels'.) Moreover, if it took the less Platonic, less authoritarian class of criticism to chart the evolution of literature and its relation to social *change*, it is no less true that the classical sort—with its idea of *decorum* of kind, character and diction—was well aware of the relation of literature to social *order* (especially the order of classes). Even the now universally condemned idea of a hierarchy of kinds can still play a useful part in critical theory. Perhaps there is no point in attempting any longer to adjudicate between tragedy and epic, but there is still some point—and supporting arguments—in asserting the superiority of tragedy as a kind over the thriller as a kind, or comedy over farce.

Above all, long abstruse wrangling has led to a pragmatic assumption that kinds are ideas, not things in themselves. Thus the conception of the *usefulness* of distinguishing kinds is gradually superseding that of *truthfulness*. Furthermore, the notion of major and minor kinds, or even of major-major and minor-minor, has been clarified, though not yet with an agreed terminology[1] for these useful distinctions.

II

The most important of the agreed distinctions—going back to Diomedes (*fl. c.* 390 A.D.), repeated in the Middle Ages, rediscovered by French critics in the seventeenth century, and occurring again in Joyce's *Portrait of the Artist as a Young Man*—is that between those kinds distinguished by what Frye calls 'the radical of presentation', and those based on other criteria. Literature originally to be presented through action (the *dramatic*) is distinguished from that originally to be sung

[1] See Allan Rodway and Brian Lee, 'Coming to Terms', who suggest 'mode' for the major-major and 'variety' for the minor-minor. (They also give grounds for preferring 'report-novels' and 'romance-novels' to 'novels' and 'romances'.)

(*lyric*) and that to be spoken (*narrative*); or, in Joyce's version, objective, subjective and medial expression are distinguished. The distinction is mainly important in a negative way. It marks off something very basic, truly 'radical', but of less importance to a practical criticism than those kinds defined less primitively. (Northrop Frye would not agree, but he means by 'criticism' something schematic and reductive: what leads to archetypes within the modes of literature, and indeed finally to 'the archetypal shape of literature as a whole'.) For those interested in criticism as an aid to the appreciation of particular works of art, these 'kinds' can obviously be given only a minor role; and in order to play it without further confounding confusion they may be marked off by the different name, *types*. This frees 'modes' and 'kinds' for the larger role they can play in aiding such appreciation. This is the one area of genre-criticism previously neglected—an area theoretically remote from that of literary history, though having pragmatic links with it; it exists somewhere between the extreme nominalism of Croce and the extreme universalism of Frye, though not as a state of compromise with both so much as a state of lesser abstraction than either.

III

Croce anathematizes all classification, all concepts of decorum, elevating instead the entirely individual and original (thus tending to appreciate only short poems or pieces of poetry, and to go rapidly from the poem itself to the 'spirit' of the author). In his view creative works can be classified only by ignoring everything that makes them works of art. This seems to be an excessive reaction against those excesses of nineteenth-century, evolutionary, species-criticism that brought it to the point of being a branch of anthropology; for classification is so much a fact of life that it seems unlikely, *prima facie*, that it must be the death of art, or of its appreciation. In life, communication itself would be almost impossible were we unable to refer to classes (men, women, children, houses, furniture) but only to each item as a laboriously described unique entity. Since good literature is the acme of communication it is scarcely surprising to find that artists, audiences and critics have been indebted to literary traditions, conventions and revolutions, which all necessarily depend on some sort of categorizing. Indeed, both ideas—that art is to be identified with originality and that classification is incompatible with the appreciation of individuality—

seem obviously false. Literary works, like the people who create them, are born willy nilly into a pre-existing society; and far from necessarily preventing individuality, these twin societies, of literature and life, are as necessary a condition for it as the laws of the game and the laws of physics are for gifted tennis. Moreover, the appreciation of a literary gift is in many cases impossible, in most more difficult, if the individual work cannot be seen in relationship to some class or classes. Against what other background would its unique qualities truly manifest themselves?

But if two millennia of critics have bequeathed us little more than 'remarkable inconsistency' (Ehrenpreis), how shall we know what classes a work should be seen in relation to? Part of the answer seems to be that it doesn't matter. The long debate has not been a waste of breath. It has made clear, first, that there is no divine truth to be re-vealed in this stony place; works of literature are multi-faceted and they can indeed be categorized in many ways, just like people. Second, that it is not how you classify that really matters (though some ways return a better yield than others, according to the nature of the particular case), but rather the fact of classifying itself. Take the least promising approach, that through the concept of type—least promising, as we have seen, because most mechanical and unsophisticated—and apply it to the least promising sort of material, something very short and very simple, where nothing seems to require critical midwifery:

Down Hall

Come here my sweet Landlady, pray how do you do?
Where is *Sisley* so cleanly, and *Prudence* and *Sue*?
And where is the widow that dwelt here below?
And the Hostler that sung about Eight Years ago?

And where is your sister so mild and so dear?
Whose voice to her Maids like a Trumpet was clear.
By my Troth, she replies, you grow younger, I think,
And pray, Sir, what wine does the gentleman drink?

Why now let me die, Sir, or live upon Trust,
If I know to which question to answer you first.
Why things since I saw you, most strangely have vary'd,
And the Hostler is hang'd and the Widow is Marry'd.

(Matthew Prior)

What type of poem is this? Well, *lyric*, of course; if Prior did not write it for music, its 'radical of presentation' is certainly that of song. We might add, moving insensibly towards other categories, that it is in the ballad mode, though it's of the 'popular' not the 'traditional' kind. But on second thoughts, *is* it lyric? Going by the radical of presentation alone, perhaps. But is it enough to go by the *radical* of presentation alone, as we can often make only an informed guess at what it was? The Joycean idea of the role of the author, speaking as it were to himself, or to an audience, or entirely through his characters is more determinate. Anyway, if we are asking, Which type? each should be at least considered. Then, *narrative*? On technical grounds, no; since there is no narration (as distinct from dialogue). The main value of the concept of type—for the criticism that regards itself as a handmaid to literature—is its technicality: it can provide a point of triangulation with the more flexible, psychologically determined concepts of mode and kind, and thus minimize the risk of stock response. So, not narrative. In fact, in the light of our definition, it is clearly *dramatic*; nothing but dialogue. But part of our pleasure—most of the aesthetic part—comes from the insolent ease with which 'lyric' structure is fused to dramatic texture. Further, there is a pleasure, akin to that of innovation or variation on a theme, for those familiar with both kinds, in seeing a method not uncommon in the traditional kind of ballad (witness *Lord Randal*, or *Edward*) skilfully appropriated to the popular kind, where it is almost unknown. Moreover, does not the most fleeting consideration of narrative raise the question of persona? Is 'the gentleman' Prior himself? Or is he not a 'character' whom we see—or almost see—being sketched in by a ghostly author who has chosen not to dematerialize entirely? Perhaps not. But at least the question has been raised and our attention directed to character, as well as form and theme. At this point, how we finally categorize the poem becomes irrelevant, for the fact of trying to categorize—even through the crudest approach—has brought us near enough to its individual qualities for genre-criticism to give way to something more subtle.

IV

The concepts of mode and kind are themselves more subtle, if only because they are imprecise; and if they are refined (respectively) to the subspecies of mood and variety—whether or not we actually name them as such—they probably lead as near to full appreciation as any methodical approach can. Further delicacy must be a matter of personal sensibility and exploration. All these concepts, obviously, can be used for non-comparative criticism (if they are taken as being of the Platonic idea class); and for comparative criticism or for clarifying 'traditions and affinities, thereby bringing out a large number of literary relationships that would not be noticed as long as there were no context established for them' (Frye) (if they are taken as being of the empirical class). And in all cases there is no reason why they should not be used with all the other basic concepts of a pragmatic criticism—form, structure, texture, tone, subject, theme, and so on.

Northrop Frye, with beautiful economy, tries to define mode solely in terms of character-status, and to reduce all literature to five modes—and what's more he nearly succeeds. These modes run, chronologically as well as logically, from the mythic (in which the protagonists are superior in kind—gods or demigods—to both men and the environment), through the romance (protagonists superior in degree—supermen, sometimes aided by magic—to other men and the environment), the high mimetic (superior to other men but not to the environment—as in most epic and tragedy), the low mimetic (superior neither to other men nor to the environment—as in most comedy or realism), and on to the ironic (protagonists inferior). The last mode might well be dropped, as irony (even structural irony, which is what Frye is talking about) is a formal means or method that could certainly be used in the high mimetic mode (witness *King Lear*) and the low mimetic (witness *Emma*), and might conceivably be used in the other two modes. Otherwise the scheme is useful as well as beautiful. But, again, its usefulness is like that of type: more evident in metacriticism (to which the study of kinds has always contributed most), less evident in intrinsic criticism (the 'one area' previously noted as having been neglected so far by genre-scholarship).

Briefly, metacriticism is centrifugal, intrinsic criticism centripetal. The one is concerned with a work's relationships, the other with its identity; the one with its significance, the other with its meaning. In short, the one moves outwards *from* the work, the other inwards *to* it. Both may use the 'background' material of diligent scholarship; it is how they use it that marks the distinction. Is the material being used to further a process of understanding and appreciating the work itself, inwardly but not eccentrically? If so, the approach is strictly literary and intrinsic. Is it, on the other hand, being used to further a process of understanding and appreciating some other topic through literature? Then the approach is metacritical. To study seventeenth-century history and to read the Old Testament as a way into Dryden's *Absalom and Achitophel* is perfectly compatible with intrinsic criticism; to use *Absalom and Achitophel* as one way into seventeenth-century history, or as part of a course in Biblical studies or 'The Social Influence of the Old Testament', is to engage in metacriticism. Both procedures are perfectly proper to English Studies; it is this fact that makes English the great liaison subject. But the former is logically primary: it is intrinsic criticism that gives specialized knowledge, and it is only that specifically literary evidence which justifies critical intrusion into other disciplines. If the metacritic is not also an intrinsic critic he cannot reasonably assume that he has anything to offer the professional historian, theologian, anthropologist, or whatever. It is this primacy that warrants the present attempt to correct the balance of kind-criticism to date—or at any rate to show that it has some part to play in the *literary* appreciation of literature.

For this purpose, Frye's concept of mode needs to be expanded. He and Croce, though on opposite sides, are in the same game; inasmuch as they use literature in the service of a metaphysic both are metacritics and need strong, rather than adjustable, construction units. Particular books, however, unlike most theories of literature, tend to have a protean nature; and the fact that the critics of two millennia have neither clearly distinguished modes from kinds nor agreed on any one definition of kind is not a reflection on their abilities but on the nature of literature. These students of genre may have been mainly concerned with its use in what were, strictly speaking, metacritical pursuits; but since such pursuits depend, as we have seen, on intrinsically literary insights they rightly found themselves, as men of taste, in disagreement, even if they were not conscious of the real basis of it. For the truth is that every way of classifying literature will be right for some books, and for some purpose (what cannot be found, as the history of genre-criticism shows, is some single demonstrably right principle of classification as a scholarly end in itself). Even similarities as broad as 'period' or 'subject', though they might include such disparates as Shaw's *Getting Married* and Lawrence's *Women in Love*, could conceivably constitute the first means towards some rather general (and probably metacritical) end. The works instanced, perhaps, might form

part of the evidence in some socio-literary or literary-historical investigation of the Edwardian revolt against Victorian conventions or the
development of wider and freer sexual reference in literature. If the end
were one appropriate to intrinsic criticism, something less vague than
'period' or 'subject' would probably be required. But *what*? The proper
answer, from a critic who considers it his function to aid potential
readers to appreciate particular works, must surely be that the nature
of the particular works should dictate what sort of kind—defined by
similarity of theme, or content, or structure, or purpose, etc.—he
should start from.

At this point, though, we are faced with a variety of the hermeneutical dilemma, which crops up in so many cruxes of critical theory:
a proper conception of 'kind', we are saying, will help to lead us to an
appreciation of the nature of the work—but to get that proper conception we seem to need to know the nature of the work already. Why
not just read the thing, and hope some aspect will stick out as clearly
more prominent than others? In practice such bulldozing may work
well enough in many cases—but not in all. And, in strict theory, it
always leads straight into another variety of hermeneutical dilemma:
you can't know the proper meaning of any part without knowing what
sort of whole it is a part of (for example, absurdities become virtues
once you see that the work is a satire and therefore start being sensitive
to, say, irony). But, since the whole is the sum of its parts, you can't
know what sort of whole it is without knowing the proper meaning
of the parts. These dilemmas are not inescapable. But their presence is
the main reason for evolving a flexible concept of mode (and indeed
also of kind).

We escape, so to speak, by edging out, tacking from evidence to
hypothesis to further evidence to renewed hypothesis. Since the
evidence offered by a literary work, however, is of more than one
sort, we need to give to Frye's technical definition of mode a psychological dimension. A work's mode, then, let us say, is whatever it
seems to be in its most general aspect—but this will depend partly on
our current concern. In certain cases, it might be most useful to take as
mode what we would more usually style 'fixed form' or even 'minor
kind'. Are we concerned first with 'The Sonnet', and only within that
framework with the qualities of various sonnets? If so, any particular
poem is first scrutinized to see if it has the characteristics that we have
decided determine the sonnet-mode. Then we may ask what *kind* of

sonnet it is, technically (Petrarchan or Shakespearean), or tonally (denunciatory, melancholic . . .), or thematically (ubi sunt, sorrow of love . . .), and so on. Are we concerned with Satire? Then our most general concern is with whatever constitutes 'the satiric', and this will be the mode. After this, the *kind* of satire—bitter, humorous, or whatever. If, however, we were concerned primarily with Humour, the case would be reversed. Thus one critic might quite properly place Pope's *Rape of the Lock* as a humorous mock-heroic kind within the mode of satire; and another, equally properly, as a satiric mock-heroic kind within the mode of the humorous. In general, though—special concerns apart—the mode of a work will be largely a matter of attitude or tone rather than style or form of writing. It will strike the reader as generally tragic, pathetic, comic, farcical, horrific, melancholic . . . We may then further distinguish *moods* within the general mode. Orwell's *1984* is *satirically* horrific; *Twelfth Night*, in its main plot, *wryly* comic. The concept of Kind must be equally flexible—to the point, as we have seen, of being interchangeable with that of Mode—in order to match the variousness of literature and the consequent variety of critical possibilities. But, in general, it will contain a larger element of technicality, being at least as much akin to Type as to Mode. *1984* we might style as narrative type, horrific mode (within the low mimetic), satiric mood; for most purposes, its major kind would be romance-novel—a technical definition[2]—and minor kinds or varieties would then be distinguished to whatever degree of elaboration was required, 'didactic' being the most obvious.

A work's mode, mood, type and kind (major and minor), then, eventually add up to what it turns out to be 'in itself', after it has been considered from various aspects; and it is in the fact of providing variables for triangulation that the value of this form of the generic approach lies. Not only is the critic prevented from going too far astray in any direction, and the later, subtler, non-generic analysis safeguarded against irrelevant ingenuity or ungoverned speculation, but also he is given navigational aids in his tacking escape from the land-locking horns of the hermeneutical dilemma.

Carefully avoiding the Intentionalist Fallacy, one would normally begin by asking what the work itself *purports* to be or do. Sometimes

[2] Refining on 'low mimetic' by indicating the existence of some uncharacteristic quality ('romance')—a not uncommon feature of literary works; Polonius's 'tragical-comical-historical' is not in principle so foolish as it sounds.

a kind established by tradition or convention is referred to in the title (*Third Satyre . . . The Lamentable Tragedie of . . .*). This gives a statement of purport, or arouses certain critical expectations, which we check by the further evidence of each succeeding line, revising and re-revising our initial hypothesis of mode or kind if these expectations are not fulfilled. In the absence of such titles, a quick read-through is necessary to obtain a very tentative hypothesis about the mode of the whole (the parts having been taken, so to speak, innocently, at the face value of first impression, to which life, the language and, cumulatively, the context, all contribute). That hypothesis is then checked and refined on second reading into an idea of kind, by the two-way process indicated—successive hypotheses about the whole interacting with the accumulation of evidence as part succeeds part. Finally one is able to say with some confidence: this work purports to be such and such, and is in fact of that mode and kind—or, perhaps, is not what it purports to be (as Blake and Shelley thought *Paradise Lost* not to be in fact a justification of the ways of God to man). In the latter case, it might be useful to speak of an ostensible purport disguising the real mode and kind. In such instances, concepts of mode and kind are evidently of particular value in helping to ensure that the escape from the hermeneutical dilemma is not bedevilled by authorial misleading (conscious or unconscious) as to the real meaning of certain parts.

Conclusions come to by such a process, of course, can claim neither logical nor empirical certainty. But the valid interpretation, as E. D. Hirsch points out in his brilliant and provocative *Validity in Interpretation* (New Haven and London, 1967), is simply the one that is most probable in the light of the available evidence; and when it comes to literature the nature of the most essential evidence can be obtained only by some two-way process, some fluid system of checks and balances, which gradually reduces the likely margin of error (if we make the necessary assumption that what is—or rather what would to the original audience have been—the most coherent interpretation is to be deemed the most probable; it is certainly, anyway, the most preferable). It may seem that traditional or conventional kinds, established by a title or other obvious indication, are an exception. But those kinds themselves, those conventions, must have been the result of some similar dialectic, for until the convention was established the nature of the kind or mode and the nature of the particular works which were to give rise to that category, stood to each other in the same dilemmatic relationship as that of whole to the parts in each particular work. This process is not restricted to literature. Induction, and indeed practically all the learning processes of life, are subject to a similar dilemma, and escape it in defiance of logic by a similar pragmatic dialectic—a spiralling or tacking progress between the particularizing of nominalism and the generalizing of universalism. Few subjects outside mathematics can avoid it; literature least of all.

Accept it, though, and genre-criticism is seen to be progressively useful. Firstly, a kind or mode may focus the literary ideal of a period (as Wimsatt and Brooks argue). Secondly, once accepted by 'tradition' or convention, it contributes metacritically not only to literary history, the sociology of literature, or its anthropology, but also as we have seen to intrinsic criticism by setting up certain expectations (an especially useful function in cases of symbolism, allegory, irony, parody and satire). Thirdly, the act of classifying a work generally by Type and Mode, and specifically by Kind, itself a dialectical process—unless predetermined by a given concern—involves us intimately and inevitably with the subtler dialectic required to establish Purport. The nature of the work should properly guide the choice of mode or kind and, reciprocally, the chosen mode and kind form triangulation points in the progress towards establishing the general purport and thence the inner nature of the work. Where the choice of mode is predetermined by an overriding concern (like 'satire') the process is affected only to this extent: that we are not less, but more aware of the existence of other aspects, other possibilities of approach, since we cannot but know that this one has been as much self-imposed as objectively discovered.

V

There is, however, a fourth use much more important to intrinsic criticism—or, at any rate, nearer to the heart of the work itself— coming into play only after the stages mentioned have been left behind.

Unfortunately, the idea of 'the work itself', so far taken for granted, faces us with another hermeneutical dilemma, not unrelated to the two already dealt with. Perhaps all three should be regarded as aspects of one problem. But at first sight this one seems to be in a class of its own,

D

as it arises from the need not to establish a work's nature but its very existence. Criticism should be objective, but literary works are not objects—or, anyway, insofar as they are their existence is insignificant; and it is their signifying but non-material existence that the critic wants to be objective about. Merely and literally as 'the words on the page' a literary work exists materially but not meaningfully. The material existence could be altered out of all recognition without affecting the meaning one iota. For instance, the pages might be of different size, shape, quality and colour, the words in Russian script or shorthand signs, but as literature 'the words on the page' would remain unaltered. The words, in short, have to be read by somebody in order to come into meaningful existence. In this field, if not in others, Berkeley has some bearing: when a book is replaced on the shelf it ceases to exist (save as an undigestible lump of matter). But if its existence as literature, not lump, is only in the critic's mind, how can he avoid subjectivity? And if he does, how does he know the work he's being objective about will exist in the same way in his reader's mind (especially as any work may be approached—that is, recreated—in various ways)? When another reader digests it, doesn't it turn into *his* reality? How do both of them distinguish between a misreading and a legitimate variant reading?

All these questions can be absorbed into one problem: how to avoid the affective fallacy (a combine incorporating as many subsidiaries as the intentionalist fallacy). One cannot assume that a work may properly be judged by its effect on the reader's mind and emotions (it might, surely, be a wrong effect due to misreading or emotional bias)—yet it exists only as an effect in the mind and therefore cannot be judged as anything else. This affective fallacy is identical with our latest hermeneutical dilemma, which seems theoretically as irresolvable as the others. But again there is a pragmatic way out—which will appear less questionable if we alter our terms somewhat, noting that 'objectivity', while admittedly easier in relation to objects, need not be confined to them; it simply combines the ideas of being unbiassed and of proceeding from the best available evidence. This means that there is no ruling of principle against being objective about literature. The difficulties are practical; therefore the solution may be too. Again, if we speak of a work's 'taking place' when read, rather than its 'existing', we both avoid unnecessary puzzles from the inherent ambiguity of the word 'exist' and also more accurately reflect the facts of reading. Moreover,

we reveal the similarity between this and the previous dilemmas—
reveal, indeed, that they are in fact only different aspects of one complex problem. For when we said that the nature of a particular work
could be discovered by a dialectical tacking between tentative hypotheses about the whole, framed and (if necessary) revised in the light
of the cumulative evidence of the parts, starting with the title (the
earlier parts of course taking a different colouring by back-reflection
from each later, revised hypothesis), we were in fact indicating that
the work was being created or, strictly, recreated as we read, though
such a form of expression as 'discovered' tended to disguise the fact.
In short, it gradually took place. The important thing to note, however,
is that the very difficulty of the process of recreation, far from being a
handicap, is in fact one of the chief means of ensuring that what does
take place corresponds to what should take place.

Attaining this correspondence seems, clearly, to be the chief task of
intrinsic criticism (and even of metacriticism, since it must rest on a
specifically literary basis): first for the critic himself, and then simply,
by leading his readers or auditors in the same direction, for the public.

The other chief means of attaining it, co-equal with the dialectical
tacking and inseparable from it, is assessment by type, mode and kind;
for that process both acts as a check on hypotheses about purport and
is itself checked during the more detailed process of assessing purport.

If the choice of a defining class-similarity, out of many possibilities,
is partly dictated by the nature of works at first only *tentatively* considered for inclusion in that class, a dialectical movement between
possible class-parts and the nature of the class-whole is instigated comparable to, and inseparable from, that aiming to establish (or recreate,
as we may now say) the nature of each work as a unique, not a class
entity. Comparable and inseparable—so it is also the case that the
nature of the works is partly dictated by some idea of a class-whole.
The common factor, of course, is the concept of 'purport'. Without
it, the parts of a particular work cannot be properly assessed. With it,
the work is provisionally assigned to a class—a mode, type or kind.

The particular nature of the work reveals itself during a taking place
that is a recreation. To be objective the revelation should be the result
of a dialectic. If it is true that during that dialectic the work will seem
to assign itself provisionally to a class or classes, it is also true that the
dialectic itself requires, as a tentative hypothesis, some idea of a (necessarily generic) whole as one of its terms. Thus generic criticism is

found, surprisingly, to be also of value in establishing the proper existence of a single work, in ensuring that what does take place is what ought to take place when it is read; that the recreation is not private and eccentric, that is to say, but as public as possible in the nature of the case. By multiple triangulation, so to speak, we fix what the 'work itself' most validly appears to be when, underpinned if necessary by scholarship, the public, reasonably discussable concepts of type, mode, kind *and purport* pushing and pulling have done their best to prevent interpretation flooding amorphously to unjustifiable lengths (or alternatively stagnating in lazy backwaters of the mind).

What safeguards the dual process from complete circularity is the presence of various links with the outside world. In the language itself at least some things are given; regardless of context, some subjects tend to delimit meanings ('spirit' in a religious work is not likely to refer to alcohol); some periods promote certain probabilities; so do some authors, some themes; and experience of life often acts as a guide even though times have changed. All these may themselves depend ultimately on a similar dialectic (of which one paradigm could be the child's progress from knowing disparate objects, to the idea of sets, and finally to concepts of abstract number that can then be applied back to concrete items at a higher level). But they have justified themselves over a long period as practically useful, and can form a ground for the second-order process. (Hence one's reasonable willingness to accept— at any rate tentatively—certain traditions or conventions as a flying start.)

However, intrinsic criticism should not merely be justifiable, on the most public grounds possible, it should also be adequately inward (though still justifiably, not as unsupported assertions of intuition). Then—to return to our main argument—has generic criticism any part to play here? Not so much, it would seem, as 'internal' concepts like structure, texture, syntax, figures, diction, and so forth; yet not so little as one might think. In fact, the part it has to play is that referred to earlier (p. 97) as its fourth and, for intrinsic criticism, most important role.

To Croce, this section began by saying, to be generically inward seemed a contradiction in terms; and it is true that generic criticism has traditionally led outward, serving, or itself being, metacriticism. It is also true that a few works—mostly short lyric poems—do not demand any reference beyond their own boundaries. On the other hand, it is equally true not only that there is no contradiction between generality and particularity, generic classification and the unique inwardness of the individual work, but also that individuality can hardly be seen to be such save when it defines itself by comparison with apparent *semblables*; only against what is common to the class will what is unique to each member stand out. Moreover, if we wish to do more than demonstrate the presence of some characteristic of a work (say mordant wit), wish to go on to its precise quality or degree, how can we possibly succeed save by comparing it with some work of the same kind—and therefore justly comparable—which possesses the same characteristic in a greater or lesser degree? Thus generic criticism turns out to be an instrument for fairly refined and precise intrinsic analysis.

Two important questions remain, perhaps. First, might not such a method still further, and possibly fatally, dehumanize the professional critic? His is already a difficult act of funambulism; he must be at once at home and abroad, feelingly immersed in the work and (in some corner of his being) objectively detached. Might not such a procedure topple him into automatism? Second, will it stifle initiative and encourage long-windedness? One answer, to both questions, is that these lamentable results might follow, but need not. It depends on the person not the method. The answer could be put more strongly. Theorizing always seems inhuman, being necessarily abstract; but the results of following a reasonable theory should be less lamentable, in any given case, than those of not doing so; for not following one simply means muddling through—that is to say, carrying out most of the same operations haphazardly (to be reasonable a theoretical procedure should not bar any useful, necessary or desirable practice). But the best answer is the test of practice.

Take this time, not an apparently simple traditional poem, but an apparently difficult experimental one by E. E. Cummings—about dehumanization, appropriately enough:

> *pity this busy monster,manunkind*
>
> Pity this busy monster,manunkind,
> not. Progress is a comfortable disease:
> your victim(death and life safely beyond)
>
> plays with the bigness of his littleness
> —electrons deify one razorblade
> into a mountain range;lenses extend

> unwish through curving wherewhen till unwish
> returns on its unself.
>
> A world of made
> is not a world of born—pity poor flesh
>
> and trees,poor stars and stones,but never this
> fine specimen of hypermagical
>
> ultraomnipotence. We doctors know
>
> a hopeless case if—listen:there's a hell
> of a good universe next door;let's go

Well, let's go. The quick, innocent first reading seems to indicate that the poem does not purport to be entirely serious. But is it serious enough to be satiric though very unlike Pope or Byron, and despite the considerable element of verbal play? Some things indicate that it might be: the positionally-emphasized 'not' in the second line, the syntactical placing of 'safely beyond', so that life and death seem beyond the victim's capacities rather than his being beyond their reach as the expected placing would have indicated; and then there's the hyperbole of 'ultraomnipotence', and one or two other things. But let us take a triangulation; first, on type, as this poem fairly insists on its technicality. Dramatic? No quotation-marks but apparently two voices; the main one being that of the doctor, whose diction—'your victim', 'we doctors know'—suggests that he shares the dehumanization he is diagnosing in the busy monster (and looks at the same advertisements); the other is that of an antithetical persona, clearly apparent only in the last line and a half. But there's really no dialogue between the voices, and anyway much of the poem seems to be in a medial relationship with the reader, the medical persona materializing and fading like a Cheshire Cat. This is narrative—but subjective, even sentimental enough here and there ('pity poor flesh . . .') to suggest a touch of the lyric type too. This is Polonius-poetry. It assigns itself to various categories, and they of course determine its nature.

Perhaps we might call it a work of mixed purport, satiric-didactic? But let us check by mode. If we are most concerned with theme, or most struck by it, we shall say Romantic, and make *comic* Romantic the kind. But the oversimple, over-Lawrentian message about man's predicament in a mathematical, mechanized world is less striking than the zing and zest of the verbal texture which is what lends new life to this familiar complaint. So let us reverse the order. Comic (not farcical), then, in mode; and a large part of the comic effect comes as much from the dramatic irony of the doctor's being what he censures as from the bracketing twists at each end, '. . . not' and '—listen . . .' or such figures as paranomasia ('manunkind'—mankind, man cruel, man unnatural), oxymoron ('comfortable disease'), hyperbole, and substitution ('bigness' significantly used where 'greatness' might have been). Mood? Well, to refine on 'satiric' how about 'ironically didactic'? Didactic on account of what is said, ironic on account of who's saying it. As for kind—technically a very *un*fixed form of sonnet. Its fourteen lines are surely meant to play against the accepted ideas of sonnet form. No further comparison seems called for. The ruin of a noble form, pretentious in blown-up experimentalism (minor kind), well matches the theme of ruined man imagining himself deified—whether or not Cummings intended this effect.

So far the method of investigation seems to be producing if anything a naturally disordered, rather than a mechanical, progress. On the other hand, it may be a little long-winded. But then, this is not a critical account, merely the preliminary jottings for one. The account itself need use none of these generic terms and could be much more compactly organized, for in considering the poem from various angles we have already found some to be angles of intersection—the same points figuring in different categories—and this is where economy could begin. What does seem to be important is that in the process of defining such basic matters as the poem's real nature and mode of existence, by a generic triangulating method designed to minimize tendencies to misreading, bias and stock-response, we have in fact been led much further into the poem than might have been expected. In this particular case, indeed, little more will need to be done—save by way of polishing and finishing with a finer set of tools the points already touched on—when we have taken the final generic step of comparison.

Comparison with what? Another comic poem? A traditional romantic poem dealing with men and mountains versus machinery? Something anti-Newtonian from Blake (as this seems to be anti-Einsteinian: 'wherewhen', 'returns on its unself')? Or should we take it more technically and use some very modernistic work to bring out by comparison, the individual qualities of its experimentalism? Something from Lawrence's *Nettles* or *Pansies* might feature most of these parallels. Any course is open to us, or all of them. But we already have enough

data for common sense to size up the degree of compulsion to act so
—and there seems to be a case for not dissecting to death a clever
harmless little poem whose complexities have shown themselves to be
all of the surface.

However, this poem does offer itself very much as a play of linguistic effects, indeed a play of eccentric usage against the expectations
of normal usage (the poem is that *variety* of experimental *kind*). We
have noted elements earlier, for instance, in the syntactical placing of
'not' and 'safely beyond', but the characteristic is especially noticeable
in the Einsteinian sentence ('lenses . . . unself') which refers us to the
inhuman, blown-up quality of a universe made unimaginable by four-
dimensional mathematics, made to 'return on its unself' by definition
—at the point where observation becomes *in principle* impossible—an
image of magnified self-imprisoned man-monster with no real self to
have a real wish. It so happens that this sentence is particularly re-
miniscent—like much of Cummings—of Orwell's *Newspeak*. And, as
we briefly categorized that work earlier but conveniently omitted
mention of its essays, we might now use it fleetingly in comparison.
Does not *1984* rightly argue in the essays, and in the narrative exemplify, the dangers and limitations of this sort of language? How *vaguely*
clever 'unwish' is!

Once attention is directed to it, this special 'Cummings' quality
might come under censure. The traditional poet, by doing something
with the language we have, adds to its resources. Cummings by doing
something *against* it (like the dictionary-makers of *1984*) impoverishes
it—or rather would be tending to impoverish it if he were trying to
substitute the new for the old. Since he is merely playing one against
the other, lesser charges are to be preferred: that his are second-order
poems (depending for their effect on a first-order of language) and
that they are often too playful for their subject. In this case, though,
the defects demonstrated by Orwell have become virtues, as such a
language perfectly enacts the theme of dehumanizing 'improvements',
and admirably supports the dramatic irony, of the persona whose very
detachment marks his involvement with 'manunkind' and whose
vocabulary all too well reflects his thesis.

Is it not, though, an outrage to the idea of 'kind' to have compared
a poem with an essay or novel? Well, both had in common satire,
didacticism, and the theme of dehumanization, as well as linguistic
experiment. But the basic answer is that 'kind' is only an idea. We

began with Ehrenpreis's assertion that kinds 'are not implicit in the nature either of literature or of the human mind'; we went on to support pragmatic usefulness against the chimera of absolute, Platonic truthfulness; and we may then logically conclude by reiterating that nothing in this particular approach through type, mode and kind need inhibit initiative or commit the critic to automatism. It even permits him, still, a modicum of eccentricity.

Note

Critical works cited for which no reference is given in the text are listed below in order of first mention; the books mentioned in both places amount to a survey of the main literature in the field. Translations from the French are mine; I have in a few places plundered my own articles for relevant examples, and have benefited from discussions with Malcolm Bradbury, Franz Kuna and Clive Scott, for whose comments I am grateful.

Bibliography and References. Etiemble, *Comparaison n'est pas raison: la crise de la littérature comparée* (Paris, 1963), especially pp. 101–3. Henry H. H. Remak's essay in *Comparative Literature: Method and Perspective* edited by Newton P. Stallknecht and Horst Frenz (Carbondale, 1961). Claude Pichois and André-M. Rousseau, *La Littérature comparée* (Paris, 1967), p. 176. David H. Malone, 'The "Comparative" in Comparative Literature', *Yearbook of Comparative and General Literature* III (1954), pp. 13–20. Marius-François Guyard, *La Littérature comparée* (Paris, 1961). René Wellek and Austin Warren, *Theory of Literature* (1963). Leon Edel's comments taken from his essay in Stallknecht and Frenz, pp. 106–7. Harry Levin, *Contexts of Criticism* (Cambridge, Mass., 1958); *Refractions* (New York, 1966), especially pp. viii, 113–15, 127, 220, 345; *The Gates of Horn: A Study of Five French Realists* (New York, 1963), especially p. 471. Erich Auerbach, *Mimesis: The Representation of Reality in Western Literature* (New York, 1957), pp. 424 and 484. Northrop Frye, *Anatomy of Criticism: Four Essays* (Princeton, 1967), p. 57. Wayne C. Booth, *The Rhetoric of Fiction* (Chicago and London, 1961). Edmund Wilson, *Axel's Castle: A Study in the Imaginative Literature of 1870–1930* (1931, reprint 1961); Mario Praz, *The Romantic Agony* (1933, reprint 1960); Paul Hazard, *The European Mind: The Critical Years, 1680–1715* (originally French, Paris, 1934). Reuben A. Brower's 'Seven Agamemnons' in his collection *On Translation* (New York, 1966), pp. 173–95. Examples of translations from *The Penguin Book of Modern Verse Translation* edited by George Steiner (1966), pp. 68, 102, 141, 267; see also p. 32. The Yeats–Ronsard translation discussed at length by Simon Jeune in *Littérature générale et littérature comparée: essai d'orientation* (Paris, 1968), pp. 110–18. Erwin Panofsky's study in *Meaning in the Visual Arts: Papers in and on Art History* (Garden City, N.Y., 1955), pp. 295–320; Calvin Evans, 'Cinematography and Robbe-Grillet's *Jealousy*', *Nine Essays in Modern Literature* edited by Donald E. Stanford (Baton Rouge, 1965), pp. 117–28; Frederic Will, 'Comparative Literature and the Challenge of Modern Criticism', *Yearbook of Comparative and General Literature* IX (1960), pp. 29–31. See also *Comparative Literature: Matter and Method*, edited by A. Owen Aldridge (Urbana, Ill., and London, 1969); Henry Gifford, *Comparative Literature* (1969), and George Watson, *The Study of Literature* (1969).

The Criticism of Comparison:
The Approach through Comparative Literature
and Intellectual History

JOHN FLETCHER

I

THERE has been in existence, for the last eighty years or so, a branch of literary study known variously as comparative literature, *littérature comparée*, and—most accurately—*vergleichende Literaturwissenschaft* or 'the comparative science of literature'. With such an appellation (especially the German, which incorporates a present participle), the subject might reasonably be expected to have developed a method which set it clearly apart from other modes of literary criticism. This it has signally failed to do: it is, if anything, characterized by the very imprecision of its techniques and the vague catholicity of its concerns. It overlaps with literary and intellectual history, with the sociology of literature and with aesthetics in so many areas that it has tended inevitably to adopt something of the methodology of each of these disciplines at the expense of evolving one of its own. It has therefore struck some people as being an unnatural hybrid with no real validity, other than the dubious one of justifying the existence of the growing number of chairs of comparative literature, the titularies of which profess throughout the world of learning courses of uncertain status ranging from state university 'Great Books' programmes to the exacting Oxford B.Phil. In the eyes of such critics 'comparative literature' is an empty tautology: to compare in literary study, they would argue, is simply to study literature. Indeed, a prominent figure in the field, René Wellek, declares—in an essay appropriately entitled 'The Crisis of Comparative Literature' (in *Concepts of Criticism*, 1963)—that it has proved impossible to establish the distinctness of the discipline's subject matter or to define a methodology which will be both specific to it and worthy of intellectual respect. He presents comparative literature as a stagnant backwater haunted by positivism and mesmerized by a preoccupation with causal explanations which keeps it stuck among the staid traditional procedures of literary scholarship. The picture is harsh but not without resemblance. It cannot be claimed that the subject has thrown up a markedly new critical method. But it can, I think, be said that it is asking some important critical questions and making some fascinating attempts to answer them.

Comparative literature, of course, *compares*; but what? René Wellek offers a depressing portrait of it working almost exclusively with the concept of 'influence' and preoccupied with plotting the literary import–export traffic which shifts the wares of Romanticism from here to there, and with assessing the volume of national profit and loss. In so doing it creates a sense of causal sequence—not content, for instance, with comparing Scott and Balzac, it seeks to *prove* that they are related —which is often insensitive to the creative process, and which in any case by-passes any serious critical confrontation with either of the artists involved. But there are other ways of approaching the subject, ways which have less in common with some of the traditional methods of literary history. The most obvious of these is that comparative literature compares literatures or smaller units: 'the practice of defining one artist or work by another is fundamental to it' (Clive Scott, *Modern Language Review*, July 1969). On this basis, it takes into its purview not a national literature which can be implicitly or explicitly explained by reference to a continuous national literary tradition, and which has its real sources in the immediate cultural environment, but an international body of literatures which can lead us towards a broader idea of what literature itself is. It thus raises different kinds of questions; on noticing that literature manifests itself in different societies and circumstances, it asks what such manifestations have in common, and how they differ from one another. Are there recurrent patterns in literature, and what is the nature of the recurrence? Is there anything to be gained by regarding the writer's milieu as being more truly an international community spread out in time and space than the human group in which he lives and works? Such questions are different in kind from those about 'influences', which tend to deal in verifiable documentary minutiae. To ask questions of this sort—questions about forms and genres; about the degree to which literature is a social manifestation and the kind of social manifestation it is; about

the way in which literature can be regarded as a perception and structure of a 'universal' human mind—is obviously not without its
dangers, but it holds out the hope of real intellectual meat. Questions
about literature lead to questions about cultures, the structures and
orders of language, the relationship between literature and society,
and the history of the human imagination and intellect.

As a result of this comparative literature has affinities with those
areas in which the results of comparative study are tangible and immediate. There is, of course, no need to create a subject called 'comparative
music' because music shows a homogeneity lacking in literature. But
comparative anatomy, comparative religion and comparative grammar
are not self-evident absurdities. They are areas in which the units compared, though diverse, have something in common, so that it is useful
and enlightening to put them side by side—in order, as the well-worn
examination formula has it, to 'compare and contrast' them. There is
no reason, *a priori*, why the effort should be a waste of time; equally
there is no reason, *a priori*, why the procedure should throw up valuable
insights. It must be judged by its results. In literary criticism this is
obviously more difficult than it is in the natural or social sciences,
since the results, finally, cannot have the same order of authority.
Indeed, the scientific analogy underlying the origin of the term 'comparative literature' is unfortunate in that it can raise too many expectations. It has led scholars (some of them eminent) to envisage the
formulation of a corpus of definitively acquired factual data to which
they could proudly point in their disputes with sceptical critics. Hence
objectors—like Wellek—have no difficulty in pouring scorn on the
ambition. In fact even where the aim has been pitched optimistically
too high, some of the scholarship produced (for instance, work on Heine
in France or on Goethe in England) still remains valid and profitable.
Nevertheless, if comparatism in literary studies is expected (by practi-
tioners or detractors) to produce tangible results, a dimension of proven
and neo-scientific data, then it will be no more successful than any other
mode of criticism, and probably less. That some of its early representa-
tives made unrealistic claims is merely unfortunate; it does not necessarily cast doubt on the principle of comparatism as such. If the ends are
set less highly and rather differently, then there is no reason why comparative literature should be a chimerical pursuit. Far from it; comparatism
has been a recurrent dimension of critical practice ever since Aristotle,
and it remains today a field that is attracting engrossed attention.

II

The commonplace justification for comparative literature has been restated recently by George Steiner:

> Literature should be taught and interpreted in a comparative way. To have no direct acquaintance with the Italian epic when judging Spenser, to value Pope without a sure grasp of Boileau, to consider the performance of the Victorian novel and of James without a close awareness of Balzac, Stendhal, Flaubert, is to read thinly and falsely. It is academic feudalism that draws sharp lines between the study of English and of Modern Languages. Is English not a modern language, vulnerable and resilient, at all points in its history, to the pressure of European vernaculars and of the European tradition of rhetoric and genre? But the question cuts deeper than academic discipline. The critic who declares that a man can know only one language well, that the national inheritance of poetry or the national tradition of the novel is alone valid or supreme, is closing doors where they should be opened, is narrowing the mind where it should be brought to the sense of a large and equal achievement. Chauvinism has cried havoc in politics; it has no place in literature. The critic . . . is not a man to stay in his own garden.
>
> (*Language and Silence*, 1967, pp. 27–8)

This generous and humane statement by a critic who did not allow his ignorance of Russian to deter him from writing *Tolstoy or Dostoevsky* is not likely to convince opponents. It relies implicitly on the continually cheated hope that somehow comparative literary studies will lead to greater international tolerance and understanding. In the age of the balance of terror a better argument than that advanced by the early comparatists must be found. Donald Davie, proceeding from more purely literary premises, is, I think, on firmer ground when he declares that 'if students of literature are to be trained alike in the structuralist as well as the historical approach to their subject . . . they need to know more of literature than just their national literature in their native language' (*The Listener*, 5 October, 1967). Inversely, Théophile Gautier must not be reserved exclusively to students in French studies but drawn to the attention of all who are concerned with 'the structure of the short poem'. The same might be said of Brecht, or Graves, or Quasimodo: it is obvious that structures of this kind transcend linguistic frontiers. Nor should we feel compelled to stay within the boundaries of any single civilization: Etiemble pushes

Davie's argument to its logical conclusion when he demonstrates that there is nothing incongruous in an aesthetic of the short story embracing both *Ugetsu Monogatari* and Maupassant's *Contes*—quite the reverse.

The detractor might still retort that this opens the door to the promiscuous pairing of anything and everything. So an attempt to define this discipline can no longer be postponed. We have the choice of two definitions; firstly, Henry Remak's:

> Comparative literature is the study of literature beyond the confines of one particular country, and the study of the relationships between literature on the one hand and other areas of knowledge and belief, such as the arts . . ., philosophy, history, the social sciences . . ., the sciences, religion, etc., on the other. In brief, it is the comparison of one literature with another or others, and the comparison of literature with other spheres of human expression.

Although the word 'comparison' seems to mean more than one thing here depending on the context (to 'compare' two literatures does not appear to be exactly analogous with the 'comparison' of literature and, say, religion), it is clear what Remak is after: the freedom to pick out significant points of contact throughout the whole field of human intellectual and imaginative activity. Our second definition is more abstract:

> Comparative literature: analytical description, methodical and differential comparison, synthetic interpretation of interlinguistic and intercultural literary phenomena, through history, criticism and philosophy, in order the better to understand Literature as a specific function of the human mind.

Apart from being more readily comprehensible than this latter one (by Pichois and Rousseau), Remak's definition is surely to be preferred in that it specifically allows for the investigation and exploitation of the points of contact between literature and the other arts (such as music and 'pure poetry', film and the novel) which many active comparatists consider as falling as much, if not more, within their province as that of general aesthetics. But Remak seems to me to be yielding prematurely to objectors when he concedes that comparative literature is 'less an independent subject which must at all costs set up its own inflexible laws than a badly-needed auxiliary discipline, a link between smaller segments of parochial literature, a bridge between organically related but physically separated areas of human creativeness'. The critics are only too ready to hear the comparatist admit that his role is of a subordinate kind. Comparatism may be an approach to a wider discipline, but it also sets out to be a discipline in its own right. David H. Malone has stated clearly the case for the dignity and autonomy of comparative literature: the comparatist, he writes, 'is a comparatist not because he wants to work in two or three literatures instead of one. Rather he wants to work in two or three literatures instead of one because he is a comparatist'. Comparatism, in other words, is a certain temperament or turn of mind: essence precedes existence. Although it may rely on analytical tools, it is essentially a synthetic turn of mind, concerned, as Remak puts it, to extend 'the investigation of literature both geographically and generically'.

For all that, comparative literature is not the same thing as 'world literature'. Donald Davie puts his finger on the difference when he warns against a superficial acquaintance with 'a handful of foreign authors through uninspected translations'. It is not that the comparatist is necessarily, or even usually, polyglot, although it is impossible to imagine a serious practitioner not fully familiar with at least one foreign language. Human limitations being what they are, however, the comparatist will have to work frequently from translations and will ensure that he has the best available, if necessary by collating two or three; and where he possesses a rudimentary linguistic knowledge which does not permit him to read a foreign text at normal speed, he will refer to the original for all passages that strike him as significant. In what ways, therefore, does he differ from the student of 'world literature' or 'great books'? In the first place, his activity is *explicitly* comparative (rather than implicitly or hardly at all): he is not just collecting masterpieces, he is seeking to relate them. Secondly, he tries to be *systematic*: he is pursuing an enquiry and is careful not to be deflected from it by the temptation of eclecticism. And finally, this single-mindedness implies a *method*, however elementary: his criteria in isolating the data of a given problem are not those of Dr. Eliot's five-foot shelf of books. It is thus an explicit, systematic and methodical approach to a basic shared material which distinguishes comparative from world literature. And in the same way, comparative literature is not exactly co-extensive with 'general literature'. If we accept general literature to cover problems and theories of literary aesthetics (such as the nature of tragedy or realism), then comparative literature will tend to merge into it. But the intensive study of a national literature may equally lead into general literature as here defined. Indeed in France (in the hands of such critics as Poulet and Barthes) it frequently does. Whether or not one finds a good deal of such French criticism abstract and metaphysical is perhaps a matter of personal taste; but one is justified in pointing out that general literature based on a single literature, albeit a central one, runs the risk of appearing blinkered and curiously insular. One would find it hard to take seriously, for instance, a discussion of the nature of the comic in drama which saw nothing incongruous about taking its examples exclusively from Molière, Marivaux, Beaumarchais and Musset; and yet such a phenomenon would not seem particularly odd in France.

If we can broadly accept Remak's definition, and if comparative literature is clearly distinguished from analogous but not identical activities, the only other theoretical problem which remains is that posed by the methodology of a so-called 'French school' of comparatism. The philosophy of this school can be exemplified summarily but not unfairly by an egregious manual by Marius-François Guyard. This is prefaced by one of the founders of comparatism, Jean-Marie Carré, who roundly asserts that 'comparative literature is a branch of literary history', a matter of 'real connections' (*rapports de fait*) and of international commerce and exchange. It is not 'literary comparison' nor even the study of influences, which Carré considers too full of imponderables to be scientifically respectable. His less sensitive disciple Guyard simplifies even further: he would limit the subject to 'the history of international literary relations', and it is soon apparent that the concern for the history of literature outweighs any interest in critical values. Guyard is fond of expressions like 'definitively established' and 'dealt with once for all'. To be fair, one must note a partial, if timid, nuancing of this position when 'future prospects' are considered, but this is not enough to remove the disagreeable impression which the unbridled positivism of the rest of the book has produced (in particular the diagrams in which blank squares indicate where aspiring candidates can write in thesis topics—from which it appears, for example, that Ronsard in England hopefully awaits the would-be Ph.D.). The following passage typifies the pedagogue's clichés, the naive *a posteriori* 'explanation', and above all a curious scale of values which puts Scott on much the same footing as Balzac:

What was Scott's contribution? Not ideas, really; a technique, rather. Because they were incapable of adapting to it writers as intelligent and gifted as Scott failed where he had triumphed. Each of them lacked one of the qualities which, in combination, made up Scott's quality: Vigny was unable, or less able, to infuse life into the crowd scenes which are indispensable in any vital historical reconstruction; Balzac chose a subject too close in time and space for the reader to be able to feel, as he should, lifted out of his everyday surroundings; Mérimée's characters lacked soul; in Hugo excess of picturesque killed the picturesque and banished life. Less of a poet than Hugo, less witty than Mérimée, less powerful than Balzac, less of a thinker than Vigny, Scott succeeded where they failed: plot and history, the exotic and the mundane, the leading actors and the crowd, none of this was sacrificed. Because they failed to understand and apply the rigorous laws governing this achievement, the Romantics were rapidly doomed to relegate the historical novel to more popular forms. Indeed, they abandoned it to Dumas.

No pedant like a French pedant; fortunately, this unsubtle rhetoric is no longer, according to Pichois and Rousseau, characteristic of French comparatism. It is true that they, too, lay stress on 'international literary exchanges' and on travellers and intermediaries—the stock-in-trade of early comparatism—but they also devote attention to the history of ideas and to literary structures. They point out that what Wellek and Warren call 'the extrinsic approach' is, in fact, a broadly conceived comparatism, and 'intrinsic' what comes under the rubric of the philosophy of literature. Comparative literature, they argue, tends to merge into this, for a close comparative study of five major European tragedies will be likely to throw up a useful definition of tragedy. In saying this, Pichois and Rousseau are clearly moving away from literary history, which aims to ascertain the complete facts by exhaustive reading, and towards literary criticism, which hopes to elicit patterns and types from a mass of data in which it takes intelligent soundings. So it is evident that the stunting ambition of definitiveness advocated by Guyard is moribund even in France.

Moribund, but not quite dead. Charles Dédéyan is still with us, a Sorbonne professor and monster of comparatism, author of multivolume studies with titles like *Rilke and France* (I, 'France in Rilke's Life', II–III, 'The Image of France in Rilke's Work', IV, 'The Influence of France on Rilke's Work'), *Gérard de Nerval and Germany* and *Italy in Stendhal's Fiction*. Dédéyan's critical approach is unrepentantly biographical; for the rest, it is not unfair to say that his books are written-up bibliographical index-cards. His colleague at Lille, Jacques Voisine, is less omnivorous. Voisine's bulky thesis *Jean-Jacques Rousseau in England during the Romantic Period* (Paris, 1956) is thorough, minute, myopic even, maintaining that 'our understanding of Rousseau cannot but gain from a better knowledge of the way our neighbours judged him.' This is a rather doubtful premise on which to base the labour of half a lifetime: does the English reception of Rousseau really tell us much about Rousseau? It may tell us quite a lot about English taste and sensibility between 1780 and 1830, but this is of interest more to the historian of English culture, and comparatism will not inspire much respect if it is content to be the handmaid of another discipline. One even wonders if Rousseau's fame in England can ever be of more than anecdotal interest. Following Guyard, Pichois and Rousseau claim that the formula '*X* and *Y*' is capable of almost infinite extension, but it is hard to see what, outside such well-researched contacts as Voltaire in England and Madame de Staël in Germany, can be contributed by the most common form of comparatism practised in France. Its extrinsic, literary history approach guides the policy of the *Revue de littérature comparée*, on the editorial committee of which Voisine sits and of which his teacher Jean-Marie Carré was one of the founders. The weakness of this approach is that, tending not to see the wood for the trees, it may fail to seize on the important link which happens not to lend itself to exhaustive documentation. It is liable to overvalue the accumulation of detail which swamps a potentially significant confrontation, as happens, for example, in Bruce Lowery's *Marcel Proust and Henry James* (Paris, 1964).

We should not go to the other extreme, however, and dismiss the study of literary transmission and influence as a waste of time. The debt one writer owes to another, if it can be established, will reveal a little about the emitter and much about the receiver and perhaps something about the creative process. It is dogmatic to maintain that if both emitter and receiver write in the same language they are the concern only of the national critic, or that the debt of a film-maker like Bergman to Strindberg, or of Malraux to the non-classical styles of Europe or Asia in the plastic arts, transcends comparative literature. If a writer does not find the stimulus he needs at hand he may well stumble upon it elsewhere, either (like T. S. Eliot) in a foreign language or, like Baudelaire with Wagner, in another medium. The comparatist does not wish to squabble over academic divisions but to follow a chain with tact and discretion. If his enquiries into Beckett's place in the European tradition lead him to suspect that he was influenced by his compatriot Swift, why should the purist object that this is English, not comparative literature?

This does not, however, answer the question what is meant exactly by influence and what evidence is considered sufficient to establish it. We are familiar with the notes which discover a book by X in Y's library, or lay claim to a garbled quotation from X buried in the writings of Y, and which assume on that basis an influence exerted on Y by X. A writer is not blotting-paper absorbing everything he reads in every book on his shelves. Influence study, like all criticism, demands sensitivity. If we can establish that Y's world has much in common with X's, that Y adopts some of X's situations or characters, quotes from him admiringly, imitates his style, and annotates his books conscientiously, then we may well be justified in invoking influence. But it is only at this point that the matter becomes critically interesting. What did Y do with what he absorbed from X? That Dante influenced Beckett, who first read him as a set-book at Trinity College, Dublin, is a fact of literary history, neither more nor less significant than any other historical fact. But the consideration of the way in which Beckett's symbolism incorporates and modifies Dante's images and situations can be literary criticism of a non-trivial kind. Why Racine failed to 'catch on' in England is probably of greater interest to the cultural historian or social psychologist than to the literary critic, since the answer is not likely to throw much light on Racinian tragedy itself. But why in his essay on Proust Beckett should emphasize certain aspects and ignore others which attracted the attention of a more professional critic like Edmund Wilson, is a question the comparatist must try to answer, since it bears directly on a central literary problem, the transmutation of forms and themes.

The point is that the comparatist, if he is to command a hearing among his literary colleagues, must concentrate on questions which are likely to interest them. There is slender justification for the erudition which recounts the fortunes of a writer in another country. This is of little concern to the literary critic and probably of less interest than is often assumed to colleagues working in the field of cultural history. French comparatism, impressive as some of it is, is vitiated by the misconception that the emitter is the significant term of the influence equation. It is clearly the 'imaginative faculty . . . and not the food it feeds upon which is all-important' (Leon Edel). But to concentrate on the imaginative faculty is to skirt the frontiers of psychoanalysis, and the positivistic thinking of French comparatism finds the unverifiable conclusions of psychoanalysis anathema.

If I have spent some time on the French school this is because it is a vigorous and well-represented branch of comparatism which must bear a fair proportion of the responsibility for the disrepute attaching to the subject in the eyes of critics like René Wellek. Indeed, for many people French comparatism *is* comparatism and its limitations inherent in the subject as such. It is this impression which I am above all concerned to dispel. If comparatism has limitations (a question I shall consider later) they are certainly not those of a misguided scientism.

Nor are the French quite alone in their approach: there is an Anglo-Saxon brand of the product, characteristically belletristic. I am not thinking of a study like Rayner Heppenstall's *Four-Fold Tradition, Notes on the French and English Literatures, with Some Ethnological and Historical Asides* (1961), which is pleasantly written magazine-section journalism. Enid Starkie's *From Gautier to Eliot* (1960) is more scholarly in ambition, but the subtitle 'The Influence of France on English Literature 1851-1939' betrays an encyclopaedic aim which, even if it were acceptable, has little hope of realization in the space of a little over two hundred pages. Reviewing Miss Starkie's book Frank Kermode felt that 'perhaps her heart was not in it.' I am not sure he was right. The way to hell in this kind of comparatism is paved with the best of intentions, but the data, such as they are, are so elusive and the tools so blunt that it is difficult to avoid shallowness. The result here is a by no means uninteresting saunter along the highways and bye-ways of Anglo-French cultural relations in the civilized company of the *doyenne* of French studies, but it is not comparative literature in any serious sense of the term. Miss Starkie's discussion of *A Mummer's Wife* by George Moore is characteristic: she shows how much Moore owes to Flaubert and particularly to Zola, but she does not see that his style and method are second-rate pastiche, both lurid and prudish. The comparatist does not necessarily limit his attention to writers of the first rank, but if he does investigate less gifted disciples, he must not be content with demonstrating a historical filiation to the exclusion of any consideration of the literary reasons for the corruption of a style into a mannerism and a vision into an affectation. This is precisely what Graham Hough is after when in *The Last Romantics* (1949) he points out that 'none of the English writers except Yeats even began to realize what an arduous discipline' was entailed by the Mallarmean notion of pure poetry, and Yeats himself 'had to work through a long and laborious development before he grasped all the implications of a poetry freed from impurities.' Hough's demonstration of the current which flows from Mallarmé to Yeats via Symons is a model of comparatist analysis: the contact was real and fruitful in this case, and the role of the intermediary tangible (Symons was expert in French literature and Yeats a poor linguist).

Writers like Hough and Kermode (who speaks in *Puzzles and Epiphanies*, 1963, of his 'limited mind of promiscuous habit') practise comparatism effortlessly in the normal course of the 'common pursuit of true judgment', and do it all the better for that. *The Picaresque Saint*, by R. W. B. Lewis (1960), is more explicitly comparative. Lewis selects a particular generation of novelists from four cultures and examines the similarities and contradictions inherent in it. Moravia, Camus, Silone, Faulkner, Greene and Malraux 'tend to communicate,' Lewis claims, 'across four countries and two hemispheres within the same world of literary discourse.' His purpose is to identify a generation (a unit actively promoted in comparative studies by Henri Peyre in *Les Générations littéraires*, 1948) by exploring the imaginative world it has created. According to Lewis, Proust, Joyce and Mann constitute an 'artistic' generation, whereas his six belong to a more 'human' tendency, concerned to discover what it means to be alive. The difficulty with the generation concept is that it pays too much attention to dates of birth (is Rimbaud, born in 1854, really most at home in that period?) and is invariably a *post hoc* category. It rarely appears to have any justification apart from serving as a pretext for grouping studies within the same covers. In Lewis's case there are two particular weaknesses. The first is that his criticism is not of a particularly incisive kind: Moravia's most characteristic quality, for instance, is defined as 'sadness'. Secondly, the occasional misquotation and inaccurate title undermine confidence in Lewis's knowledge of western literature. On the credit side, he does suggest some interesting cross-fertilizations, such as Mann's probable influence on Silone.

Moreover there is no doubt that in certain circumstances the cosmopolitan phases in literature are of considerable importance. Bohemias and avant-gardes must obviously be seen as international phenomena.

Attitudes spread more rapidly and widely than styles: the rapid diffusion of the 'Theatre of the Absurd' is a case in point, and Dada, characteristically, was a widespread revolt that merged into a more narrowly national stylistic revolution, French surrealism. The meeting of like minds is clearly of more significance and has a more tangible impact than the fortuitous coincidence of dates of birth. Are the French 'new novelists' a generation? Beckett was born in 1906, Simon in 1913 —the same year as Camus—and Butor not until 1926. If by 'generation' movement is meant, this should be made clear, and more rigorous methods of investigation and comparison applied accordingly. This kind of study will then tend to merge into a particularly interesting form of the sociology of literature.

This relatively new discipline takes several forms; at its most basic it is concerned with questions of penetration and readership and relies on systems analysis and techniques of market research. An institute of the University of Bordeaux, run by Robert Escarpit (who came to the sociology of literature from English studies via comparative literature) is engaged on advanced research in this field and has already produced concrete information about fiction and the reading public. But Escarpit is the first to admit that this activity is at best only an auxiliary to literary studies. A more theoretical approach is practised by Lucien Goldmann and Roland Barthes. For Barthes the 'unity of classical literature' has been replaced by a 'plurality of modern forms of writing', and this break-up corresponds to a crisis in history itself. Language is basic to literature and it is the language of literature which reflects the times: 'classical writing was obviously class-writing,' as Barthes tersely puts it in *Writing Degree Zero* (1965). Goldmann, who concentrates more specifically on the novel, sees it in a 'dialectical relationship' with the class for which it is written: it is a dynamic reaction to a certain socio-cultural situation of crisis, without becoming a mere tract for the times (as Trotsky mistakenly read Malraux's *Les Conquérants*). The tensions and contradictory pulls in Malraux are what makes him profoundly representative, because in his best work they are held in balance. From this and other concrete examples Goldmann is able to reach an enlightening principle.

The same can hardly be said of the sociological approach using broader comparative methods as seen in *Literature and the Image of Man* (1957) by Leo Lowenthal. This application of socio-political criteria to imaginative literature is the apotheosis of the extrinsic method, in itself not a matter for complaint. The impact of meta-physical concepts and political mythology on literature has been too tangible for all but the prejudiced not to take account of its effects. But to investigate the enthusiasm Yeats felt for Nietzsche, or the mark Babbitt left on Eliot, or the influence Maurras exerted on Drieu la Rochelle, or the impression the figure of Saint-Just made on Mal-raux, is one thing: to apply categories like 'rightist' or 'leftist' to literary manifestations that transcend them is another. In its despair and anarchy the Theatre of the Absurd may well be potentially reactionary, but literary history shows that contemporary ways of viewing works of art tend to appear inadequate later. Unlike seven-teenth-century critics, we no longer find the 'pleasurable castigation of common foibles or vices' a useful category in evaluating Molière's originality as a comic dramatist. Similarly for a modern critic to say that Ibsen represents the dilemma of liberalism or that Arrabal's *a*-politics are rightist politics is to impose criteria that are too close to us to be comfortable and to partake of what I would like to call the 'relevance heresy', which traps Sartre into thinking that Flaubert must be irrelevant because his reactions to the Commune were timid and bourgeois. To practise this kind of criticism on a comparative scale is to indulge in cultural pseudo-history.

III

So far I have been examining largely the debit side of the compara-tist ledger, not with any polemical intention but in order to clear the way for a more positive balance-sheet. Comparative literature has not yet displayed its letters patent of nobility to everyone's sufficient satis-faction for it to be able to envisage *mésalliance* with equanimity. Among the acknowledged members of the aristocracy the name of Harry Levin figures prominently, and rightly so: his theoretical statements as well as his practice have done much to make the discipline respect-able. The practice looms larger than theory in his contribution to the 'Harvard Studies in Comparative Literature', *Contexts of Criticism*, being illustrated by essays in definition such as 'What is Realism?' and by studies like '*Don Quixote* and *Moby Dick*'. The collection is notable for its refusal to accept dogmatic limits to the purview of comparative literature: Levin clearly has little time for those who would exclude an essay in confrontation like 'Balzac and Proust' from such a volume.

His reasons for this attitude are made clear in *Refractions*, emphatically subtitled 'Essays in Comparative Literature':

> The discipline of comparative literature . . . has tended to focus its interest on interrelationships—traditions and movements, the intellectual forces that find their logical termination in -*ism*—rather than on the contemplation of individual masterpieces.

This, he continues, is because the 'special illumination' of the comparatist perspective 'derives from its way of looking at all literature as one organic process, a continuous and cumulative whole. . . . There are grounds for hoping that the comparative method can throw light upon the aesthetic and formal aspects, the styles and structures of literary craft.' This is rightly ambitious: only the concerted attempt to illuminate the essence of the art of writing will establish the uniqueness of comparatism as a form of literary criticism. For 'the organic totality of literature itself, insofar as it can be comprehended through its dynamic processes and its related configurations, must—in the last analysis— prove greater than any single author' if only because 'a literary object owes its existence to a network of relationships.' An approach which seeks to 'illuminate the means by which imagination renews itself, the permutation and transmutation of themes' is at the opposite pole to the eclecticism of a Saintsbury: comparatism is a tool, not a branch of connoisseurship. Nor is it impersonal literary historiography in the manner of the *Oxford History of English Literature*, here unfavourably contrasted with the less impartial Pelican *Guide*.

Levin's practice does not quite fulfil the expectations raised by his theoretical formulations, which offer a blueprint for an ideal comparatism. His own way is urbane and civilized, which has its dangers, particularly that of anecdote; perhaps the need to entertain in the lecture and occasional essay is to blame here. Certain key-books, moreover, keep cropping up; not in itself a defect, this leads one to suspect that Levin has his pantheon like anyone else. He is particularly astringent on the post-Joyceans; his taste seems to end at 1940. This does not prevent one admiring insights that are of the essence of comparative literature, like this one:

> Others have always turned to them [the French] for precepts and examples of refinement, while their more robust spirits have frequently sought to escape from the effeteness of their own conformities.

Like Leavis ('we shall not find Swift remarkable for intelligence if we think of Blake'), Levin is fortunate in the gift of a feeling for terse paradox.

He is seen at his best in a full-length study like *The Gates of Horn*, which characteristically eschews dogmatism by establishing a firm base in one literature. This is the most satisfactory survey extant of the French realistic novel, because the specialized analyses of the five individual authors are framed by chapters which bring out their general relevance, and which only a comparatist could write. Levin's general thesis, applied to his five examples, is that literature is itself an institution. The realistic novel is at once an expression, a critique, and an achievement of bourgeois society, one of its 'monumental glories'. With Levin, as with Goldmann, we see that the forms of art bear some relation to the kind of social change which tends to make the world into a 'global village' by producing similarities between one society and another. The realistic novel, free and relatively detached, held up a mirror to middle-class society; insofar as the image was not a flattering one, it was instrumental in forcing it to change. Totalitarian societies can only have sycophants, not the critics who, paradoxically, alone bring them credit.

The best comparative literature, like this, will tend, as I said before, to merge into general literature. This is especially true of the classics in the field, such as Auerbach's *Mimesis*, which, on the basis of a relatively small number of texts analysed in detail, demonstrates that the imitation of everyday reality in western literature has usually found expression in a comic style, 'high' style being reserved for ideas and feelings, and that the achievement of Balzac and Stendhal was 'the entrance of existential and tragic seriousness into realism'. It is significant that, like Spitzer, Auerbach came to literary study from Romance philology, which no doubt enabled them to avoid the literary-history approach of the French pioneers. Eschewing 'anything in the nature of a history of European realism', Auerbach let himself 'be guided by a few motifs' tried out on a series of texts. If the motifs are correctly perceived they 'must be demonstrable in any random realistic text'. If the general law is true, in other words, it will be verified in each individual instance: the aspiration here towards a theory of literature is plain.

There are not many critics who share this aspiration. Northrop Frye is an exception. Frye would probably not think of himself as a

THE CRITICISM OF COMPARISON 123

comparatist, but *Anatomy of Criticism* represents the best kind of comparatist criticism, ranging widely for its examples and illumining the known with a fresh dimension, as in this characteristic remark:

> Of all fictions, the marvellous journey is the one formula that is never exhausted, and it is this fiction that is employed as a parable in the definitive encyclopaedic poem of the mode, Dante's *Commedia*.

(Yet another manifestation, not surprisingly, is Beckett's *Molloy*.) Frye's book is a 'theory of literature'—whatever one may think of the theory—in a way that Wellek's and Warren's volume is not ('Introduction to the Theory and Practice of Literary Criticism' would be a more apt title, as the authors recognize, tacitly, in their preface). In a more restricted field of theoretical investigation, Wayne C. Booth has sought to establish a 'rhetoric of fiction' based on an impressively eclectic set of examples. Significantly the ultimate origin of the book was a more traditional piece of comparatist scholarship, a Ph.D. dissertation on *Tristram Shandy* and its precursors in 'self-conscious narrator' fiction. In the ablest hands comparative literature is thus a tool towards general theory.

One of the points made by Northrop Frye is that critical insights follow in the wake of creative innovations such as Symbolism. The outstanding example of this is Edmund Wilson's *Axel's Castle*, a classic study of an international literary earthquake the shock-waves of which are only now dying away. Another study which falls within the field of comparative literature without necessarily seeking to do so, *The Romantic Agony* by Mario Praz, traces 'a literary tradition of erotic cruelty, hysterical enjoyment of horror and perverse admiration of crime' (Edmund Wilson). Praz moved from the chair of Italian studies at Manchester to a chair of English at Rome; his references are almost exclusively to English, French and Italian sources. Nevertheless his book illustrates an important tendency in comparatism to merge into the history of ideas, a remarkable example of which is Paul Hazard's *The European Mind*. As one might expect, this tendency is more popular in continental than in Anglo-American comparatism which, in its pragmatic fashion, feels wary of ideological syntheses that are liable to treat works of the imagination in much the same way as periodicals and pamphlets, and to lump writers of the first rank with secondary figures as manifestations of the *zeitgeist*. In the hands of sensitive scholars like Praz and Hazard, however, such essays in intellectual history can illumine a movement or generation from within by revealing the ideas that swayed it, often unawares: that sadomasochism, for example, informs much nineteenth-century writing, is a perception we owe to Mario Praz. When that has been said, it is only reasonable to add that such investigations are a useful and sometimes invaluable companion to literary studies rather than criticism in their own right.

Nevertheless there is one area where comparative literature and intellectual history clearly overlap, and that is in the consideration of broad modes like the tragic and the comic. The comic has attracted less attention than the tragic, and even then tends to be viewed as partaking of tragic seriousness (in such books as J. L. Styan's *The Dark Comedy*, 1962, or Walter Kerr's *Tragedy and Comedy*, 1967). Studies of the tragic mode tend to see it more as an element of contemporary consciousness than as a mere genre: for example, Murray Krieger's *The Tragic Vision* (1966), Raymond Williams's *Modern Tragedy* (1966), and above all George Steiner's *Death of Tragedy* (1961), which closes on the 'remote possibility that the tragic theatre may have before it a new life and future.' In somewhat similar vein Jan Kott's notorious *Shakespeare our Contemporary* (1964) attempts, as the title implies, to relate the great tragedian to an age of camps and dictators, and *King Lear* to *Endgame*. All these studies, to a greater or lesser extent, use some of the methods of comparative literature to pursue notions that transcend it, and belong rather to the field of political and cultural reflection and existential philosophy than to literary criticism proper.

I should like to conclude this brief survey by considering some contemporary examples of 'pure' comparative literature. They are not necessarily the best in the field, but they are fully characteristic. A recent use of the comparatist method known as *stoffgeschichte*, for instance, is *The Ulysses Theme* (1954) by W. B. Stanford, which plots the metamorphoses of Ulysses from Homer to Joyce. Ulysses, according to Stanford, is an adaptable figure: 'sometimes the hero seems to impose his personality on the author', and 'sometimes the author shapes the traditional outlines of the hero to resemble himself.' Precisely how and why the person of Ulysses should cause 'a mutually energizing power' to be exchanged between the author and the hero Stanford does not claim to be able to determine, but thinks Jung's theory of archetypes might offer an explanation. It would have been interesting if he had followed this up.

In *Widening Horizons in English Verse* (1966) John Holloway draws attention to the often fruitful contact between an exotic influence and an indigenous tradition in poetic creation: here the forces working at different moments on English verse are Celtic, Saxon and Norse, Islam, India, the Far East and Egypt. Holloway's concern is that of the comparatist at all times: 'to comprehend the general nature of literary culture and literary creativeness, and of their continuance over extended periods of time.'

Leon Edel, for his part, makes one simple but cardinal point in *The Modern Psychological Novel* (1964): that nineteenth-century fiction explored the external world, whereas the modern novel has concentrated more on the inner world of consciousness. A particular type of fiction, the portrait-of-the-artist novel, is the subject of Maurice Beebe's *Ivory Towers and Sacred Founts* (1964). By examining artists' self-portraiture Beebe hopes to throw light on 'the artistic temperament, the creative process, and the relationship of the artist to society'. In the first and last of these he succeeds: the writer is a kind of secular priest who takes his role seriously and, after a time-lag, is usually venerated for it. But Beebe is no more capable than anyone else of explaining what it is that makes the artist. Nevertheless he fulfils, like the other authors I have just mentioned, the aim of comparative literature which Harry Levin sets out in *Refractions* and which, despite its banality, is worth quoting: 'to counteract one's innate provinciality, and to obtain a more objective view of what one may know, by relevant comparisons with whatever one can learn.'

IV

To the objection that he is a jack of all trades but master of none the comparatist can reply that he is concerned with recurrent structures. It may be that comparative literature—until now the most widespread, democratic, imprecise and perhaps primitive of approaches to literary study—could imitate structural linguistics, and discern formal structures which will resemble the old genres no more than transformational grammar embraces Latin categories. Tragedy, for example, may show up in the basic form of the inward-turning spiral, and comedy as a continuous wavy line. Man's faculty to interpret experience in a certain manner may be structure-based, and his imaginative reactions may be reducible to a finite number of fundamental modes. It is perhaps possible to isolate a given aesthetic—the tragic aesthetic, for instance—and classify certain novels, plays and poems according to it, thereby exploding the category of genre, which long ago revealed its inaptness. There is no doubt that there are in fiction, for example, stock situations that recur continually, such as the giant adrift, from Gargantua in Paris to Gulliver in Lilliput, or the figure of the 'fallen woman' ensnaring gullible youth in nineteenth-century novels. Of course there are sociological explanations for such phenomena as the persistence of the adultery trauma in the last century, but we often come across situations in fiction, some of them quite trivial, which we recognize from a previous encounter elsewhere (in both *Pantagruel* and *Scarlet and Black*, for instance, the populace marvels at the hero's learning). Our aesthetic response resides partially in the satisfaction of a half-conscious expectation, and partially in the pleasurable surprise of novelty. This is, I take it, what Etiemble means when he says that comparatism inevitably leads to a comparative poetics, the elucidation of the structural *sine qua non* of any literary work. If there are basic patterns in literature (and the many fragments of evidence point to that conclusion) it should be the ambition of comparatism to unearth them.

The fundamental issue is this: what can comparative literature do, and what can it not hope to do? Let me try to answer the first half of this question. Through the explicit and deliberate study of a number of phenomena, the comparative method can hope to illuminate certain things about literature. It can, for example, look into cultural transmigrations, such as the impact of the American novel on French fiction in the inter-war years, or into cosmopolitan manifestations such as bohemias. The interaction between individual writers is another obvious focus for investigation (this of course includes 'influence' study but is not necessarily limited to it). A third centre of interest is translation and mistranslation: the translator has been the ubiquitous factor in the emporium of culture. He used to conceive his role as being to smooth out the linguistic asperities of his text in conformity with the tastes of his public, as Reuben Brower's study of 'Seven Agamemnons' has entertainingly demonstrated, and the bizarre fortunes of Desdemona's 'handkerchief Spotted with strawberries' exemplify. Urquhart's Rabelais is one of many brilliant non-translations which have been remembered. Today the translator values fidelity above all else and seeks, if anything, to expand the resources of the recipient language (Bonnefoy's translations of Shakespeare, and Leishman's of Rilke, or Beckett's of his own French, are cases in point). But the comparatist is more interested in the infidelities of the past: he treats translations 'as rare and precious test-cases, as microcosmic dramas in which are acted out the rituals and disputes of different linguistic, generic or ideological forces' (Clive Scott). A contact in the past is kept embalmed in a translation, which is of course a form of creative criticism. By examining it, the comparatist can practise his own form of textual criticism. He will notice that Yeats's rendering of Ronsard's 'When you are old . . .', a fine poem in its own right, alters the tone of the original fundamentally. Ronsard is confident that his verses will immortalize the lady but chides her for her improvident coyness; Yeats eliminates the arrogance. By contrast, Pound's version of Du Bellay's 'Rome' exploits archaisms ('seek'st') to reproduce the original conceit. Scott Fitzgerald's translation of 'Voyelles' makes characteristically explicit and trivial the closing image which Rimbaud, also typically, left enigmatic:

—O l'Oméga, rayon violet de Ses Yeux!

O equals
X-ray of her eyes; it equals sex.

And Richard Wilbur translates Tartuffe's hypocrisy with a glance over his shoulder at *Prufrock*:

But I'm no angel, nor was meant to be

In the first case, a great poet takes a theme from another great poet and recasts it in a subdued manner entirely his own; and in the second, a 'master jackdaw' pulls off a virtuoso trick. The third and fourth flaunt modernisms. But each of these translations constitutes what Scott calls an 'explosive contact', and as such is of interest to the comparatist.

A fourth object of attention is the interaction between literature and the other arts. One kind of interaction is the influence of one art on another: Panofsky has shown how a painter (Poussin) was instrumental in changing the 'thinly veiled moralism' of the dictum *et in Arcadia ego* into 'undisguised elegiac sentiment', thereby provoking the reinterpretation of a theme in European civilization. Then one may look at parallel manifestations: Gombrich, for example, has pointed out similar devices used by Daumier the cartoonist and Swift the satirist, and Calvin Evans has noticed that Robbe-Grillet uses cinematographic techniques in narrating one of his fictions. Lastly, one may use the jargon of another art as a critical term, like 'staffage', or 'zooming' (Flaubert can be said to 'zoom' on the Tetrarch's palace at the beginning of *Hérodias*, for instance). There is no doubt that the different arts are continually and fruitfully affecting each other: Liszt wrote music inspired by Dante, Mallarmé and Valéry were fascinated by affinities between poetry and dance, and Beckett's *Godot* owes much to Laurel and Hardy.

A fifth area for investigation is the promiscuous commerce between literature and ideas. This is so obvious that one or two examples will suffice: Goldmann proposes to study the influence of Marxist and existentialist thinking on French writing, and Hugh Kenner has demonstrated the Cartesian roots of Beckett's vision.

Through the study of these various phenomena, then, comparative literature can hope to throw light on certain things. It may, for example, be able to reveal aspects of the creative process, especially those connected with the genesis of the work of art and its fertilization by contact with others. Wölfflin has pointed out that every picture owes more to other pictures painted before it than it owes to nature, and this is even truer of works of literature: nothing springs *ex nihilo*, but from a corpus of books, a kind of 'library without walls' as Malraux might put it. The comparatist ranges freely within that library in the steps of the artist or movement he is interested in.

In the second place, comparatism can throw light on literature as an institution, not (like Taine) as a product of race, milieu and moment so much as an institution in its own right, acquiring its own developing body of practices and procedures which are to some degree independent of a particular social environment.

Thirdly, the comparative method may illuminate literature as a universal phenomenon—Milton (for instance) being seen as an epic writer among several working within a tradition. It will seek the patterns that a broader perspective may permit, without concerning itself with actual historical contact: the dramatic technique of the Elizabethan and classical Chinese theatre, for example, can be fruitfully paralleled. Or it may notice that as Beckett's tramps wait for Godot, Balzac's financier Mercadet waits for Godeau, a long-lost partner whose return will save him from bankruptcy and dishonour; since there is no evidence of influence here, the shift from the commercial to the existential plane in a century can receive undivided attention.

These are some of the things comparative literature can do; what can it not hope to do? It cannot be expected, except in the comparison of translation and original, to illuminate texts minutely. Comparatism is irremediably extrinsic: 'the privacy, the inner silence where a literary work turns on the axis of its value, is not open to the comparatist, as comparatist' (Frederic Will). The discipline overlaps too much with intellectual history and is too much interested in movements and currents, the *extra* dimensions of an individual work. It does not ignore the uniqueness of the literary act, but it does see it as being produced in a cultural context—a context which is, to a greater or lesser extent, international, but always aesthetic rather than ideological or social. And although the genetic method had value in establishing firm bases of fact, the positivist comparatists were mistaken because they were mesmerized by chronology, simultaneity and the flow of time into the impossible hope of eventual omniscience. Of course chronology cannot be ignored, but to be blinded by it is to miss the significant parallel across time and space, and the interesting *differences*. In other words, the prime concern of comparative literature should not be diachronic but synchronic, not historical but formal: it should concentrate on the abiding and the constant, on common funds from diverse origins.

To sum up, then, comparative literature is the branch of literary study which concerns itself with the basic structures underlying all literary manifestations, of whatever time or place; so it is concerned with whatever is universal in any particular literary phenomenon. There is therefore no limit in theory to its field of investigation, since literatures in all languages, and their relations with each other and with other art-forms, come within its purview. It aspires to be a dimension of criticism with the final aim of throwing one kind of light on what Gombrich has termed those 'multiform crystals of miraculous complexity which we call works of art', since 'even shapes and colours acquire their meaning only in cultural contexts'. It deals with the many-faceted relation between work and context, seeking to steer a middle course between dogmatic formalism on the one hand and blinkered historicism on the other. T. S. Eliot has said that 'comparison and analysis are the chief tools of the critic.' In giving proper weight to the second, we should not allow ourselves to neglect the first.

E

Note

For literary purposes, psychoanalysis works best when it is concrete, close to a text. Given this need for concreteness, the best introductory readings are Freud's case histories: e.g. 'Wolf-Man' ('From the History of an Infantile Neurosis', 1918). Anyone with verbal interests should proceed to *The Interpretation of Dreams* (1900) and *Jokes and Their Relation to the Unconscious* (1905) (see the new Strachey translations). The works of Erik H. Erikson, particularly *Childhood and Society* (second edition, New York, 1963), offer an excellent statement of today's developmental model of man (as used in the present essay). Otto Fenichel's *The Psychoanalytic Theory of Neurosis* (1945) still serves well as an encyclopaedia of psychoanalysis.

Turning to psycho-literary essays, Frederick C. Crews, 'Literature and Psychology', in *Relations of Literary Study* (New York, 1967) provides a firm correction of misconceptions, a strong appeal for the careful use of the method, and an introductory bibliography. Simon O. Lesser's *Fiction and the Unconscious* (Boston, 1957) remains the most flexible and humane introduction. Ernst Kris, *Psychoanalytic Explorations in Art* (New York, 1952), though hard reading, is indispensable as theory. My own *The Dynamics of Literary Response* (New York, 1968) develops a comprehensive model of the interaction of a literary work with a reader's mind; but this way of working with a text can also be applied to the author's or a character's mind (as I try to show in this essay and in the closing, theoretical chapters of *Psychoanalysis and Shakespeare*, New York, 1966).

Since there are many bad psycho-literary studies, I simply suggest anthologies and let the reader select. Very good are *Art and Psychoanalysis* edited by William Phillips (New York, 1957) and *Hidden Patterns* edited by Leonard and Eleanor Manheim (New York, 1966); of second rank are *Psychoanalysis and Literature* edited by H. M. Ruitenbeek (New York, 1964) and *Psychoanalysis and American Fiction* edited by Irving Malin (New York, 1965).

A total search of the literature for studies of a particular text or author means reference to the exhaustive, thoroughly indexed, annual *Psychological Abstracts*. The successive volumes of Alexander Grinstein's *Index of Psychoanalytic Writings* (New York, 1956–) are focussed on psychoanalysis alone; Norman Kiell's handy bibliography, *Psychoanalysis, Psychology, and Literature* (Madison, Wis., 1963), on literature alone. The journal *Literature and Psychology* carries annual bibliographies with abstracts and evaluations.

For illustration of my argument here, I have used Robert Frost's poem 'Mending Wall' from *Collected Poems of Robert Frost* (New York, 1949). It has attracted many non-psychoanalytic commentators. The following approximates a complete list. (To minimize footnoting, I give references here and mention them in the text by the author's name.) Joseph W. Beach, 'Robert Frost', *The Yale Review* XLIII (Winter, 1953), pp. 210–11. John C. Broderick, 'Frost's "Mending Wall" ', *The Explicator* XIV (1955–6), Item 24. Babette Deutsch, *This Modern Poetry* (New York, 1935), p. 42. John R. Doyle, *The Poetry of Robert Frost* (New York, 1962), pp. 72–3. Northrop Frye, 'Literary Criticism', in *The Aims and Methods of Scholarship in Modern Languages and Literatures* edited by

VI

The 'Unconscious' of Literature:
The Psychoanalytic Approach

NORMAN N. HOLLAND

I<small>F</small> we trust what is often said and take literary criticism to mean the valuing of different literary works, then psychoanalysis and literary criticism have little or nothing to do with each other. If we try to bring psychoanalysis into evaluation, we meet right away the logical barricade of Moore's naturalistic fallacy: one cannot proceed logically from descriptive statements to evaluative ones. Psychoanalytic psychology, like other kinds, aspires to the condition of a science: it tries to be a system of descriptions and explanations of the real world. Logically, no values can be derived from it. By contrast, much literary criticism seems to aspire only to the expression of the critic's own values, impulses, and credulities. If so, the critic becomes a mini-poet and criticism a kind of self-expression to which descriptions and explanations are as irrelevant as Captain Shaw's brigade to the flames of true love.

There is, however, one procedure in which the critic behaves in an almost purely descriptive way: explication is the old-fashioned term for it. In effect the contribution psychoanalysis can make to literary criticism begins with explication to which it can add a second dimension—unfolding what might be called the 'unconscious content' of the work.

James Thorpe (New York, 1963), p. 65. Carson Gibb, 'Frost's "Mending Wall" ', *The Explicator* XX (1961-2), Item 48. John McGiffert, 'Something in Robert Frost', *English Journal* XXXIV (1945), pp. 469–71. Marion Montgomery, 'Robert Frost and His Use of Barriers: Man vs. Nature Toward God', *South Atlantic Quarterly* LVII (Summer, 1958), pp. 349–51. George W. Nitchie, *Human Values in the Poetry of Robert Frost* (Durham, N.C., 1960), pp. 7, 8 and 92. M. L. Rosenthal and A. J. M. Smith, *Exploring Poetry* (New York, 1955), pp. 3–6. Also, *The Case for Poetry: A New Anthology, Poems, Cases, Critiques* edited by F. L. Gwynn, R. W. Condee, and A. O. Lewis, Jr. (Englewood Cliffs, N.J., 1954), p. 147 and *Teacher's Manual*, p. 28.

To see it, let us consider a text, one of manageable size which is well known already: Frost's 1914 meditation, 'Mending Wall'. Certainly a number of non-psychological critics have already explicated the poem well, so they can serve as a check to any psychoanalytic extravagancies. Perhaps most important, it is about taking down walls, like the one between respectable literary criticism and psychoanalytic psychology.

Mending Wall

Something there is that doesn't love a wall,
That sends the frozen-ground-swell under it
And spills the upper boulders in the sun,
And makes gaps even two can pass abreast.
The work of hunters is another thing:
I have come after them and made repair
Where they have left not one stone on a stone,
But they would have the rabbit out of hiding,
To please the yelping dogs. The gaps I mean,
No one has seen them made or heard them made,
But at spring mending-time we find them there.
I let my neighbor know beyond the hill;
And on a day we meet to walk the line
And set the wall between us once again.
We keep the wall between us as we go.
To each the boulders that have fallen to each.
And some are loaves and some so nearly balls
We have to use a spell to make them balance:
'Stay where you are until our backs are turned!'
We wear our fingers rough with handling them.
Oh, just another kind of outdoor game,
One on a side. It comes to little more:
There where it is we do not need the wall:
He is all pine and I am apple orchard.
My apple trees will never get across
And eat the cones under his pines, I tell him.
He only says, 'Good fences make good neighbors.'
Spring is the mischief in me, and I wonder
If I could put a notion in his head:
'*Why* do they make good neighbors? Isn't it
Where there are cows? But here there are no cows.
Before I built a wall I'd ask to know
What I was walling in or walling out,

And to whom I was like to give offense.
Something there is that doesn't love a wall,
That wants it down.' I could say 'Elves' to him,
But it's not elves exactly, and I'd rather
He said it for himself. I see him there,
Bringing a stone grasped firmly by the top
In each hand, like an old-stone savage armed.
He moves in darkness as it seems to me,
Not of woods only and the shade of trees.
He will not go behind his father's saying,
And he likes having thought of it so well
He says again, 'Good fences make good neighbors.'

When we explicate a literary work in the regular way, we proceed, I take it, in a series of three steps. First, we go through the text noticing particular words, images, phrasings, incidents, and the like. For example, in 'Mending Wall', as Carson Gibb points out, one thing we must notice if we are not to misread the poem is that the wall not only separates the two men; it brings them together, too.

I let my neighbor know beyond the hill;
And on a day we meet to walk the line . . .

Moreover, it is the speaker, the narrator, who for all his scepticism about the wall is the one to call this annual meeting. John Broderick shows how speaking of 'spring mending-time' gives the act of rebuilding the wall a special, magical, ritual quality, as does the statement,

The gaps I mean,
No one has seen them made or heard them made, . . .

We should notice that the poet is trying to take a wall down as did the frozen-ground-swell—another kind of 'Frost', I suppose, which adds a complication to the sentence, 'Spring is the mischief in me'. And so on. In explication, the critic's first move is to collect as many of these individual insights as he can.

The second is to group these individual *aperçus* into themes. For example, we would notice here several phrases that refer to seasons, particularly in a repetitive, cyclic way: 'spring mending-time', 'frozen-ground-swell', 'once again', 'spring is the mischief in me'. For such a group of phrases, a critic ordinarily uses the term 'theme', and he might conclude, 'the cycle of the seasons is one of the themes of "Mending Wall".'

Another theme that brings together a number of particular lines and images is parallelism or the lack of it. Sometimes this takes a physical form, associated with the wall, as we imagine the two men walking parallel paths: 'We meet to walk the line', 'We keep the wall between us as we go', 'One on a side'. But it is mental as well as physical, and the gaps signify a meeting of minds as well as of lands and bodies. Closing the gaps means closing off points where the two men might meet physically or mentally. As the poet says, 'If I could put a notion in his head'; but he can't, and the two men will remain parallel, on opposite sides of a wall.

This parallelism shows in the language as well, in phrasings like, 'To each the boulders that have fallen to each', 'And some are loaves and some so nearly balls', 'Walling in or walling out'. Most importantly, 'Good fences make good neighbors', the parallelism of which contrasts in our minds with the tangled, redundant syntax of 'Something there is that doesn't love a wall'.

As the parallelisms in phrasing suggest, speech and language are themselves important themes. We hear phrases like, 'I tell him', 'He only says', 'I'd rather he said it', 'his father's saying', 'He says again'. The neighbour speaks 'his father's saying' twice; the poet also speaks twice, and the repetition marks a hardening of position. Speech takes on an almost ominous quality when we hear about those yelping dogs or when the poet spells out the spell he uses to balance rocks.

No doubt there are many other themes one might formulate to which various phrasings and images might be relevant, but these three —or four, really—will do to start: the cycles of nature and the seasons; parallelism; speech; physical and mental. One arrives at such themes by saying such and such an image 'fits under' or 'contributes to' or 'has relevance to' such and such a theme. Thus we could look at some of the puzzles in the poem and ask, for example, what is the significance of Frost's taking a line to say, 'We wear our fingers rough with handling them'. We might conclude that this line treats the skin as another boundary being firmed up and that therefore this line 'fits under' or 'is relevant to' the theme of walls and parallelism. In theory we could continue to fit under one or another theme every phrasing or image in the poem.

Similarly, if we are really thorough-going explicators, we will also use this notion of 'fits under' or 'is relevant to' to bring our four themes under one central theme or meaning. What idea would unite: seasons; parallelism; physical and mental; speech? Northrop Frye suggests for 'the whole design of the work as a unity', its 'centre',

> not the question whether good fences do or do not make good neighbours: the [central] theme is the identity of the 'something' with which the poem begins. We are not told definitely what it is, except that it is not elves, but whatever it is, the contrast of the two human attitudes towards the wall and the two directions of the seasons, towards winter and towards spring, radiate from it as the centre of the poem.

Thus Frye brings together parallelism, both in a physical and in a mental sense, with its representation in the seasons and in the speaking of the poet. He has defined a 'centre' for the poem. He has in effect said those four themes 'come together', 'find a mutual relevance', 'are unified by'—however you would phrase it—a 'centre' or 'central meaning', namely, 'something' from which dualism comes.

Whether or not one agrees with Frye's precise formulation,[1] one should be able to use such a centre to see the relevance of parts of the poem that would otherwise sit oddly. For example, the poem spends one of its forty-five lines to tell us of the fallen rocks, 'Some are loaves and some so nearly balls'. How does this line contribute to the unity of the whole? One could say it suggests a dualism right inside the wall itself, a wall within a wall, a division within a division. Similarly, why does the speaker start talking about 'elves'? We might conclude that 'elves' are nature-spirits and have to do with the 'something' that takes the wall down, hence 'fit under' or 'contribute to' the theme of the seasons. On the other hand, what is the significance of Frost's spending a line to introduce non-existent cows? Or most puzzling of all, what is the rationale behind the phrasing of these four lines?

> There where it is we do not need the wall:
> He is all pine and I am apple orchard.
> My apple trees will never get across
> And eat the cones under his pines, I tell him.

To give a detailed explanation of

[1] A number of explicators, for example Professors Doyle, Gibb and Montgomery, have disagreed with readings such as Frye's that assume the poem approves of the spring-like attitude of the narrator and disapproves of the neighbour's wintry view. Rather, they say, the poem recognizes that both attitudes have their claims on us. I have settled for Frye's simpler view only to spare space and complication.

There may be hidden a pun on 'pineapple' because it is a traditional emblem of hospitality, but somehow I'm not convinced. The 'central theme' or 'nucleus of meaning' we have found does not seem to me able to give these lines sense or relevance. Perhaps I am wrong, but, in any case, this bizarre image cues us to try a second mode of explication, the psychoanalytic.

When one looks at a poem psychoanalytically, one considers it as though it were a dream or as though some ideal patient could speak from the couch in iambic pentameter. As in regular explication, one proceeds in steps.

First, one looks for the general level or levels of fantasy associated with the language. By level, I mean the familiar stages of childhood development—oral, anal, urethral, phallic, oedipal. Just as a first guess I'd say this poem was rooted primarily in the oral stage, because of its references to speech and eating, both associated with the mouth. I do not find the imagery of dirt or smell or money that would signal an anal fantasy, the fire and water of the urethral stage, the risking of the body I associate with phallic writing, or the realistic portrayal of triangles of love and hate that would make me think I was dealing with oedipal material.

If the underlying fantasy of the poem be in a general way, oral, then, more precisely, What is that fantasy? This is our second step, and to know what to look for, we need to know more about the oral stage, the first period in child development. 'Think of the baby's first year this way,' says Dr. Spock,

> He wakes up because he's hungry, cries because he wants to be fed. He is so eager when the nipple goes into his mouth that he almost shudders. When he nurses, you can see that it is an intense experience. Perhaps he breaks into perspiration. If you stop him in the middle of a nursing, he may cry furiously. When he has had as much as he wants, he is groggy with satisfaction and falls asleep. Even when he is asleep, it sometimes looks as if he were dreaming of nursing. His mouth makes sucking motions, and his whole expression looks blissful. This all adds up to the fact that feeding is his great joy. He gets his early ideas about life from the way feeding goes. He gets his first ideas about the world from the person who feeds him.[2]

[2] Benjamin Spock, *Baby and Child Care* (New York, 1957), section 76. This is the usual American and British edition, sold in supermarkets for 2 a.m. comfort.

In this oral phase, the infant must learn two things or, to use current terminology, he confronts two 'tasks' or two 'crises'. As Dr. Spock says, with an arch pun, 'He's wrapped up in himself the first two or three months.'

> In the period up to two or three months, a baby hasn't much contact with the outside world. Most of the time he seems to be listening to what his insides tell him. When they tell him that all is well, he is very peaceful. When they tell him about hunger, or indigestion, or tiredness, he feels wholeheartedly wretched because there's nothing to distract him.[3]

His first job in this world is to learn that he is not at one with the world, that there is an inside and an outside, a self and a not-self. In other words he must become individuated; he must learn his own separateness and identity. *secret*

There is, by the way, nothing esoteric about this notion of individuation and identity. In as prosaic a source as the pediatrics column of *The New York Times*, James Kleeman refers

> to the time in a baby's life (symbiotic period) when he experiences 'oneness' with his mother, that is, he cannot distinguish her as separate from himself, and to the process (individuation) by which the baby learns that he is a person—and that his mother is another.
>
> . . . . in the symbiotic phase, ending at about five or six months, baby cannot tell where he ends and mother begins.
>
> The normal separation-individuation phase leading to healthy individuality takes place between five months and three years. . . .
>
> Differentiation of self starts when the infant recognizes his mother as a special person and begins to grow away from the state of oneness with her.
>
> [At three years] The capacity to tolerate separation from mother for longer periods is strengthened by the progression of speech, fantasy, and knowledge about reality. . . . A sense of time evolves at this period and aids the toleration of delay [in] satisfactions. This fosters greater endurance of separation. Around the end of the third year the child can distinguish himself from non-self, inside from outside, animate from inanimate.[4]

[3] Spock, *op cit.*, section 343.
[4] James A. Kleeman, 'Hatching Out', *The New York Times Magazine* (February 9, 1969), pp. 67-9.

Individuation is an important concept, doubly so in this essay, and we must be clear on it.

The crucial factor is feeding. In the beginning the newborn child thinks of himself as at one with the world around him, chiefly with his mother. As she gratifies his hunger, he merges or fuses with her, or at least he feels as though he and she are one thing. As he feels the discrepancy between his inner needs and the outer satisfaction of those needs, he learns that he is not the whole world. He finds that he is not autonomous, that there is an outside something, a not-self, an Other who feeds him or, more generally, on whom he is dependent. As he learns that Other is a separate being, he necessarily learns he himself is separate, and he becomes aware of his own identity. In other words, his—our—whole sense of identity is predicated upon having to wait, expect, endure delay, and trust that that Other will come.[5]

Managing that delay sets up the second developmental task of oral infancy: the mastery of ambivalence, which is closely related to individuation. 'The infant's first social achievement,' says Erik Erikson, 'is his willingness to let the mother out of sight without undue anxiety or rage, because she has become an inner certainty as well as an outer predictability.'[6] He must learn to tolerate the frustrations inevitable in his passive state without being overcome by fury or panic. Dr. Spock described the frustration and real rage the infant feels when his feeding is interrupted or delayed—yet it is precisely by tolerating that delay (and anger)—that he achieves his own identity and makes his mother 'an inner certainty as well as an outer predictability'. Were there no delay, were his wishes gratified before he could ever feel them not being gratified, he would pay a terrible price in development: the loss of a sense of himself. Conversely, if the delays and frustrations are too much, he pays another way: by being overwhelmed by an anger he cannot deal with, by investing his mother and therefore his own sense of separateness with terror and rage. The mother must be 'adequate' or 'sufficient' if the child is to learn to tolerate the mixture of love and resentment he feels towards her. He must learn to accept his ambivalence if he is in later life to accept ordinary relationships with others

---

[5] Some of the most important work on early infancy and individuation is by the English pediatrician, D. W. Winnicott. See, for example, his 'Theory of the Parent–Infant Relationship', *International Journal of Psycho-Analysis* XLI (1960), pp. 585–95.

[6] Erik H. Erikson, *Childhood and Society* (2nd edn., New York, 1963), p. 247.

(which will inevitably both frustrate and gratify him as his first relationship did).[7]

Now, all this pediatric material must seem odd in a literary essay, but perhaps not for long. I have used Dr. Spock and the Sunday supplement, hoping you will agree that we are talking about familiar, well-known, widely experienced things: people—children—really *are* this way. I am not proposing psychoanalysis as a 'system' or 'philosophy' or a 'myth', 'structure', 'Weltanschauung', 'science de l'homme', 'theory of being', or whatever. I am using psychoanalysis for its knowledge of the way human beings are, particularly of what adults retain from childhood, for I think the psychoanalytic explication of poems ought to be grounded as much as possible in experience as visible and tactile as poetry itself.

I said a psychoanalytic explication proceeded in steps. Our first was to note that the poem seemed to contain a fair number of images having to do with the mouth, with eating or speech—for example, 'the yelping dogs', stones which are 'loaves', the speaking of a spell, the neighbour's twice saying 'his father's saying', 'I tell him', 'He only says', and so on. I concluded that the poem probably dealt with a fantasy from the oral stage of development. The second step was to consider some data about the oral stage, derived ultimately from psychoanalytic work with and observation of very young children.

We can now take our third step, namely, using this knowledge of the oral stage to hypothesize a nucleus of fantasy that will bring together the separate themes and images of the poem with reference to the unconscious mind, as the 'central theme' did with reference to the conscious. Our excursion into pediatrics showed that our first 'wall' —the boundary between self and not-self—came about by means of the mouth. This poem involves mouth imagery, and it is also a poem about setting up and breaking down boundaries, particularly boundaries between people. Quite obviously, I think, the poem works with some infantile fantasy about breaking down the wall which marks the separated or individuated self so as to return to a state of closeness to some Other.

Once we have hypothesized this nucleus of fantasy, we can see why a poem about a wall has so many images of eating or why, though

[7] Elizabeth R. Zetzel, 'Symposium on "Depressive Illness": Introduction', *International Journal of Psycho-Analysis* XLI (1960), pp. 476–80. See also Erikson, *op. cit.*, pp. 72–80 and 247–51.

Frost and his neighbour are grown men, the poet should begin to explain things by 'elves'. The poem itself offers something of a clue: 'Spring is the mischief in me.' Elves are nature-spirits, and the poet seems to be allying himself with a natural force, the 'something' that takes walls down. Here again, we come to an oral characteristic. 'Psychoanalysis assumes,' writes Erikson, 'the early process of differentiation between inside and outside to be the origin of projection and introjection which remain some of our deepest and most dangerous defense mechanisms.'[8] As the speaker in the poem contemplates the letting down of those boundaries between inside and outside, he regresses to a stage in which he projects onto nature his own human characteristics. 'Something there is that doesn't love a wall,/That wants it down.' The verb 'love' calls for an animate subject and thus makes 'something' more than some *thing*. Besides, the frozen-ground-swell is really Frost, and that concealed pun again mixes up self and outer world as does 'Spring is the mischief in me.' The regression shows in the way he calls himself a child-like elf or uses a magic spell to keep the stones balanced.

This whole section of the poem where he entertains the possibility of just letting the wall fall down involves a faintly paranoid[9] loss of boundary between himself and his neighbour: 'I wonder/If I could put a notion in his head', 'I'd rather/He said it for himself.' Thus, too, the puzzling image of the cows introduces oral themes: milk and motherhood, most obviously, a note of femininity, but we should also

[8] Erikson, *op. cit.*, pp. 248–9.
[9] There is a link, widely recognized in psychiatry, between paranoia and the projection of homosexual impulses. In this context, the tone of the poem matches its underlying fantasy of merger, not with a mother, but with another man. More generally, one of the striking confirmations of a psychoanalytic approach to literature is that occasionally a literary insight will lead to a psychological discovery. Here, the paranoid tone in a relatively oral poem tends to confirm a purely psychoanalytic hypothesis, namely, that paranoid projection builds anal and phallic anxieties on an earlier, more primitive failure of an oral kind, depressive or schizophrenic. This was early suggested by Karl Abraham, *A Short Study of the Development of the Libido, Viewed in the Light of Mental Disorders* (1924), Part II, *Selected Papers* (1927), and more recently by Melanie Klein, 'A Note on Depression in the Schizophrenic', *International Journal of Psycho-Analysis* XLI (1960), pp. 509–11. These purely psychoanalytic writings would lead us, in turn, back to the poem and additional levels of fantasy, anal and phallic, in the boulders: as mess, as 'balls', 'handling them', and so on.

remember the cow is an eat-and-be-eaten animal: we feed her but then we feed on her.

In this poem, the primitive rage of the oral stage comes through in 'the work of hunters':

> they have left not one stone on a stone,
> But they would have the rabbit out of hiding,
> To please the yelping dogs.

Still more ominous is the picture of the neighbour holding a stone in each hand, 'like an old-stone savage armed', and the palaeolithic reference images in yet another way regression to a primitive, violent, savage state of mind.

Knowing something about the sources of this oral rage helps make sense out of what are, to me, the oddest lines of the poem:

> He is all pine and I am apple orchard.
> My apple trees will never get across
> And eat the cones under his pines, I tell him.

In a manifest way, the speaker is simply being sarcastic: you only need a wall if you think immovable trees will cross over and eat inedible seeds. Even so, the phrasing seems extreme to me—until I take into account the unconscious oral fantasy latent in these lines. In the poem, as in the human mind itself, boundary and eating and identity all go together. The speaker imagines the boundary down, and with it he imagines that both he and his neighbour lose their human identities: 'He is all pine and I am apple orchard.' The next lines say, in effect, the to-be-eaten will never move to eat the not-to-be-eaten. Knowing something about oral frustration, we can understand these terms as, the to-be-eaten (the infant fearing being devoured) will never move (being helpless) to eat the not-to-be-eaten (the Other whose withholding has mobilized overwhelming needs). We have entered the range of what Erikson would call 'undue anxiety or rage', though the unconscious anger shows consciously only as sarcasm. Just the chaos comes through unchanged, as though to say, if the wall comes down, a psychotic fantasy will break through.

Obviously I do not mean the poem is literally psychotic, only that the oddity of Frost's language at this point matches what we know about orality. The most severe mental disorders get their start in the oral stage. As Erikson says, 'the bizarreness and withdrawal in the behaviour of many very sick individuals hides an attempt to recover social mutuality by a testing of the borderlines between senses and physical reality, between words and social meanings.'[10] Indeed one of the poem's non-psychoanalytic explicators, Marion Montgomery, picked up precisely this motif: 'Something wants all walls down so that individual identity may be destroyed. The wise person knows that a wall is a point of reference, a touchstone of sanity, and that it must be not only maintained but respected as well.'

Evidently, when we look at this or any poem psychoanalytically, we find in it a nucleus of fantasy that corresponds to the nucleus of meaning regular critics discover: when 'something' takes the walls down between self and other, a chaotic, violent, irrational, primitive aggression appears.

I do not wish to suggest that the poem in any sense 'reduces' to this fantasy—just the opposite, in fact. The poem has *both* this nucleus of fantasy *and* the central meaning regular explication points out. If it didn't have both, it wouldn't be a poem, for a literary work is just that—work. It is a transformation rather like the dream work in which the nucleus of fantasy shapes and informs the central theme and the central theme shapes and informs the nucleus of fantasy. Each is transformed into the other through the writer's choice of words. And if we have properly explicated the poem we should be able to see this process of transformation from fantasy to intellectual significance.

For example, Frye sees the conscious theme of the poem as the identity of the 'something' from which, as from the centre of the poem, radiate two human attitudes towards the wall corresponding to two seasons, winter and spring. It is not difficult, I think, to see that the warm, spring-like (but dangerous), walls-down feeling in the conscious content of the poem corresponds to a cosy but risky return to symbiosis at the fantasy level; or that the neighbour's wintry walls-up sense of privacy and separateness corresponds to the cold, hard reality of individuation. In short, the conscious theme Frye finds in the poem represents a *transformation* of the unconscious. The poem is not one or the other but the *process* of each becoming the other. Similarly, a well-known textbook offers as a reading: 'The subject of the poem is the subtle tolerance and humaneness of the speaker' (*Case for Poetry*). Again we can recognize a transformation, this time a reversal of the hidden rage into 'subtle', that is, hidden, tolerance and humaneness.

[10] Erikson, *op. cit.*, p. 248.

Often, as in this last comment, one can hear in the critic's phrasings of the conscious issues of the poem faint echoes and traces of the nucleus of unconscious fantasy. In 'Mending Wall', the fantasy has to do with the on-again-off-again boundaries established between mother and child. Thus one critic (Gibb) says the poem deals with walls 'that *both* divide and unite men.' As we have seen, in the poem as in the oral stage of childhood, there is a fear, if the boundary comes down, of being devoured or engulfed by the symbiotic unit. Two explicators tell us this poem has to do with a New Englander's cold sense of how 'it is never safe to commit himself inescapably' (Rosenthal and Smith).

Still other phrasings bring a faint image of the mother to mind. One critic sees the poem as about different 'means of propitiating a deity', ways of giving 'worship to that indefinite "something" that does not love a wall, that, in fact, "wants it down"', a 'primitive worship' which constitutes 'acceptance' of things 'which have been handed down from a preceding generation' (Broderick). Two readers describe the poem as dealing with 'ideas from the past that still haunt the present'; the conflict, they say, 'dramatizes the irrationally firm hold that in-herited, half-forgotten beliefs have over the minds of men' (Rosenthal and Smith). Sometimes the mother comes out symbolized simply as something big, the world, as in this phrasing: 'Something in the world doesn't like a wall between a man and the world' (Montgomery).

The point is that when we look closely at the wording of the poem or the wordings of critics' associations to the poem, we find that it comes to a focus around an unconscious fantasy just as it does around a conscious theme. Indeed we find that there is every reason to believe that the conscious meaning is a transformation of the unconscious fantasy. If so, then the next question is obvious enough: what is the agent of transformation?

In a psychological sense, of course, it is the mind and hand of the poet that transform an unconscious oral, anal or phallic fantasy into a poem with conscious themes and meaning. In a more literary sense, we can identify two such agents. The first is the press towards meaning that we have already seen, a kind of sublimation or symbolization of the unconscious material in which, for example, the boundary between the symbiotic unit of mother and feeding child is transformed into a wall between two farms; in which the child's hostility in that relation, or the mother's, becomes 'an old-stone savage armed'; in which the trust and expectation developed by mothering become the regularity and ritual of closing the gaps, and so on.

The second agent of transformation is that tired old warhorse among literary concepts—form. Here I am using the word in a large sense and a small. By form in the smaller sense, I mean a displacement to language which tones down the emotional power of the raw fantasy. The basic psychological issue of the poem—the establishing of an ultimate boundary of self—becomes translated into verbal games like the pun in:

> Before I built a wall I'd ask to know . . .
> to whom I was like to give offense.

By form in the larger sense, I mean the arrangement of the parts of the poem. Partly that means just the sequence, so that after we have the noisy, violent hunger of 'the yelping dogs' we get the stealthy and mysterious gaps, which 'No one has seen . . . made.' But partly I also mean the very selection and choice of material—the strategy of the poem—which plays the most important part of all in pressing the unconscious fantasy towards meaning. We can see this kind of form best by contrasting 'Mending Wall' to some other literary works that happen to build on the same oral fantasy of aggressive merger but use quite different strategies towards it.

I am thinking, for example, of Swift's *A Modest Proposal*, where this fantasy of a hostile merging with a parent-figure gets very direct expression: the mother-country is eating her colony up; Irish babies should be raised like cattle and butchered for food. Swift is building his satire on a very common oral fantasy: the wish to eat mother or the fear that mother will eat you. It survives in the familiar nightmares of ferocious animals or monsters, and it shows its closeness to infantile love in such terms of endearment as 'Sweetie' or 'Honey' or in statements to children like, 'You're so cute, I could eat you up.'

In growing up, we all developed a 'reaction-formation' against expressing love by simply and directly eating the loved one up. By 'reaction-formation', the psychoanalyst means the defence mechanism by which impulses to be messy get reversed into compulsive cleanliness or impulses to be cruel into exaggerated charity. In psychological terms Swift's satire presents us with the impulse to devour babies and then builds on our pre-existing reaction-formation against that impulse. The form of Swift's satire, its *reductio ad absurdum*, and his straightforward, numerical calculation of the feasibility of his scheme as though it were all really going to happen, strengthens still more the audience's reaction-formation. We then react to Swift's apparently serious suggestion with revulsion and horror, so much so that Swift makes us feel quite generally disgusted with such 'scientific' projects, disgusted at the way England once fed on the Irish, disgusted at man's inhumanity to man, and we cast about in our minds for better ways of identifying with the Irish than eating them. (And you will notice that all unconsciously, with the word 'disgust', this critic, too, slipped into an oral metaphor.)

For a quite different way of handling these oral fantasies, let me turn to a different sort of literary work, an elegy on the death of Billie Holiday by the childlike American poet, Frank O'Hara, who was killed in an automobile accident in 1966. It is called,

The Day Lady Died

It is 12:20 in New York a Friday
three days after Bastille day, yes
it is 1959 and I go get a shoeshine
because I will get off the 4:19 in Easthampton
at 7:15 and then go straight to dinner
and I don't know the people who will feed me

I walk up the muggy street beginning to sun
and have a hamburger and a malted and buy
an ugly NEW WORLD WRITING to see what the poets
in Ghana are doing these days

                       I go on to the bank
and Miss Stillwagon (first name Linda I once heard)
doesn't even look up my balance for once in her life
and in the GOLDEN GRIFFIN I get a little Verlaine
for Patsy with drawings by Bonnard although I do
think of Hesiod, trans. Richard Lattimore or
Brendan Behan's new play or *La Balcon* or *Les Nègres*
of Genet, but I don't, I stick with Verlaine
after practically going to sleep with quandariness

and for Mike I just stroll into the PARK LANE
Liquor Store and ask for a bottle of Strega and
then I go back where I came from to 6th Avenue
and the tobacconist in the Ziegfeld Theatre and

casually ask for a carton of Gauloises and a carton
of Picayunes, and a NEW YORK POST with her face on it

and I am sweating a lot by now and thinking of
leaning on the john door in the 5 SPOT
while she whispered a song along the keyboard
to Mal Waldron and everyone and I stopped breathing

As with Frost's poem, certain images tell us we are dealing with an oral
fantasy about taking in—food, the mysterious dinner party, the hamburger and the malted, then the liquor, the highly flavourful cigarettes
to be inhaled, breathing, finally the Lady's whispering voice. O'Hara
is dealing with the same kind of return to at-oneness with a gratifying
mother, here, Lady Day (as she is still called), but the boundaries he
will break down are different. His poem insists on the flow of ephemera,
the very minute the trains leave, the name of a bank teller, who 'for
once in her life' doesn't question him, his momentary decisions in a
bookstore, leaning on a door, his half-anonymous friends, Billie
Holiday's accompanist's name. As against this transiency of experience
are various permanences: books, like the classics Richmond Lattimore
translates, banks who, permanent themselves, record the ebb and flow
of O'Hara's balance, the permanence of Bastille Day, even though the
Bastille itself did not survive.

   In short, the boundaries O'Hara's poem deals with are those of time,
and in the last lines of the poem we hear how great art holds a moment
frozen forever. At an unconscious level, the fantasy is a return to an
at-oneness with the Lady, felt as forever. The form by which O'Hara
achieves the poem is a complicated reversal, signalled by the change in
the title of Lady Day to Day Lady. His momentary fusion with her
whispered breathing makes the ephemera of his 17 July, 1959, forever
permanent, gives him and his friends identity. Yet it is their identities
and his ephemera, which the writer of lyrics can capture, that make
forever permanent her art, the most ephemeral of all, the singing, the
very breathing, of jazz. The poem works by reversal, building out of
the young poet's impermanences and the mature woman's impermanences, a paradoxical moment of immortality. Each impermanence
makes the other immortal to create one of the most astonishing elegies
of our time.

   As Lionel Trilling pointed out long ago, in the great line of English
poets, it is Keats who most markedly reveals unconscious content from

the oral stage of development. Consider these well-known lines from the 'Ode on Melancholy':

> Ay, in the very temple of delight
> Veil'd Melancholy has her sovran shrine,
> Though seen of none save him whose strenuous tongue
> Can burst Joy's grape against his palate fine;
> His soul shall taste the sadness of her might,
> And be among her cloudy trophies hung.

He fantasies a fusion with the maternal might of melancholy and with it the typical oral themes of having all or nothing, total depression or total elation, that to taste joy is to be engulfed by melancholy—alternatively, that not to have all is to have nothing, as in these lines from the late sonnet, 'To Fanny':

> O! let me have thee whole—all—all—be mine!
> That shape, that fairness, that sweet minor zest
> Of love, your kiss,—those hands, those eyes divine,
> That warm, white, lucent, million-pleasured breast,—
> Yourself—your soul—in pity give me all,
> Withhold no atom's atom or I die,
> Or living on perhaps, your wretched thrall,
> Forget, in the mist of idle misery,
> Life's purposes,—the palate of my mind
> Losing its gust, and my ambition blind!

Keats reaches always for the total, the ineffable, the transcendent, and it is in passages such as these that we see the unconscious meaning of his quest for the ideal. We can see, too, the unconscious significance of the ending of *Endymion*: to have achieved a compromise, an imperfect part, like the Indian Maid, is an unstable position; she must become either nothing or all—the unattainable moon goddess. Keats's dominant psychological pattern is one of identification. By tasting a small satisfaction—or a small sorrow—taking it into himself, he becomes able to identify with, really to lose himself in, a total, all-encompassing reality. Thus he can speak of the 'camelion Poet' and say of the poetical character, 'It does no harm from its relish of the dark side of things any more than from its taste for the bright one; because they both end in speculation.'

Keats, O'Hara, Swift—I chose them because they all deal with the same unconscious oral fantasy, a more or less aggressive fusion with the nurturing mother. Yet each brings a different strategy to that fantasy, and each of these strategies, if it happened in a person rather than a poem, would look like a defence mechanism well known from clinical experience: Swift uses reaction-formation; O'Hara, reversal; Keats, identification.

Frost, too, uses a poetic form that resembles a familiar defence mechanism—projection. That is, he starts with a wall but it turns out not to be 'just a wall'. He builds its significance by stressing that 'something' doesn't like it; its gaps have a mysterious quality ('No one has seen them made or heard them made'); it seems to be engaged in a struggle between beings. In effect, Frost is projecting human or other attributes onto the inanimate world, to the point where one critic finds the wall engaged in a supernatural, religious confrontation (Broderick) —and certainly a paranoid quality shows through in the magic spell the poet speaks to keep the boulders balanced.

When the wall becomes something mental as well as physical, Frost himself is taking down a wall. He is breaking up the received categories with which we live to reveal a world underneath of 'eternal things', to use Miss Deutsch's phrase. But those 'eternal things' (which, psychoanalytically, we would understand as having something to do with the mother) turn out to be primitive, savage, chaotic and dangerous. Frost's form acts like the defence mechanism of projection—he attributes dangerous wishes and fears within himself to the inanimate world around him; then his poem explores those mental states in the guise of physically (phallically—in an unconscious sense) dealing with the physical realities of a New England farm.

With that uncanny selfknowledge of the artist, Frost seems almost to have recognized this tendency in himself to project, as when he wrote, 'Like giants we are always hurling experience ahead of us to pave the future with.'[11] Or, in the poem, 'For Once, Then, Something',

> Others taunt me with having knelt at well-curbs
> Always wrong to the light, so never seeing
> Deeper down in the well than where the water
> Gives me back in a shining surface picture
> Me myself in the summer heaven, godlike, . . .[12]

The poem ends, explaining its title, by describing how once he did

[11] *Collected Poems*, p. vii.   [12] *Ibid.*, p. 276.

see a vague 'whiteness'. 'Truth? A pebble of quartz? For once, then, something.' Often Frost's poems leave his projections still in the air that way, and those are the poems that end in strangeness and fear, at their headiest, a kind of paranoia. Other Frost poems, like 'Mending Wall', make the whiteness solid: they take down the paranoid structure and leave us a (more or less) reassuring solidity. 'He says again, "Good fences make good neighbors." '

In short, a psychoanalytic look at Frost's poem enables us to discover the infantile fantasy at its core and, further, what happens to that fantasy both as it is transformed towards meaning by the poem as a whole and as the poem progresses from its beginning to its end. Nevertheless there is always the nagging question, so what? It seems to me are three *so that's* which can or do follow from this kind of psychoanalytic study of a literary text.

First, one often finds unexpected connections and unities within the text. For example, in Frost's poem, the odd idea of the apple trees crossing the boundary to eat pine cones, the curious introduction of cows and elves, the description of the rocks as loaves and balls—none of these would fit in the poem for me until I was able to use a psycho-analytic reading as a clue. Similarly, so astute an observer and critic of the current poetic scene as Paul Carroll says of the O'Hara poem that its images occur without any organic reason, that it is like an action painting: the poem *is* the act of writing it and nothing more.[13] Now, it may be true that the poem resembles an action painting—I think it *is* true and a good insight—but it is not true that the poem lacks a traditional organic unity. While an ordinary reading for that unity did not work, a psychoanalytic understanding quickly showed how the dinner in Easthampton, the Gauloises, the hamburger and the malted all relate to the singing of Billie Holiday. Then, once we have seen the connection at the fantasy level, we were able to see it in a more traditional way and find that 'The Day Lady Died' is not only an 'action poem' but a highly unified poem in the long tradition of the English elegy, which adds to that tradition by making the act itself, the momentary act of living and writing the poem, part of the poem's mourning for all momentary things.

By the same token we may understand the two speakers in 'Mending Wall' as two aspects of the basic psychological issue of the poem: given a violence that appears when the wall is down, the two characters

[13] Paul Carroll, *The Poem in its Skin* (New York, 1968), pp. 160-3.

suggest different ways of dealing with it. The neighbour speaks for an aggressive distancing, the narrator for a loving closeness. This approach leads to an understanding of literary characters in general as functions of drive and defence within an overall psychological process which is the literary work. We can then understand how literary characters, who are patently not real and sometimes not even realistic, nevertheless often feel like real people. We might go still further to understand how these two characters might represent different aspects of Robert Frost. Indeed, C. L. Barber tells me that Frost himself said to someone who took this poem to mean he had become an 'internationalist', 'As if I weren't on *both* sides of that wall!'

In general, I would make a second answer to 'so what?' A psycho-analytic analysis of a poem often enables us to see new unities between the writer and his writing. For example, recognizing the orality and projection in Frost's poems makes more probable the depressions and panic states his posthumous biographers have revealed. We can under-stand, too, his tenacious regionalism as in the poem paraphrased by Joseph Warren Beach: 'Sent as a greeting on Independence Day, his sentiment is one of regret that the Atlantic Ocean has not proved a more effective wall between us and Europe.' The same theme of dis-tancing shows in his description of 'The Figure a Poem Makes': 'It begins in delight and ends in wisdom . . . in a momentary stay against confusion.' 'It finds its own name as it goes and discovers the best waiting for it in some final phrase at once wise and sad—the happy-sad blend of the drinking song.'[14]

Similarly, recognizing the strongly oral colouration of Keats's per-sonality and his use of identification as the defensive strategy in his poems, we can see the importance in Keats's life of such things as his over-large mouth, his fondness for 'concerts' in which he and his friends would mouth the sounds of the various instruments, his tendency to depend on older friends, his systematic setting out to 'be a Poet', his identification with earlier or older poets. We can in turn see connections between these biographical data and Keats's critical concepts of negative capability and the sympathetic imagination or, in his poems, the linking of sleep and poetry or the imagination and trance, his recurring tendency 'To cease upon the midnight', to 'drink, and leave the world unseen,/And with thee fade away.'

In short, we are seeing what Yeats called that 'some one Myth for

14 *Collected Poems*, p. vi.

every man, which, if we but knew it, would make us understand all he did and thought.'[15] 'Our *Humour*,' wrote Congreve, describing what a psychoanalyst today would call 'character' or 'life-style', 'Our *Humour* has relation to us and to what proceeds from us, as the Accidents have to a Substance; it is a Colour, Taste, and Smell, Diffused through all. . . . So the Natural sound of an Instrument will be distinguish'd, tho the Notes expressed by it are never so various, and the Divisions never so many.'[16]

Finally, in addition to understanding the work better and the writer better, the psychoanalytic approach helps in understanding the audience better, both in general ways and in highly specific and technical ways—that is, the large secular trends in what Proust called the 'literary stock market' and also the specific understanding of particular responses, as, for example, the eerie feeling so many of Frost's poems give. To understand and to see the very sweeping implications of such a view of literature, we need to introduce one final concept. We have seen how a literary work has a central meaning that traditional explication finds for us and how it has a nucleus of fantasy that a psychoanalytic analysis discovers. Further, we have seen that the literary work looks like a transformation of unconscious fantasy into conscious meaning and vice versa, with form and the press towards coherence and meaning as the two principal agents of transformation. The next question is, how does this process enter into a particular individual's response?

To answer, we need to know how we get entranced or absorbed, a feeling I suppose we are more familiar with in cinema or television than in poetry or fiction. We are two kinds of reader: we are an intellecting reader, to the extent we are thinking about 'high art' or non-fiction, interpreting, searching for meaning; we are also an absorbed, rapt, drugged reader when we are wholly engrossed in reading.

Robert Gorham Davis has phrased this deeper sensation and the mechanism behind it quite beautifully:

> When a man is 'absorbed' or 'immersed' in a story . . . he is not primarily thinking *about* what he reads. That implies separation, externality. The work, rather, is thinking *him*. His ego has become

[15] 'At Stratford-on-Avon', *Ideas of Good and Evil* (1903), p. 162.
[16] '*Mr.* Congreve *to Mr.* Dennis, *Concerning Humour in Comedy*' (1695), in *Critical Essays of the Seventeenth Century* edited by Joel E. Spingarn, 3 volumes (Oxford, 1907), III, pp. 248-9.

object, not subject. We speak of being 'absorbed' and 'immersed' in the work but actually it is the other way around: we take the work into ourselves, introject it. What the ego is immersed in—sometimes with oceanic raptness—is its own larger, profounder self, which the work, as a series of excitations and counterexcitations has set in motion and directed.[17]

In technical terms, we introject the literary work: we take its psychological process into our own ego so that the transformation it embodies feels as though it is happening within us or, more exactly, neither 'out there' nor 'in here' but in some undifferentiated 'either'. I say 'undifferentiated' because the process involves a blurring of the boundaries between self and other which derives ultimately from that same symbiotic at-oneness with the mother, that same loss of self that makes the nuclear fantasy at the core of 'Mending Wall'. In being gratified, we merge with the source of gratification as once feeding child and nurturing mother formed a unit. We take in like food the process of transformation which is the literary work, feeling, for example, Keats's ecstatic mergings or the creation and undoing of Frost's eerie projections as though they were happening in our own heads.

The psychological process of the work, then, may match a reader's normal processes or it may clash with them or it may simply co-exist. His response to the poem will come from the relationship between the two. We have already seen how critics' phrasings of their reactions to the poem will sometimes reveal the unconscious material beneath the surface of the poem. Now we are coming to a second-order version of that same idea: that the *differences* in readers' phrasings must somehow reflect the *differences* in the readers' personalities, for the poem, even the poem considered as a transformational process, remains the same. In this sense, a psychoanalytic approach to literary criticism leads us to fundamental human issues: how do different personalities react to the same event? Or, borrowing a somewhat fuzzy term from recent French criticism, we could phrase the issue, how do different subjectivities interact? For a 'subjectivity', I take it, is what a psychoanalyst would call a character, a personality, or a life-style, and we have seen how the fantasy-defence structure of a poem looks like the structure of a personality.

In short a psychoanalytic approach to literary criticism has led us quite quickly to the most basic questions we can ask about art and

[17] 'Literature's Gratifying Dead End', *Hudson Review* XXI (1968), pp. 774-5.

human beings, and this is not surprising. Morse Peckham states the reason in its most drastic form, namely, that the humanities are really a branch of the social sciences:

> The humanities are concerned with investigating certain kinds of human behaviour, particularly artistic behaviour and culturally transmitted value behaviour. All aspects of literary criticism, for example, purport to talk about a particular kind of verbal behaviour. To my mind, literary criticism, except for evaluation, properly belongs to the behavioural sciences.[18]

Lest this sound too horrendous, it might be well to remember that Aristotle, father of us all, was not uninterested in psychology, nor were Longinus, Lessing, Goethe, Hazlitt, Coleridge, the Schlegels, Poe, I. A. Richards or Edmund Wilson, to name only a few. In fact I think one could fairly say it is more traditional to link literary criticism to the social sciences than to divorce them. Surely there can be no harm in seeing literature as part of the great continuum of human activity.

At any rate, that is inevitably what a psychoanalytic approach must do. Though the first move may be traditional explication, the second adds a distinctively psychoanalytic element—the recognition of a central unconscious fantasy which the work transforms into literary meaning. The third step is also wholly psychoanalytic—the recognition that the state of being 'rapt' or 'absorbed' or in a 'willing suspension of disbelief' takes us back to the original undifferentiated state of being gratified in the oral stage of infancy. It is by fusing with the literary work as we once fused with another source of nourishment that we take its process of transformation into ourselves. We achieve a timeless moment of at-oneness, transforming our deepest wishes and fears into meaningfulness. And when we do, we necessarily transform literary criticism from the study of literature alone to the study of literature in the mind of man.

[18] Morse Peckham, *Man's Rage for Chaos: Biology, Behavior, and the Arts* (Philadelphia, 1965), p. 119n.

Note

My article describes several socio-cultural and sociological approaches to literature but one in particular—that associated with the Centre for Contemporary Cultural Studies, University of Birmingham.

References. Section I: for the English 'culture and society' debate see Raymond Williams, *Culture and Society* (1958). The most available introduction to *Scrutiny*'s contribution is the recent two volume selection (Cambridge, 1968). Among the important books which belong to this cultural tradition in criticism, or contrast usefully with it, are: L. C. Knights, *Drama and Society in the Age of Jonson* (1937); Ian Watt, *The Rise of the Novel* (1957); and Lionel Trilling, *Beyond Culture* (1966). Among European critics the work of the Hungarian Marxist George Lukacs (e.g. *The Historical Novel*, 1962) is pre-eminent; for more extensive references, see the bibliographies to the essays in the present volume by W. K. Wimsatt and Graham Hough. From the sociological side, see Leo Lowenthal, *Literature and the Image of Man* (Boston, Mass., 1957). There is a very useful exploration of the historical background in Jacques Leenhardt's article, 'The Sociology of Literature: Some Stages in Its History', *The International Social Science Journal* XIX(4) (1967) (UNESCO).

On the analysis of more popular forms of literature, see Q. D. Leavis, *Fiction and the Reading Public* (1932); George Orwell, *Collected Essays, Journalism and Letters of George Orwell* (4 volumes: 1968); F. R. Leavis and Denys Thompson, *Culture and Environment* (1933); Richard Hoggart, *The Uses of Literacy* (1957); Stuart Hall and Paddy Whannel, *The Popular Arts* (1964). On mass media, the best short guides to the studies of effects are J. D. Halloran's two studies, *The Effects of Mass Communication* (Leicester, 1965) and *Attitude Formation and Change* (Leicester, 1967). See also Charles R. Wright, *Mass Communication: A Sociological Perspective* (New York, 1959) and the biography therein. For any understanding of the distinctive nature of television one must mention Marshall McLuhan, *Understanding Media* (1964).

In Section IV, where I discuss the links between literary-cultural analysis and the social sciences, I would refer to P. Rickman, *Understanding and the Human Studies* (1967) for a clear, shrewd and useful first guide. For contacts with psychology, see Norman N. Holland, *The Dynamics of Literary Response* (New York, 1968) (and his essay in the present volume) and the following essays by D. W. Harding: 'Psychological Processes in the Reading of Fiction', *British Journal of Aesthetics* II (1962), pp. 133–47; 'Reader and Author', in *Experience into Words* (1963), pp. 163–74; 'Raids on the Inarticulate', *The Use of English* XIX(2) (1967); and 'The Notion of "Escape" in Fiction and Entertainment', *The Oxford Review* IV (1967). On structuralism and semiology, see in particular the work of Lucien Goldmann, Umberto Eco and Roland Barthes (references to their work given in the bibliography of the articles in the present volume by W. K. Wimsatt and Graham Hough). Goldmann's essay 'The Sociology of Literature: Status and Problems of Method', in the 'Sociology of Literature Creativity' issue of the *International Social Science Journal* XIX(4) (1967)

VII

Contemporary Cultural Studies:
An Approach to the Study of Literature and
Society

I

In one sense most if not all literature can be said to be engaged with its society. The statement seems virtually self-evident. But its implications are varied and complex; they differ from period to period and from country to country.

The literary tradition in Britain—especially in the two centuries since urbanization, industrialization and democratization got under way—has had a distinctive record of direct and specific engagement with questions facing the society of its time. The engagement has been carried on both by creative writers and by critics, and often by men who were both. What Raymond Williams has called the 'culture and society debate' runs from Blake to T. S. Eliot through Coleridge,

---

is particularly relevant; so are Barthes's *Writing Degree Zero* (1967) and *Elements of Semiology* (1967). The special issue of *Communications* IV (Paris, 1964), 'Recherches Semiologiques', and the 'Structuralism' issue of *Yale French Studies* 36/37 (1966) are illuminating. On mass culture and content analysis, see B. Rosenberg's and D. M. White's anthology *Mass Culture* (Glencoe, Illinois, 1957); and on the sociology of knowledge, Karl Mannheim, *Essays in the Sociology of Knowledge* (1952). For essays on several aspects of the whole field, see Richard Hoggart, *Speaking to Each Other* (2 volumes, 1970).
The Centre for Contemporary Cultural Studies has produced both reports and Occasional Papers surveying the field. Reports 1–4 (1964–7, inclusive) contain fuller bibliographies. In this essay I refer particularly to three of the Occasional Papers; Alan Shuttleworth, *Two Working Papers in Cultural Studies* (No. 2, 1966); Richard Hoggart, *The Literary Imagination and the Study of Society* (No. 3, 1968); and Tim Moore, *Levi-Strauss and the Cultural Sciences* (No. 4, 1968). A more recent Occasional Paper is also relevant—Rolf Meyersohn, *Society and Cultural Studies* (No. 5, 1969).

Arnold, Carlyle, Ruskin, Morris and many others. 'Culture' there means the whole way of life of a society, its beliefs, attitudes and temper as expressed in all kinds of structures, rituals and gestures, as well as in the traditionally defined forms of art. We are looking now, I should stress, not at the way such writers explored their society in creative work, but at their direct, discursive engagement in questions of the day, in the analysis of the 'quality of the life' of their culture.

When we do turn to British creative writing itself, we find again a characteristic tone of social and moral concern. This isn't to say that social and moral concern doesn't figure in American and European writers; obviously it does. It is to stress that the shape and pressure of this concern differ with different cultures. In England it shows most often as a kind of concrete, pragmatic, humane insistence. There is a long-standing belief, not much examined but powerful and shared by many writers, critics and serious general readers, that 'good literature' offers a key to understanding societies better, a way of apprehending better their 'moral life'. Here again, the line of specific statements by creative writers runs strongly from Blake through Wordsworth and George Eliot to D. H. Lawrence.[1] In the last few decades it was best continued, in critical writing, by *Scrutiny*; and thence it moved out into English teaching at all levels. By this tradition it is claimed that good literature can reveal a society to itself in unique ways if—and the proviso is very important—we learn how to read it properly and do not try to use it for external ends.

Some critics have also, especially in the last thirty years, been willing to try to analyse the social and moral significance not just of 'high' literature but of 'low' literature or mass literature. Or they have tried to assess the cultural meanings of forms of mass art which are not simply verbal, such as advertising or film or popular music. Here one thinks again, for instance, of *Scrutiny*, of Mrs. Leavis's *Fiction and the Reading Public* and of a few brilliant essays by George Orwell. Orwell did not have time before he died to do much in this area, but he saw the possibilities:

> What you say about trying to study our own customs from an anthropological point of view opens up a lot of fields of thought, but one thing to notice about ourselves is that people's habits etc. are formed not only by their upbringing and so forth but also very

[1] For example, George Eliot and D. H. Lawrence write in strikingly similar terms about the moral function of the novel.

largely by books. I've often thought it would be very interesting to study the conventions etc. of *books* from an anthropological point of view. I don't know if you ever read Elmer Rice's *A Voyage to Purilia*. It contains a most interesting analysis of certain conventions —taken for granted and never even mentioned—existing in the ordinary film. It would be interesting and I believe valuable to work out the underlying beliefs and general imaginative background of a writer like Edgar Wallace. (*Collected Essays, Journalism and Letters of George Orwell* I, p. 222)

II

I have mentioned these main lines at the start so as to suggest the peculiar character and strength of the British tradition in literary-cultural thinking. It has tended to stick close to human beings and to the direct experience of literature; it has been on the whole non-aesthetic and non-abstract, not fond of making intellectual patterns, rather homely, decent and concerned.

Its limitations are the reverse of its strengths. In some respects it seems unintellectual, suspicious of ordering its own thoughts, wilfully amateurish, over-wary of 'disciplines' or 'methods'. It has assumed more than it has proved, and has not always been willing to listen to people who ask for more evidence or a more logical line of argument. It has tended to be rather parochial. I have mentioned the 'culture and society debate' as it was carried on discursively by English creative writers throughout the nineteenth century. But the tradition of nine-teenth-century continental (and especially German) philosophical writing, which is addressed to similar questions, is little known to literary students in Britain.[2] Yet it has a great deal in common with the English debate and, where it differs, is especially challenging. Max Weber, for instance, uses many of the skills of a literary critic, often brilliantly, sometimes in a way a literary critic will question; and he

[2] I think it is also true to say that the *British* culture and society debate, let alone the continental, is not sufficiently well known to literary students in Britain. The continental tradition includes Saint-Simon, Comte, Durkheim, Marx, Weber, Tönnies and Mannheim. For a discussion of this tradition and of the British literary-cultural tradition see Alan Shuttleworth, *Two Working Papers in Cultural Studies*. Shuttleworth suggests that yet another tradition should be associated with the two above: that of Anglo-American social anthropology.

has a complex rigour in teasing at his definitions which is rarely seen in discursive writing about society by literary students.[3]

It is especially easy for literary people to be suspicious of some modern social-scientific work. Suspicious of its abstracting character, since our work stresses the particular, the individual, the unique. But this is one reason why the social sciences can be good for us. When put to the test by the generalizing, 'objective' disciplines of the social sciences our truths ought to be confirmed, or they are shakily held.

Yet we do in fact move out from particular instances and particular works into making general statements about society. We do it a great deal; most of us, and often rather cavalierly. We use large words (like 'moral') and large concepts very easily. We have a number of large social and cultural assumptions at the back of our minds. Even further back, supporting the assumptions, we have a whole picture or patterned view of the nature of society and the place of literature within it. Thus we have largely undusted assumptions about the nature of élites or minorities, their roles in society, the ways in which their values are transmitted; or about relationships between class and cultivation and power and authority.

We tend, if we draw upon other disciplines at all, to use only those which are most immediately sympathetic to us or appear to be so, and then to use them selectively. We are quick to take off from a few particular instances into general rhetoric. We ought to have a more realistic sense of the cost of, the necessary rules for, such moves outwards; and the social sciences can help here. They wouldn't deny the genuinely new insights from literature; they could help us to grasp them better.

We insist, as I said earlier, that one has to learn to read works of literature in and for themselves; that only by doing this can one learn what they have to tell about society; and that what they tell is irreplaceable, available from no other source. I think all this is true. But I am struck by the contrast between the size of the assertions and the failure to do more than propound them as selfevident truths. It is as though we are talking to ourselves, to the converted, almost all the time. The relations of the fictions of literature to knowledge, to 'truth', are fantastically complicated. In a sense they can never be conclusively demonstrated or 'proved', but only experienced. Still, we

[3] See particularly Max Weber, *The Protestant Ethic and the Spirit of Capitalism* (1930).

could do more to help others to see just what we are claiming, to see better how the revelations of literature about society are brought to bear.

For instance, we use the word 'significantly' frequently, as when we say that such-and-such a man has shown a 'significant' movement or a 'significant' detail about society. We say, again quite confidently, that a good writer 'sees further', sees 'representatively', 'stands outside his society', conveys more 'truth' about its nature and so on. Though all these claims may be true, they are harder to prove than most of us think, and are not proved or forwarded by assertion and re-assertion.[4]

When we examine popular literature, we retain our self-confidence by reversing our approach. We have claimed that 'good' literature will only yield what it has to tell about society if it is read in and for itself, each work as a unique object; by contrast we assume that popular literature can be read in large generic groups, very quickly; and then boldly generalized about. It is, after all, merely 'symptomatic', we say. Hence we tend to use and abuse it; we oversimplify its relation to society and so fail to see what it can tell us about the nature of a culture, what symptoms it really indicates.

It follows that our views about the effects of good or bad literature on individuals and society tend to be large but under-nourished. We claim too quickly that both good and bad literature are in direct relationship to a society's moral condition, that good literature is an index to a society's health and a nourishment to it, and mass literature a sign of its corruption which will even further debase it. All this may be in some senses true but, if so, it is true in very complex ways. So again we could do with less assertion and more patient consideration. There is by now a good deal of social-scientific literature about effects. Most social scientists would agree that it doesn't get past, say, letter C in the alphabet of the problems. But at least it does get to letter C; so it would be as well, before we talk about effects, to go that distance with people from another discipline.

The point again is that, though good literature may well be valuable in the ways I have just described, in the insights it offers and the moral growth it can prompt, all these things are harder to demonstrate, especially to people who aren't themselves professional students of literature, than we usually think. I do not believe that it is sufficient

[4] These questions are outlined in Richard Hoggart, *The Literary Imagination and the Study of Society*.

for us to reply that this is because such people are insensitive or because they 'haven't learned to read a book *properly*'. Often they do try to read the book with all the care it demands, and they do listen to us and they do seem as sensitive as we are. But still they can't quite make our great leaps; they still seem like leaps in the dark. We do not help them to understand what we are doing and saying by repeating the instructions or incantations in what has become a set of almost closed languages. Bad literature or mass literature or processed literature may be as corrupting as we often say. But we have not made the claim convincing even to sympathetic outsiders; and, whatever the effects of bad literature, we shan't ourselves know them for what they are unless we read that literature with more care than we commonly give it. There is more to it, a good deal more, than most of us think.

III

If what I have said so far is right, then two main developments need to be made by literary students who have a special interest in understanding their culture. They need to improve literary-cultural analysis in itself; and they need to make better links with other disciplines.

Everything must start with the experience of literature 'in and for itself'. Without that kind of attention to the uniqueness of the works, that constant concern for the integrity of their individual natures, we shall be led into premature pattern-making, genre-generalization and structural type-casting—all gained through some infidelity to the works themselves. There is a place, as I shall mention later, for ideal-type abstraction across a genre; but it is more limited than we think and should come fairly late.

We have to attend to the work as peculiarly itself if we are to show why we say, and what we mean when we say, that literature can make a unique contribution to the understanding of a culture. Then we have to learn how to move outwards into statements about the nature of the culture, of a sort which can be discussed with other disciplines.

So the first task is to improve the literary-cultural reading *in itself*, as a preparation for learning how to express its cultural meanings. At the Birmingham Centre for Contemporary Cultural Studies we call this 'reading for tone' and 'reading for value'. The phrases aren't satisfactory, but it is difficult to find better ones. The former means trying to grasp as fully as possible the texture of the writing. It means paying attention in the first place to all sorts of elements in the language, to stress and lack of stress, to repetition and omission, to image, to ambiguity and so on. It means moving from there to character, incident, plot and theme. All the time one has to keep in mind the three major elements in a work of literature: the aesthetic, the psychological and the cultural. Briefly, the first points to those characteristics which have been predominantly decided by aesthetic needs, by the work of art as a formal structure, a type of 'fiction' or gratuitous 'making'. The psychological elements are those which seem pre-eminently to have been decided by the make-up of the particular individual who wrote that particular book. The cultural elements are those which seem chiefly to have been decided by the fact that this book was written in a certain kind of society at a certain period. But, of course, the first two elements are to some extent culturally conditioned; and none of them is strictly separable from the others.[5]

We have to make and then to justify 'significant selection', the choice of what seem like 'critical incidents'. If we do not, we shall be making no difference between the relative pressures, convincingness and importance of different passages and scenes; and it is this dimension which is the first crucial gain from a full reading. Otherwise, one might just as well simply count references and recurrences, cross-tabulate and generally make elaborate quantitative manœuvres with them.

The aim is to find eventually what field of values is embodied, reflected or resisted, within the work. What, in assumed meanings or counter-meanings and whether the writer knows it or not, is in play? One is 'reading for values', but the phrase doesn't mean that one is at this point trying to make a 'judgment of value' about the work in itself; one is trying to describe as sensitively and accurately as possible the values one finds within the work. Admittedly, one can never be quite as 'objective' or outside the work as that sounds. One is part of the scene being observed. In any reading for cultural meaning, one must start with some hypotheses, acts of selection, prior judgments of certain kinds—or one could never choose between the multitude of possible hypotheses. One can't avoid in some ways making at the least implicit value-judgments; but one can try all the time to be clearer about one's own involvement, and try to keep 'reading for values' separate from 'judgments of value'.

[5] A rather fuller description of 'reading for tone' can be found in Richard Hoggart, 'The Voices of Lawrence', *New Statesman* (14 June 1968).

So, one isn't at this point specifically asking questions about the value of the work, but is trying to understand better what Weber called 'the relationship of the object to values'. One is trying to find, from as internal a reading as possible, what this kind of work tells you about its society, about what that society believes, about its self-identity. It is in this sense that we can be willing to go on using that often suspected phrase 'the quality of life'. It is suspected because people often think that one is saying (and sometimes critics are loosely saying this) that one has a scale of merit for different attitudes to experience and is giving marks for quality according to that scale. But good literary-cultural analysis, in describing 'quality of life', aims to explore better the texture or fabric or feel or temper of the life embodied in a work (and though, as I said just above, that is at bottom a subjective matter, it need not be so self-justifiedly impressionistic as we often make it).

Behind all such attempts at cultural reading are a set of major assumptions, some obvious, some not quite so obvious. Such as: that a society bears values, cannot help bearing values and deciding their relative significance; that it makes what seems like a significant or ordered whole out of experience, a total and apparently meaningful view of life; that it embodies these structures of values in systems, rituals, forms; that it lives out these values expressively, in its actions and its arts; that this living out of values is a dialectical process, never complete, always subject to innovation and change; and that no one individual ever makes a perfect 'fit' with the dominant order of values of his culture.

For our purposes, the crucial idea here is that literature (and the other expressive arts) is a bearer of the meanings within a culture. It helps to recreate what it felt like to believe those things, to assume that experience carried and demanded those kinds of value. It dramatizes how it feels on the pulses to live out those kinds of value and, in particular, what stresses and tensions come from that living out. This helps to define the 'what' that is believed. To have a better sense of the form and force of an outlook on life helps to define that outlook. By creating orders within itself, art helps to reveal the orders of values present within a culture, either by mirroring or by resisting them and proposing new orders. Yet that makes the relationship sound too logical. Orders or anti-orders cannot be interpreted 'straight' from literature of any depth. To use structuralist language: 'the coherent universe of the literary work is not the same as the coherent universe of the culture outside.' And indeed a work may aim to destroy all order, to suggest a state of anarchic non-order, against not only the order of its society but against all order except that of art (and that, too, may be denied). Yet just there is its cultural meaning—which can only be understood by experiencing the work directly and seeing through its eyes.

This is why we say that the expressive arts are guides of a unique kind to the value-bearing nature of societies. We also claim that they affect the nature of the values held within a society and the way they are held; that, for example, writers may purify the language and educate the emotions of the tribe. But that is harder to prove.

It is important that some critics continue to insist that a work of literature is an autonomous artefact. This reminds us that the 'coherent universe' of a work is, first and foremost, itself and not something else to be used for other purposes. It underlines the singularity of each work of art and the sense in which the expressive arts are free, pointless acts. The claim for autonomy has a heuristic value and in the last decade or two has done a great deal to sharpen and make more subtle our understanding of literature. But it is at bottom a limited and mistaken claim. A work of art, no matter how much it rejects or ignores its society, is deeply rooted within it. It has massive cultural meanings. There is no such thing as 'a work of art in itself'.[6]

So far this discussion of 'reading for value' has been based on the close tonal reading of single works. And this is right: we have to begin with the single text and work outwards from it. When one starts to read for cultural meanings in groups, by genres or over a period, a whole new range of problems arises. It can be heady work, this hunting for trends or sketching in of great secular movements—by watching the change in the role of the hero or leaping across the mutations of meaning within a word. But it is justified and needs to be done. At Birmingham, though, we have not yet tried to do it, on the grounds that a grasp of how to read for value in individual works is an indispensable preliminary and that we do not yet know how to do that well.

Most of the foregoing applies to the analysis of mass art or lowbrow art as well as to high art. But I said earlier that literary students who

[6] One of the most easily available and cogent brief statements of that view of literature which I am challenging here is to be found in chapter 9 of René Wellek and Austin Warren, *The Theory of Literature* (1949).

move into the examination of non-traditional literature usually work too quickly. Their preconceptions lead them astray. I also noted that it is difficult enough to make, convincingly, the case that good litera-ture 'stands outside its age so as to illuminate and judge it'; difficult but worthwhile and necessary. But it is unhelpful and inaccurate to say that the mass arts or lowbrow arts are merely symptomatic, mirrors of conditions within their society, never in an oblique relation to it, simply reflectors of its conventional wisdom or folly.

Even the apparently most processed forms of mass art are more complex constructions than the usual formulations suggest, complex in themselves and in their relations to their readers or audiences. James Bond, the Archers, Andy Capp, Mrs. Dale, science fiction, Coronation Street—these do not all belong to a single group of phenomena. Mass art can mirror conventions, be a response to the need for change and innovation, be a catalyst of regressive desires or shape-less fears, act out at one level—usually unconsciously—some of a society's quarrels with itself.

Some mass art has more life than the formulation, 'mass, processed, conventional, dead' suggests. And sometimes what offers itself as, and is accepted as, 'high art' (individual, alive, disinterested, engaged) is dead. Because it has some of the formal characteristics of high art—for instance, thematic pattern—we fail to notice that it lacks any per-ceptive life. It is better not to start with a priori divisions between types of art (high, middle, low or any of the others). It is better to start as if from scratch each time. This procedure doesn't lead to a loss of standards or a shapeless relativism. It throws us into the search for more valid distinctions between good art and poor art, and out of that there can only be gain.

Lowbrow art or mass art won't yield its cultural meanings without effort. If we make that effort, we find that it can be more revealing than we would have thought; not as revealing as high art (here is where valid distinctions really do come into play—about integrity, complexity, perceptiveness) but certainly not easily read or dismissed. At Birmingham we have learned this most of all by working in long weekly seminars over two or three months on a single short story from a women's magazine.[7] And one of our graduate students has

[7] The record of this enquiry, as it moved from stage to stage, will be pub-lished shortly as an Occasional Paper by the Centre for Contemporary Cultural Studies, University of Birmingham.

had a similar experience from three years' work on Ian Fleming's James Bond novels.

Much the same is true of the other mass arts, whether or not they are predominantly verbal. The popular press, in itself and in its relations to society and its readers, is more difficult to understand than we have usually assumed and more rewarding when it is read carefully. Advertisements are even harder to read, since they are visual as well as verbal. Literary students have spent most time looking at the words of advertisements, and even then have looked sketchily. On the cultural meanings carried visually by advertisements hardly any work has been done. Those in the business who write about advertisements usually produce technical descriptions which don't discuss their inner meanings; or their attempts at discussing meanings are perfunctory. There seems to be no adequate vocabulary for describing the cultural meanings carried by the shape and layout of advertisements, let alone for describing the interactions between copy and text. Again, a graduate student at Birmingham is trying to produce a first vocabulary for discussing the cultural implications of the visual and verbal impact of modern advertisements. In television one can say much the same: we are only just beginning to understand the complex nature of the more distinctive television productions; nor do we yet know much about the relationships between television and its overlapping audiences. In analysing popular song we have habitually given most of our attention to the words, and it has not been difficult to prove that those are banal. Any pop-song writer in Denmark Street in the twenties, thirties or forties could have told us that in advance, since he paid little attention to the words. But if you approach pop music in the sixties in this way, you get a predictable answer and blind yourself to more useful lines of approach. Pop song today is best approached as a whole musical 'event' in which the words are only part and, it may be, a small or almost irrelevant part (though some pop song in the late sixties is paying quite serious attention to *what* is being said). And, once more, we know little about the relationships of pop music to the people who listen to it, or play it for themselves.

Outside the arts (high or mass) as usually recognized there are in any society a great range of other expressive phenomena. For instance, types of gesture which appear at certain times in certain parts of society, styles of dress, linguistic habits, all kinds of manners. How does one 'read' these, using the word 'read' to mean interpret or understand their cultural meanings? One can decide that the job is too difficult, too amorphous, that one can't separate the phenomena from the epiphenomena. One can decide to leave such regions to popular journalists or Colour Supplement trend-hunters. Or to a more firmly structured discipline, such as one of the social sciences. Yet most literary people, when they are not being professionally literary, do make quite large generalizations about phenomena of this kind, without any recognizable discipline. Much more important, if we are justified in claiming that literary criticism can show one how to 'read' the meanings of a society through tone and style in its officially recognized expressive arts at all levels, if this is true and if we want to continue that tradition of direct social observation set by some of our great forbears which I recalled at the start of this essay, then there is scope here to modify and adapt literary criticism to the 'reading' of these non-formal but nevertheless richly expressive phenomena of contemporary culture.

IV

About the relationship of literary-cultural analysis to other disciplines for the study of society whole volumes wait to be written, and will eventually be written. As I said much earlier, none of these interconnections needs to weaken our sense of the importance of literature and may strengthen it.

I shall mention briefly a few disciplines with which closer connections would clearly be valuable. First, history, since a dialogue with historians seems easiest to arrive at as well as obviously interesting. But there are no easy routes in this work and an effective dialogue between historians and literary students (many, many miles past the point at which one is setting Blue Books side-by-side with Dickens) is not soon reached. The irony is that historians do often use literary approaches without calling them that, and literary people use historical approaches in the same unnamed way. Whether they use the other's approaches well or ill depends not on a training in the other discipline, but on general intelligence and imagination. But that kind of almost accidental taking in of each other's washing doesn't necessarily build a bridge across which other traffic can pass. The Birmingham Centre has discussed with sympathetic historians the way one should 'read' contemporary popular journalism so as to bring out its relationship to its culture. It was difficult for the historians to see how we arrived at our statements; and we felt that they generalized too quickly from the overt content of the newspapers and paid too little attention to the meanings carried by their inner tone.

Psychology and social psychology can cooperate with literary-cultural studies in at least three ways: in exploring the psychic characteristics of individual authors and the links between them and other aspects of their work (I referred to this earlier), in studying the social anthropology of a period (Steven Marcus's book *The Other Victorians* (1966) is a good example of this kind of reading of 'low' literature), and in considering the psychology of readers and the act of reading (a handful of scattered essays by D. W. Harding are particularly suggestive in this respect).

Other kinds of cooperation are fairly obviously possible. For example, at Birmingham we are just finishing a three-year study of changes in the British popular press, its attitudes to its readers and its sense of its own corporate personality, as these are indicated by tone and manner and style within the papers themselves. It may be that this work will be carried further by a group of social psychologists, who will use their methods to see how far there is consonance between what seems to be indicated by a reading of the newspapers and what the journalists themselves think they are doing and saying. We want to know what causes changes in tone and style and attitude—objective, political and economic and social changes—or myths about social changes, and about the newspapers' public personalities, held by the journalists.

Even more briefly, there is a lot to be learned from anthropology. Much of the hold of mass art or popular art takes place at the level of folklore or myth, and some understanding of the way in which an anthropologist reads the meanings of myths in primitive societies and relates them to beliefs and tensions within those societies can help with the reading of television soap-operas as much as of earlier folk-literature.[8] The case for more interest in structuralism follows naturally. It was the Italian critic Umberto Eco who called structural analysis 'an investigation into the reciprocal implications of a rhetoric and an ideology'. Even more urgent is the case for semiology, since we do not have languages or codes to discuss many of the expressive phenomena of mass society.

[8] On Lévi-Strauss and the analysis of popular literature, see the discussion in Tim Moore, *Levi-Strauss and the Cultural Sciences*.

The case for greater links with sociology is plain and the gains can be considerable. To speak personally and from a limited reading in sociology, I have learned something from the disciplined systematizations as well as from the brilliant insights of good sociology. I have been struck, in reading in the sociology of knowledge and the nature of ideology, by their connections with some literary critical approaches. Weber has been interesting in more ways than one—by his 'insistence on the subjective-meaning complex of action', by *verstehen* sociology (which has useful links with what we call 'quality of life'), by the similarities between his discussion of 'rationality' and elements in the literary debate about culture, and by his use of ideal-type analysis. Contemporary American sociologists in particular have been useful in their discussion of mass society and mass culture, and, more precisely, in communications research of various kinds (the group around the French journal *Communications* has been useful in this connection too).

One particular area where the two disciplines come close together and yet are not the same lies in what sociologists call 'content analysis', the reading of a work so as to bring out as many as possible of its meanings. Literary people tend to underrate such sociological work since it is at bottom—it must be—quantitative; whereas the literary reading of a text is, we claim, essentially 'qualitative'. But content analysis can be subtle and valuable. It needn't quarrel with a qualitative or tonal cultural reading, as I described such a reading above, but each can complement and learn from the other.

Or, as with social psychology, there could be useful joint operations between literary-cultural work and sociology. In, for instance, understanding better the nature of 'youth culture'. Such a project would marry sociological enquiry with the 'reading for cultural meaning' of the main expressive phenomena within youth culture. This has not, so far as I know, been done anywhere and would give a much fuller understanding than we have at present.

V

In all this, the special contribution of literary-cultural analysis is its stress on the expressive elements of a culture, and on the importance of 'reading' expressively before interpreting in any other way. It is natural for social scientists (and even for historians, to some extent) to be tempted to read instrumentally or operationally, to ask: 'what does this kind of thing *do* to people?' or 'what do people *do* with this kind of thing?' In communications studies the movement has been from Lasswell's input/output model ('who says what to whom, where and with what effect?'—which, for a student of literature, recalls I. A. Richards) to two-step flow analysis and uses-and-gratifications studies which have led to a closer examination of audience differences ('what do different kinds of people do with the media?') and so to the study of communications as only one element in much more complex leisure and societal settings. The process needs continuing into expressive reading, in the literary critic's sense.

The literary student asks first: 'what is the thing in itself?' Thereafter, although some of the questions he goes on to ask may be at bottom quite close to those of the social scientist, he doesn't put them in quite the same way, and this is important. He asks not so much: 'what do people do with the object?' but 'what relationship does this thing in itself, this complex thing, have to the imaginative life of the individuals who make up its readers or audiences?' Then whole new sets of questions begin to appear. Does it reinforce an accepted pattern of life? Or does it seem like a form of play? Or is it oblique, drawing upon deep psychic needs, perhaps running counter to the assumptions of its society? Or does it celebrate, stand in awe before, what one might call fundamental mysteries about human life? These questions have to be asked if one is to understand a work of art 'in itself' and so its relationship to its society; however they are answered, they will tell us something about that society, not just about the work of art.

So I come back to the claim that a literary-cultural critic is not in any way 'using' literature. He will do nothing to define better the contribution which literature can make to understanding society if he does not focus himself first and foremost on the work of art 'in and for itself'. If he does that, its special contribution to cultural understanding may be released. It is important to say this clearly today since so many other disciplines are analysing society. The literary-critical contribution tends to go by default, just at the time when it needs to be heard, through failing to define its own character and then to make the right kinds of intellectual connections. The literary contribution lies, when it succeeds, in its integrity and sensitivity of response to the objects studied (again, one thinks of a phrase of Weber's: 'empathic understanding'). It is concerned always with reading for value. Works of literature at all levels are shot through with—irradiated with—values, with values ordered and values acted out. What literature does all the time and what, therefore, the handmaid of literature, literary criticism, must do is to insist and demonstrate that, in Coleridge's words, 'Men ought to be weighed, not counted.' At the points where the complex, value-laden structures of societies most interact with the value-heavy, psychic life of individuals—at these points an expressive culture is born; and it is at these points that we have to listen and try to read most carefully.

I have not been writing about what is usually understood by 'the sociology of literature'; nor about 'literature, life and thought'.[9] That latter phrase in itself, in its disjointed, aggregatory quality, suggests how far removed is the idea it describes from the more organic study I have been discussing. I have not been describing 'background studies' —nor, finally, 'the history of ideas'—another over-mechanical phrase. I have been talking about literary-cultural studies, chiefly contemporary cultural studies, which begin in close cultural reading and can lead out, in conjunction with other disciplines, into better cultural analysis.

[9] Some studies in the sociology of literature are simple and mechanistic; some are subtle and imaginative; most seem to fall in between these two poles. At its best the sociology of literature can throw light on the way in which the nature of the work of literature has itself been qualified by all kinds of social factors. Studies of this kind can cover the mass arts just as much as the high arts and are particularly valuable (and particularly needed) on some contemporary mass arts such as television—on which, during the whole process of creation, a range of different forces (financial, physical, professional) are brought to bear. I would, of course, prefer to call studies like these a branch of contemporary cultural studies, since both social scientific discipline and an imaginative sense of the literary work have to be brought to bear in them.

Note

My argument concerns contemporary literary criticism and theory, contemporary linguistics and anthropology, and the relation between linguistics and literature. In the first area, about the practice of the New Critics and the Chicago Aristotelians, see Cleanth Brooks, *The Well Wrought Urn* (New York, 1947), for an example of the former, and R. S. Crane's *The Languages of Criticism and the Structure of Poetry* (Toronto, 1953) and the selection of some of his and his colleagues' most famous essays in *Critics and Criticism* edited by R. S. Crane (Chicago, 1957)—which includes Elder Olson's essay 'An Outline of Poetic Theory'—for the latter. Some of the more useful books on the 'theory' of literature are I. A. Richards, *Principles of Literary Criticism* (1924), which examines the process of reading and the responsibilities of criticism; René Wellek and Austin Warren, *Theory of Literature* (third edition, 1963), a conservative but very eclectic introduction, and W. K. Wimsatt's *Hateful Contraries* (Lexington, Ky., 1965) and *The Verbal Icon* (Lexington, Ky., 1954), both containing collections of theoretical and practical essays on literature, (note especially the essays with Monroe C. Beardsley, 'The Intentional Fallacy' and 'The Affective Fallacy'). Also see Beardsley, *Aesthetics: Problems in the Philosophy of Criticism* (New York, 1958). On language and structure, see, notably, David Lodge, *Language of Fiction* (1966), and his essay 'Towards a Poetics of Fiction, 2: An Approach Through Language', in *Novel* I (1968), pp. 158–69; and Winifred Nowottny, *The Language Poets Use* (1962). Also see Donald Davie, *Articulate Energy* (1955), which analyses the modes of meaning of syntax in poetry; and Frank Kermode, *The Sense of an Ending* (1967).

Reading in linguistics alluded to in the essay includes the work of Noam Chomsky and his associates: see his *Syntactic Structures* (The Hague, 1957); *Aspects of the Theory of Syntax* (Cambridge, Mass., 1965); and a lucid introduction to the theory, 'The Formal Nature of Language', Appendix A in E. H. Lenneberg, *Biological Foundations of Language* (New York, 1967). A modern selection from American linguistics is J. A. Fodor and J. J. Katz, *The Structure of Language* (Englewood Cliffs, N.J., 1964). Relevant British publications include J. R. Firth, *Papers in Linguistics, 1934–51* (1957); Randolph Quirk, *The Use of English* (second edition, 1968); Roger Fowler, 'On the Interpretation of "Nonsense Strings" ', *Journal of Linguistics* V (1969), pp. 75–83.

In linguistics, see also Ferdinand de Saussure's brilliant classic, *Course in General Linguistics* (translated by W. Baskin, New York, 1959); and, in the tradition set by Saussure, Roland Barthes, *Elements of Semiology* (1967). A very suggestive (if controversial) work on the relation between language structure and conceptual structure is Benjamin Lee Whorf, *Language, Thought and Reality* (Cambridge, Mass., 1956).

Several anthropologists have made notable contributions to this field. *Language in Culture and Society* edited by Dell Hymes (New York, 1964) presents a selection; see also J. J. Gumperz and Hymes, *The Ethnography of Communication*, special publication of *American Anthropologist* (1964); and Edmund Leach,

VIII

The Structure of Criticism and the Languages of Poetry: An Approach through Language

ROGER FOWLER

I

THERE are some statements by critics which, however vague and rudimentary, at least give the impression that, with a little more logical care, they could be derived directly from axioms in the theory of literature. These two assertions are of this kind; though woolly in expression, they are 'safe' and, I think, could be paraphrased to give incontrovertible truths:

> In considering the language of poetry it is prudent to begin with what is 'there' in the poem—'there' in the sense that it can be described and referred to as unarguably given by the words. (Winifred Nowottny, *The Language Poets Use*, p. 1)

> The novelist's medium is language: whatever he does, *qua* novelist, he does in and through language. (David Lodge, *Language of Fiction*, p. ix)

'Anthropological Aspects of Language: Animal Categories and Verbal Abuse', in *New Directions in the Study of Language* edited by E. H. Lenneberg (Cambridge, Mass., 1964).

In recent years there has been a growing body of writings on literature by linguists. For a representative selection, see *Essays on the Language of Literature* edited by Seymour Chatman and S. R. Levin (Boston, 1967); also Roger Fowler, *Essays on Style and Language* (1966); and 'New Attitudes to Style', a special volume of *Review of English Literature* VI (April 1965); and *Linguistics and Style* edited by John Spencer (1964). For more specialized or detailed arguments, see R. Fowler and P. Mercer, 'Criticism and the Language of Literature: Some Tradition and Trends in Great Britain', *Style* III (1969), pp. 45–72; S. B. Greenfield, 'Grammar and Meaning in Poetry', *PMLA* LXXXII (1967), pp. 377–87; G. N. Leech, *A Linguistic Guide to English Poetry* (1969); S. R. Levin, *Linguistic Structures in Poetry* (The Hague, 1962).

Others seem to proceed from the axiomatic by a much less direct route:

> There are four parts in this poetic composite [the lyric]: choice, character, thought, and diction. For choice is the activity, and thought and character are the causes of the activity, and diction is the means. The choice, or deliberative activity of choosing, is the principal part, for reasons analogous to those which make plot the principal part of tragedy. Next in importance comes character; next thought; and last, diction. (Elder Olson, 'An Outline of Poetic Theory', p. 21)

Can both kinds of statement be tolerated? I suppose this question would, conventionally, be answered affirmatively: after all, it is empirically evident that there are in existence many diverse critical 'metalanguages', the speakers of which operate happily and productively in their own literary fields—indeed the present volume would seem to celebrate a multiplicity of critical schools, a healthy diversity of opinion and interest. Again, tolerance of different critical metalanguages seems to be justified on *a priori* grounds: the plea for pluralism, like pleas for religious or political toleration, is self-evidently reasonable and attractive. The range of literature—in this context I hardly dare to say the range of *kinds* of literature—is enormous, as is the range of readers, motives for reading, performances, audiences, markets for publications, teachers and studying communities. In these circumstances diversity of method and interpretation is inevitable and, if the alternative is repressive and authoritarian bigotry, desirable. Freedom of interpretation, if responsible, can only be laudable; so also flexibility of method. This much admitted and approved, one begins to have doubts. In practice, twentieth-century pluralism has meant discord, intolerance and mutual ignorance. One of the benefits of a true pluralism, one would think, would be healthy and productive interchange of views, informed agreement to differ, and certitude on what it is one is differing about. This is certainly not the case with contemporary criticism. It would be a grave mistake to regard the 'schools' as simply possessing alternative descriptive terminologies which could, in the last resort, be translated one into another. Critical discourse saturated with a distinctive and highly developed functional vocabulary is not merely in a situation of using certain special terms; it is conditioned by the terms it uses. As Olson and Crane make clear, a framework which is superficially a set of terms is more exactly a system of assumptions, attitudes and expectations—to use a specialized vocabulary is to commit oneself to a specialized attitude. At the very least, learning a specific metalanguage may unfit one for understanding any other. (See, for example, Elder Olson's failure to understand Empson's language and method.)[1] It is a sad state of affairs if critic A cannot understand critic B, and the logical independence of A and B (the truth of A cannot disprove B) justifies neither A nor B, does not excuse their egocentricity, and certainly does not encourage our toleration of either. Since criticism, like literature, 'belongs to the public', the critic (as opposed to other, less reputable, sorts of commentators on literature) should earn his right of free speech by openness and clarity; willingness to understand and to be understood.

Ultimately a pluralism of critical frameworks is a multiplicity of exclusive doctrines about the nature of literature. Most disputes reduce to this sort of question: whether poems are 'autonomous'; whether or not poetic language and ordinary discourse are to be distinguished; whether literature is language, or language just one of a number of 'elements' of literature. Judging by the writings of the critical theorists, there is a small range of central aesthetic questions about which passionate discord is inevitable, and about which there is not even the possibility of 'informed agreement to differ'. Often the friction between aesthetic theories is a consequence of failure to define stock terms—symbol, word, structure, image—or of dependence on terms of a necessarily highly abstract and therefore potentially vague character—plot, tone, realism. The metalanguages employed in criticism of the arts and theorizing about the arts are notoriously slovenly, and they could easily be tidied up, to the benefit of harmony and constructive argument in general. But the incompatibility of competing poetics is not simply a mechanical result of the confusion of terms employed. It stems from the lack (despite appearances) of careful ontological discussion. We are offered *a posteriori* arguments proceeding from the critics' demands on literature rather than fundamental enquiries about what can be known about literature and stated formally. I would argue that we do not need a justificatory ontology, nor a speculative, quasi-logical ontology, but a scientific ontology; that is to say, an ontology founded on a set of carefully controlled concepts derived from appropriate sciences and generating a wide range of descriptive

[1] 'William Empson, Contemporary Criticism, and Poetic Diction', *Critics and Criticism* edited by R. S. Crane.

terms available to critics with many different interests in the study of many different kinds of texts. An ontology so stable, so easily taken for granted, that it can be implicit in criticism, not demanding continual overt defence: an invisible theory which will tacitly inform, not restrict, the various compatible 'kinds' of criticism that can derive from it. This ontology should be of a kind which will serve *all* criticism; which should relieve critics of the necessity of redefining fundamental concepts for every new article and book. It should establish concepts which are not redefinable in an *ad hoc* way.

(There are several predictable objections to this proposal for a single, unified, scientific theory of literature: for example, that it is unreasonable to expect critics to agree completely in their aesthetic presuppositions; that no science is absolute, but all are relativistically dependent on their 'frameworks'; that science and art are by definition alien and must be kept apart. No one who believes that these are disqualifying objections is going to be convinced by a digression here on pertinent issues in the philosophy of science.[2])

II

To return to the quotations with which this essay opened: it should now be clear that they are not harmless alternatives simply employing different kinds of descriptive terms. As I implied at the outset, they hold quite different positions relative to the ideal unperplexing theory of literature. The first two seek to present literature in terms of categories which are basic and which can be empirically justified—language, medium, words. The third operates with categories which claim to be fundamental but which either are not basic or are establishable empirically only with the greatest difficulty—thought, character, plot. These terms are secondary *at least*: they are not close to human behavioural reality and cannot be set up unless the primary terms have been defined. (The difficulties caused by a lack of primary terms—in this case not having an adequate semantic theory—are illustrated by Olson's vacuous note 8 in 'An Outline of Poetic Theory'.) This is not to say that statements containing non-primary terms cannot be tolerated in literary criticism—most critical and theoretical statements are such—but that these secondary statements make little sense unless they

---

[2] *Cf.* my comments on the issue of 'art *versus* science' in *Essays in Criticism* XVII (1967), pp. 327–8 and XVIII (1968), pp. 168–9.

rest on a solid empirical base. Let it be understood that the 'scientific ontology' provides a base only; the secondary—and even further distanced than secondary—terms depend on it but are not replaced by it. No criticism can exist without secondary terms; but these secondary terms must have their conceptual content supplied by the primaries. My strictures against the secondaries—plot, realism, fiction, theme, structure, style, decorum, etc.—allege that they are too often employed in a conceptual vacuum (hence inefficient criticism) or confusingly used as if they were primaries (hence meaningless word-play posing as aesthetic theory).

It is of course no guarantee of theoretical or practical wholesomeness that a writer employs lots of words like *language, communication, concept, set, culture, semantic,* etc. The empirical bases of literary aesthetics have not yet been revealed so clearly that anyone can use primary terms with confidence. Let us consider again the quotations from Nowottny and Lodge (the first sentences of their books, as it happens). Both begin with a large assumption: that one can invoke a workable, common-sense, usage of the term 'language' without tortured definition. There is such a common-sense usage, I believe, and the general drift of both books suggests the authors intend it (as Empson does, but not, for example, Cleanth Brooks, whose 'paradox is the language of poetry' uses 'language' metaphorically). However, to turn the common-sense term 'language' of practical criticism into the stable and overt term 'language' of axioms in critical theory needs much effort, as anyone familiar with the turmoil of linguistics in this century might predict. Our two critics add qualifications. Nowottny asserts that there is an 'unarguable' quality in, or dimension of, language—an assertion that has to be squared with Empson's cornucopian polysemy and with the semantic arbitrariness of Humpty-Dumpty's sect. She implies—as does Wimsatt with his 'explicit meaning' (*Hateful Contraries,* pp. 221–2)—that all words have stable and stateable meanings: this must be so, or we would not be able to communicate at all, but it is as well to realize the relativity of this fact. A workable theory of denotation and connotation, and some psycholinguistic studies of the facts of misunderstanding, would seem to be valuable projects in this connection. Lodge characterizes language as a 'medium', but does not make it clear whether he means the sculptor's marble or bronze or the communications engineer's telephone cables, air, bones, or whatever. In the indecisive 'in and through' he tries to suggest both definitions at once.

Progressing further into Lodge and Nowottny, we find other important qualifications. Nowottny acknowledges that the structuring to be found in poems is not 'discontinuous with linguistic processes in ordinary life' (p. 82); this is a massive and essential concession to the empirical facts of linguistic usage. The language of poems is, however, 'more highly structured' than 'language outside poems' (p. 72). To judge by Lodge's methodological conclusions and by those sections of his criticism which deal with word-patterning, high structuring would appear to be, for him, important in novels too. But he does not regard structure—or 'verbal arrangements' as he calls it, quoting C. H. Rickword—as merely independently beautiful or interesting. It also 'creates' other elements such as character and plot. Perhaps structure as structure is 'medium in which' whereas structure as creation is 'medium through which'.[3]

The general implications of Nowottny's and Lodge's remarks may be expressed in a series of propositions: that language is central to literature; that the description of the language of literature is central to criticism; that such description can be an objective process; that such description confers objectivity on literary criticism; that (to complete the circle) its linguistic character defines what kind of object a literary text is. There is a good deal of evidence (including the fact that much excellent criticism exists which seems to be founded on these ideas) that these propositions are true and essential. They also assume a general framework that is widely accepted today: the argument that a literary work is independent of its origins and its effects, an argument inaugurated by I. A. Richards and developed by Wimsatt and Beardsley. Richards's exposition is marred by basic contradictions concerning affectism, and Wimsatt's and Beardsley's articles are not without untidiness—chiefly flaws in the classification of genetic materials—but the general drift is clear enough. A poem is free of an author's intentions and his experiences, and of a reader's responses, because these are variable, irresponsible, undiscoverable, demonstrably erroneous, etc., while the poem remains stable. We cannot locate the poem in the author's state of mind at the moment of creation because this is inaccessible and may be changed by the act of writing—i.e. it may be an effect rather than a cause of the poem; we cannot allow the poem to

---

[3] Creation by structure is much more interestingly discussed in Lodge's article 'Towards a Poetics of Fiction: An Approach through Language', *Novel* I (1968), pp. 158–69.

reside in the individual reader's experience as he reads, because that would be tantamount to saying that there are as many poems as there are occasions of reading, whereas we know very well that there is only one poem. If a poem is not subjective in either of these two ways, it is objective: it is an object, with defining characteristics independent of the characteristics of poet and reader.

Having said that a poem is an object, it is essential (and extremely difficult) to specify what kind of an object it is. It is not a physical object, everybody agrees: it can be memorized and 'recited' silently; it can be printed in different typographies on different papers, and remain the same poem; some or all printed records of it may be destroyed, yet the poem can survive (contrast paintings). There are other related arguments; all conspire to make the point that a poem is not to be identified with any physical record, manifestation or performance of it. Nor is it a perceptual object, despite Beardsley (*Aesthetics*, Chapter 1), who regards all aesthetic objects (musical, graphic, dramatic, poetic, etc.) as perceptual objects. In fact, the usual gestures made towards the marbled page in *Tristram Shandy*, Herbert's 'Easter Wings', concrete poetry, etc., are gestures towards a poetically uncentral existence as perceptual objects. A particular printing of 'Easter Wings' is a physical object, an arrangement of letters; the reader or beholder *perceives* the object as a representation of a pair of wings. So poems are not basically perceptual objects (though they *may* exploit a perceptual dimension), whereas sculptures, for example, are essentially perceptual objects—forms perceived under the stimulus of physical artefacts.

A printed text is not a poem; a musical score is not a symphony. Is the likeness of music and poetry implied in this popular comparison illuminating? I would deny that it is. Certainly a score, like a text, implies both an underlying abstract formal structure and an acoustic realization. But whereas acoustic performance is vital to the symphony, it is quite accidental as far as the poem is concerned. Undoubtedly Beethoven experienced the works he composed after he went deaf, and undoubtedly many musicians can experience pieces of music very adequately by reading scores. But this internal music entails imagining acoustic performance, whereas silent reading, or recollecting, of poetry, may not involve internal vocalization. It seems inescapable that musical scores exist as directions for physical performance, whereas texts of poems, and oral performances of poems too, exist as directions for the recovery of meanings.[4] A literary object has semanticity, *pace* Cleanth Brooks; very little music attempts to create this dimension, *pace* the post-Romantic composers of what are called, significantly, tone-*poems*. (And classical representational music, like Vivaldi's *The Four Seasons*, is stylized away from the reality it pretends to imitate.)

This comparison with music fails to illuminate the nature of poetry, because it attempts to establish music and poetry as variants of the same thing, the same kind of aesthetic object, while semanticity differentiates them absolutely. However, one analogy (rather than equation) of music and poetry does help, if we take it as an analogy only.

Haydn's *String Quartet in D Major, Op. 64 No. 5 (The Lark)* opens with a theme of great melodic simplicity stated in an impressively detailed and complexly symmetrical arrangement:

[4] In 'Suprasegmentals and the Performance of Poetry', *Quarterly Journal of Speech* XLVIII (1962), pp. 366–72, Samuel R. Levin offers an ingenious, and I think rather convincing, case against the oral performance of poetry.

We have eight bars of common time, a series divided into units of 2, 2, and 4. The two two-bar units at the beginning each divide into 1 plus 1. In bar 1 the second violin begins a simple and basically falling tune which progresses by no more than one whole tone at a time; this is answered by a rising sequence in the same rhythm to be played by the cello. In bar 3 the tune of bar 1 is repeated slightly higher up throughout, but this time (in bar 4) the cello responds by a falling series. Bar 5 opens up the intervals between the elements in the second violin tune, but retains the basic shape, and, through bars 5–8, the falling sequence is repeated three times in a general melodic descent. Throughout the passage the viola matches the second violin note for note in a subtle counterpoint in which the viola traces a tune sometimes moving in the same direction as the violin tune, and sometimes (as in bar 5, where the viola rises as the second violin falls) contradicting it. It is all mathematically very tidy, simple yet involved, and very characteristic of Haydn's style. It is well known that eighteenth-century England yields poetic analogues of this style. The couplet as turned by Pope is a close parallel to the treatment of the eight- (and four-) bar theme by Mozart and Haydn. To avoid wasting space on gratuitous analysis I will quote a passage which has been discussed in these terms by Mrs. Nowottny:

> Where-e'er you walk, cool gales shall fan the glade,
> Trees, where you sit, shall crowd into a shade,
> Where-e'er you tread, the blushing flow'rs shall rise,
> And all things flourish where you turn your eyes.[5]

Here the 'themes' and the counterpoint are a play of syntax and metre. As in the Haydn passage, the structure is one of units of almost algebraic abstractness—sentence-types and other structural components in regular and determinate relationships. It just happens that Haydn and Pope in these passages reveal their grammar with great clarity. These are no more than convenient examples; we are not for the moment concerned with the style itself. The grammar is an abstract system of materials out of which works are constructed. Of linguistic artefacts, such as poems, we may say that they are built with abstract, non-physical, formatives to which we give names like 'sentence', 'noun', etc. If we ignore the distracting level of physical performance, the answer to the question 'what kind of object?' is, 'an abstract object'.

[5] Pope, *Pastorals* II, 73–6; see *The Language Poets Use*, pp. 11–12.

III

In order to state why any particular linguistic (or musical) object has the structure it does have, one has to take into account two sorts of facts. A text is structured in a certain way because it is a distinct use of certain distinctive materials given in advance. We need to make a fundamental division between the musical or linguistic materials available (grammatical facts) and the use made of them (stylistic facts). To take the available materials first: Haydn had at his disposal a simple but very productive system of rules of pitch, harmony and rhythm, the system stabilized largely by Bach and basic to most Western music ever since. The system is different from that, for example, on which Indian classical music is based, or the serial system of pitch conventions on which some twentieth-century music depends. The basic musical conventions known (and used) by Haydn could be seen as a kind of musical grammar, strictly analogous to the linguistic grammar possessed by Pope. This grammar distinguishes Haydn from Schoenberg as Pope's grammar distinguishes him from Racine. The rules of the linguistic system, like those of the musical, are abstract, finite in number but virtually infinitely productive, and conventional. This system of linguistic rules Ferdinand de Saussure called *langue* (*parole* being concrete use of the rules in a specific linguistic situation); Noam Chomsky, refurbishing this famous distinction, refers to the linguistic materials as *competence* (as opposed to *performance*). The status of this competence, this set of linguistic rules in which Pope is competent, must be determined very carefully. Sometimes grammar is thought of as a set of rules or patterns derived from texts by analysis. Such a view obliterates the distinction between the grammar of a language and the use that is made of it in constructing any particular text. A linguistic analysis of the language of a text (including literary texts) reveals less what is uniquely possessed by that text than what properties it has by virtue of being a use of a certain grammar: the grammar is external to the text and prior to it. This grammar, and therefore the texts founded on it, is the public property of all speakers of the language. I am a native speaker of English. Like Pope, W. K. Wimsatt, Winifred Nowottny, Queens Elizabeth I and II, and many hundreds of millions of others, I acquired linguistic competence in English in my infancy. Apart from certain superficial differences caused by historical, geographical, social and personal factors, my command of English is much the same as Pope's. I could converse with Pope with no greater linguistic difficulty than conversing with an Irishman or Cornishman. The grammars of natural languages being what they are, any sentence of English that Pope might write is my property just as much as his: though I may never have uttered the sentence 'cool gales shall fan the glade', I know its meaning all the same, and know its meaning in advance of reading it in Pope.

To understand this assertion, it is necessary to grasp the principle of the *creativity* of natural languages. Apart from quotations and trivial standardized utterances like 'Good morning', 'Dear Sir', speakers are constantly producing (and understanding) new sentences. Although for obvious reasons this can never be proved as an empirical fact, it seems that the number of sentences possible in any language is infinite. Repetition is the exception rather than the rule. It would be a mistake to believe that each individual acquires, as he matures linguistically, a vast store of completely formed sentences from which he selects, from moment to moment, appropriate off-the-peg utterances. Contemporary linguistics suggests rather that each speaker of a language learns a finite system of rules (*langue*, competence) which enables him to produce an infinite number of sentences, i.e. the infinite set of grammatical sentences that constitutes the English, or whatever, language. (It is not possible to defend this hypothesis here, but many of my readers will see the point if I say that we propose a finite grammar with recursive properties, for example a grammar containing some rules which can be applied over and over again to form sentences of theoretically infinite length.) Pope uses this creative grammar to produce something which is unique, but not untypically unique or untypically creative, and not cut off from all other uses of English. A poem of his is not a quite selfcontained assemblage of sentences, and not to be regarded as his personal property to the exclusion of his readers. We must adopt this position if we do not want to reject such analytic truths as 'speakers of English speak the same language' and 'readers of English can read Pope.'

This theory of linguistic competence has two immediate and fundamental implications for literary theory of the kind we are considering. First, it gives clear support for those who, like Empson and Nowottny, have claimed that the language of literature is not different in essence from language at large. Since nobody has ever managed to devise any workable criteria for distinguishing 'poetic language' from 'ordinary language', it seems foolish to retain a spurious terminological distinction which effectively denies common sense. From the point of view of the present theory, those texts commonly regarded as literary are not to be differentiated from those regarded as non-literary, at least not by the invocation of any absolute criterion at the level of linguistic competence, the level of the available materials. Nor is any absolute distinction forthcoming in the study of linguistic performance, consideration of the use made of the materials. This is not to say that descriptive statements of variability among literary texts at the level of performance are impossible: such description is central to criticism. The second implication for criticism of contemporary linguistic theory is that it makes nonsense of the cruder assertions of the 'autonomy' of single works of literature. The extreme of the New Critical aesthetic, developed by argument and by the pressure of metaphors such as 'icon', 'urn', and 'monument', maintains that each poem is a self-sufficient symbolic object, by the act of poetic creation severed from its roots in language, culture and personality, with the power to teach the reader its own unique context and language—hence that no appeal is desirable or possible to anything except 'what is "there"' in the poem. It is of course sound advice that the evidence of the page should be given priority over evidence off the page; some kinds of non-textual evidence are not evidence at all, or inadmissible, or misleading. But accepting this advice does not entail believing that poems are utterly free, linguistically, culturally or psychologically. Certainly, authors can control and restrict the meanings of words by manipulating collocations; and to some extent poems, especially long poems, can enforce a new variety of the language. (Milton's syntax is a case in point.) But ultimately, in the experience of readers, poems are unequivocally in a language which exists independently outside the poems, and this fact guarantees 'reference out', connection with the outside world. Poems do not create out of nothing their own meaning and logic; the language they use imports from outside concepts and organizations of concepts as firm and demanding as the grain in the sculptor's medium. It is only a superficial paradox that 'what is "there"' in a poem, i.e. its language, ensures that the poem is linked essentially to the outside world.

IV

Criticism not being linguistics, critical statements are not statements about grammar (materials available) as such. However it seems to me that they cannot but be improved by knowledge of what grammar is. Insofar as critical statements make reference to language, they make reference to particular *uses* of the grammar, i.e. they are concerned with linguistic performance. Of course reference to language may be only implicit and indirect, but it is nevertheless unavoidable: criticism cannot do without a sense of the functioning of language. I am aware that that is a provocative assertion, even with the concession that criticism is not concerned with grammar as such. It can be justified only if we are equipped with a sufficiently rich theory of linguistic performance. Now I must make it clear that the construction of a theory of linguistic performance is a task that a linguist *qua* linguist cannot carry out alone. Chomsky has very little interest in linguistic performance, rightly defining the role of the strict linguist in terms of competence. We must look to the anthropologist for help, and we ought also to be able to consult critics who are well informed about language, but in practice find little assistance in the critical literature. The anthropologist rather than the linguist is the key figure because the 'unit' of linguistic performance is not the sentence but the language situation defined culturally, or communicative event, that gives sentences a function and a characteristic shape. I am now rephrasing the distinction between competence and performance, grammar and use of grammar, in the following terms. About any sentence, we can make two quite different kinds of statement. We can say 'This sentence is generated by a grammar of English' and then proceed to identify its structure; say whether it is grammatical, or, if deviant, in what way it is deviant; if it is ambiguous, state its alternative meanings; if it is a paraphase of some other sentence, point this fact out. All this is simple observation and description, dependent merely on accepting the sentence as being in existence and bearing a definable relationship to the grammar of English. On the other hand, we could seek to answer the question 'Why this sentence? Why have all the other possible sentences been rejected?' It is obvious that grammar in itself, the individual's ability to produce English, or French, or Russian, sentences, gives no reason at all for the production of one sentence rather than another—a speaking machine programmed just with a grammar of English could produce English sentences only in an utterly unmotivated fashion. But sentences do not occur randomly: there are always good reasons why in normal linguistic performance a certain sentence should be produced rather than some other. These reasons have to do with topic, style, social etiquette, tradition, rhetorical design, and so on—factors external to language but central to the structural organization of the culture that employs the language. As a general rule, we may say that the formal linguistic characteristics of every text or discourse are determined by the role it plays in the network of communicative conventions which defines a culture. 'Every particular *use* of English is to some extent reflected in and determines the *form* of the language that is used for that particular purpose,' as Randolph Quirk puts it (*The Use of English*, p. 21). So a 'sufficiently rich' theory of linguistic performance demands not merely a cataloguing of the types of sentences that occur in texts but also a powerfully explanatory model of the culture (or relevant parts of it) which makes texts the way they are. Texts must be seen as possessing certain internal formal characteristics as a consequence of performing a certain role within a conventional type of communication situation.

It is not difficult to demonstrate that there is correlation between the uses to which language is put and the form it assumes. The sentences used for advertising are immediately recognizable as different from those used for reporting Parliamentary business; the style of the instruction book for a car is distinct from that of romantic stories in women's magazines; the conventions for lecturing are different from those adapted to light conversation; and so on. These usages are easily explicable by reference to the external circumstances of linguistic performance. There is a growing body of studies by anthropologists and linguists (see many of the papers in Hymes, *Language in Culture and Society* and Gumperz and Hymes, *The Ethnography of Communication*) of patterns of discourse in culturally institutionalized speech situations. The more we think about these patternings, the clearer it becomes that *all* linguistic performance makes reference to recognized cultural conventions of a very regular and restrictive kind. The overall structure of performance in a language seems to be isomorphic with the network of communicative relations which maps a culture: one could draw a diagram of the structure of a community by making a classification of its modes and styles of linguistic performance.

Learning to be a mature participant in a community means primarily learning flexibility in an enormous range of 'registers' of language, acquiring the skill to perform linguistically according to the situation one is in, the role one is playing, the function of one's speech, one's audience or interlocutor, etc. One has to learn the way to perform linguistically as a father, son, colleague, neighbour, customer, husband, lover, and so on. There are also corresponding passive roles: it is as vital to be able to recognize significant differences in the character of linguistic performance as it is to be able to produce them. A mature member of the English-speaking community might be said to have attained 'sociolinguistic competence' as well as 'grammatical competence' in English. An habitual and successful reader of literature broadens and refines his sociolinguistic competence—his sensitivity to and skill in the patterned variability of English. Learning to read late Henry James is not an activity different in kind from learning to recognize and understand some equally circumscribed variety outside literature, for example the language of scientific articles. We have now provided another angle from which the common opposition of literature and non-literature, or literary language and non-literary language, appears less than sensible. The communicative activities of a society are not duolithic, split gigantically into two masses; they are split again and again and again with great delicacy and complexity into perhaps thousands of functional adaptations—commercials, sonnets, workshop manuals, recipes, odes, metaphysical lyrics, obituaries, specifications, political speeches, textbooks, academic articles, sermons, newscasts, short stories, labels and notices, dirty jokes, classical plays, Mozartian libretti, meteorological reports, epics, sports commentaries . . .

I have brought the argument to this point for theoretical and cautionary, rather than practical and methodological, ends. The practical benefits of accepting this model of intra-language variety are simple and perhaps trivial. Much of the spadework in literary studies has always consisted of constructing taxonomies of styles and genres. The above theory—suggesting external causation of verbal distinctiveness by distinct cultural situations—allows for varieties of language in literature to be sifted by a categorization of situational types, thus making stylistic categories intrinsically more interesting by imparting cultural content to them. Methods for this kind of classification are readily available. One thinks of, for example, J. R. Firth's (ultimately Malinowski's) notion of 'context of situation', designed as a schematic representation of the influencing circumstances in which language functions, and useful for the classification of situations, functions and forms. Nils-Erik Enkvist has proposed a literary adaptation of this device (Spencer and Gregory, *Linguistics and Style*, pp. 30-1). The methods of anthropologists, especially their treatment of ritual situations and oral folk-literature, would also assist in the development of procedures. The simplicity and cultural responsibility of this approach to stylistics and generic study recommend it highly. The theoretical gains are higher still, however. This proposed model of linguistic performance in society removes some of the most obsessive oppositions in modern poetics: language *versus* society, text *v.* context, internal *v.* external, autonomous *v.* dependent, linguistics *v.* sociology; language *v.* literature, ordinary language *v.* poetic language; static *v.* creative, convention *v.* innovation, habit *v.* invention; conformity *v.* licence, regularity *v.* deviation. All language is language, all language is creative, all language interpenetrates with culture.

V

The above is a fragmentation model, an analytical model, adapted to stylistics. The thesis is: every bit of linguistic performance has its associated bit of culture. There is also a synthetic paraphrase of the theory: language is culture. (That is exaggerated, but not grotesquely: language is the most potent systematic base of a culture.) Someone who attempts to come to terms with a society but knows *nothing* of its language is a profound alien indeed. His alienation embraces three degrees of severity: he cannot talk to others; he does not know the appropriate sociolinguistic rules, as above; he is perceptually paralysed. The last of these three handicaps—or its positive converse—is of the greatest interest to the critic: language is essentially, and not only in literature, a fiction-making device—a capability consequent upon its having a semantic dimension. I invoke here a commonplace belief, that language conditions perception. The belief has been prominently asserted in many quarters. There is Wittgenstein's dictum that the limits of one's language are the limits of one's world; Benjamin Lee Whorf's theory (developed from Sapir) of linguistic relativity, that speakers of languages with different semantic organizations have different world-views; the principle in the psychology of learning that concept-formation depends on language. Undeniably we are here moving into a field that is rife with confusion, absurdity, and metaphysical speculation. Whorf committed himself to an extreme and untestable doctrine; others—chiefly those who have debated the priority of language and thought—have descended to a chicken-and-egg dilemma. Nevertheless, it seems clear that man is a fiction-making animal, and that language assists the making and stabilization of fictions. Man has always been a great cataloguer and segmenter, a designer of calendars, numerical systems, units of measurement, and so on. Adam's first task was to name all the beasts and fowls, bestowing order and relationship on their collective presence. That myth is a myth of creation and security as well as of ownership: what is amorphous, contingent and undifferentiated is made into something manageable by imposing a conceptual structure on it. We understand our universe by naming its parts—or so we like to think. Of course what we really do is partition our universe fictionally by an imposed grid of language: the parts are created by the separateness of the linguistic symbols. Edmund Leach postulates that

> the physical and social environment of a young child is perceived as a continuum. It does not contain any intrinsically separate 'things'. The child, in due course, is taught to impose upon his environment a kind of discriminating grid which serves to distinguish the world as composed of a large number of separate things, each labelled with a name. This world is a representation of our language categories, not vice versa. ('Animal Categories and Verbal Abuse', p. 34)

A culture is one set of people's particular organization of the chaos of physical universals. The organization is made largely (not wholly) through language, and in this sense language is culture. Whatever 'reality' is, we do not think directly in terms of it, but in terms supplied by language. I segment the continuously gradated series of light frequencies into a set of colours structured by my colour vocabulary; manufacturers of paints, fabrics, etc., attempt to increase the size of my set of colours by extending my colour vocabulary. Or, to adopt Leach's example, I distinguish trees and bushes—there is no absolute distinction in nature—because I possess the terms 'tree' and 'bush'. The fictional concepts symbolized by 'tree' and 'bush' are items in a structured network of concepts, the semantics of my language. The semantics of my language comprise a matrix of logical oppositions and relations by which I chop up the flux of the world. Syntax allows me to juggle with concepts, and thus to demand that my audience attempts

G

to follow my conceptualization as I speak. Every sentence is a fiction. And so the interrelationship of syntax and semantics in poems becomes peculiarly interesting. The semantics of a poem do not constitute a bald, extractable, 'content' divorced from the mechanical forms of syntax and phonology: they are a fragment of a society's linguistic conceptualization of its experiences, actively arranged by the syntax to induce novel fictional perceptions in a reader.

Fictions are language-reinforced conceptualizations. Where the need for order is overwhelmingly powerful, myths and sensory percepts are created. Frank Kermode's *The Sense of an Ending* (1967) is a stimulating discussion of the fictional ordering of time. The bulk of the argument concerns apocalypses as examples of man's imposition on continuous temporality (*chronos*) of the significant but unempirical moment (*kairos*), bestowing crisis on mere flow. Put into language, artificially structured time becomes plot. As the paradigm of plot he alludes to the primitive fiction of 'what the clock says': *tick-tock*. It is a fact, presumably biologically determined, that, presented with a sequence of equispaced acoustic stimuli, people perceive them not as equally spaced out but as grouped into pairs with longer alternate intervals. This perception transcribed linguistically—*tick-tock*, with the *tock* indicating elongation of the second, fourth, etc., interval—becomes an emblem of fictionality, a micro-novel.

We are to view language, then, as the way fictional orderings of experience are created. Such a view is more promising for criticism than that which considers language as having two rather mechanical possibilities: making patterns ('medium in which') or acting as a transparent channel for the passage of ideas ('medium through which'). We avoid any hint of the form/content dualism which, though denied, has bedevilled New Critical practice. With this development of the theory of language in mind, let us return to Pope. When I introduced the quotation from the *Pastorals* (using it because it displays its grammar very clearly) I suggested that the abstract materials of the grammar were organized into structural patterns which could be characterized as partaking of a certain style. Later, methods of integrating such stylistic conventions of linguistic performance in a cultural framework were touched on. Now it becomes apparent that such an exposition would fall short of the potential of a criticism founded on an organic model of the reciprocity of language and culture. I shall refer briefly to Pope's *Essay on Man* to suggest what might be done. This 'general

Map of Man' is a reasoned assertion of man's place and function in relation to the rest of created nature. It is thus fair game for the historian of ideas, and also happens to be excellent quarry for materials on Augustan syntax, metre and imagery. A way of combining these two concerns is offered by Pope's own justification for writing these principles of philosophy in verse rather than prose: 'I found I could express them more *shortly* this way than in prose itself; and nothing is more certain, than that much of the *force* as well as *grace* of arguments or instructions, depends on their *conciseness*'. We must ask, then, how the poetic style enforces the argument. The basic premiss is that nature is ordered on the 'great chain' principle (I, 34, 245, etc.): man is a 'system' in a vertically ordered set of interdependent systems gradated 'justly' from inconceivably high to lowliest low. But though the poem is eloquent on the dependency of chains, it is silent on their linearity, extension, continuity. It presents no catalogue of systems, no survey, no explanation of each, one after the other. Rather it insists on the 'middle state' of man (II, 3) and in a rather odd way. Simple paraphrase might affirm that Pope sets man comfortably midway between angels and beasts, telling the reader that we may have grounds to be contented with the convenience and justice of our position. But the language is not contented: it rages with oppositions and paradoxes so severe that man can at one point be addressed as 'Vile worm' (I, 258), a slur superficially quite at odds with the philosophy as a whole. Man is not in the middle as, say, the digit 5 is in the middle of a series of nine, stable and symmetrical; he is in the middle as a piece of iron between two magnets is—being pulled and wanting to move two ways. His position is defined by negations and oppositions: not angel, not brute; reasonable, but passionate; physical, yet weak; wise, yet blind; neither one thing nor the other, and at the same time all things. The language is dense with syntactic and metrical opposition and antithesis, imagery in terms of absolutes (light and dark, etc.), opposed processes (rise and fall), oxymoron, paradox. The habitual discords of Pope's grammar and metre, the internal and external tensions of the couplet and its parts, contribute in a major way to inducing our conception of man through this poem: man occupies a state of just the same tension and contradiction as the poetic style itself. The language creates the fragile order of the great chain of being: an ordered and firmly conventional form so full of basic conflict that it is continually on the point of losing its fictional equilibrium (but never does).

Consider another kind of example. At the end of chapter 9 of *Washington Square*, Morris demands a private interview with Catherine; she asks him to come to the house and he exclaims 'I can't enter your house again . . . Your father has insulted me.' Nevertheless, he acquiesces, and chapter 10 opens:

> Catherine received the young man the next day on the ground she had chosen—amidst the chaste upholstery of a New York drawing-room furnished in the fashion of fifty years ago. Morris had swallowed his pride, and made the effort necessary to cross the threshold of her too derisive parent—an act of magnanimity which could not fail to render him doubly interesting.
> 'We must settle something—we must take a line,' he declared, passing his hand through his hair and giving a glance at the long, narrow mirror which adorned the space between the two windows, and which had at its base a little gilded bracket covered by a thin slab of white marble, supporting in its turn a backgammon-board folded together in the shape of two volumes—two shining folios inscribed, in greenish-gilt letters, *History of England*.

Morris's 'line' is then suspended for two pages, and it is this last sentence that 'causes' the suspension. He entered confident: confidence derived from his self-bestowed judgment of magnanimity—he had set aside his honour to enter the house for Catherine's sake. But the chosen ground of Catherine asserts itself: a casual (vain?) glance at himself in the mirror leads his eyes through a train of objects epitomizing the inescapable material presence of the Sloper household and its master. As the sentence drags out, and the objects it presents become more extraordinary (I think there is no specific symbolism in them), the dissipation of his will is dramatized before us. The perception is so powerful that it destroys his 'line'; it is Catherine who makes the decision, two pages later when the suspended action begins again.

A rather more complicated example of the structure of a sentence presenting to the reader the fictional ordering of an environment comes in chapter 16 of *Mansfield Park*, at the end of an account of the history and contents of the East room, just before Fanny enters it to 'try its influence on an agitated, doubting spirit':

> The room was most dear to her, and she would not have changed its furniture for the handsomest in the house, though what had been originally plain, had suffered all the ill usage of children—and its greatest elegancies and ornaments were a faded footstool of Julia's

work, too ill done for the drawing-room, three transparencies, made in a rage for transparencies, for the three lower panes of one window, where Tintern Abbey held its station between a cave in Italy and a moonlight lake in Cumberland; a collection of family profiles thought unworthy of being anywhere else, over the mantle-piece, and by their side and pinned against the wall, a small sketch of a ship sent four years ago from the Mediterranean by William, with H.M.S. Antwerp at the bottom, in letters as tall as the main-mast.

The complexity here is all in the ambivalence of the narrator's inter-vention: the sentence ostensibly gathers a set of physical objects, about to be seen and reflected on by Fanny, but in actuality juxtaposes all kinds of judgments. Far from being a nest of comforts, it is a concrete précis of all Fanny's conflicting affiliations, from the cruelty of Mrs. Norris to the love and security of her thoughts of William. She thinks to go to a room with objective characteristics from which she can learn; in fact she goes to a room in which her own and the novel's dilemmas are jostled together by the language of 'description'.

A language is a structured repository of concepts, and every use of language is a particular ordering in a (partly language-dependent) cir-cumscribed cultural situation. This ought to be a tacit principle for criticism, because it is an inevitable fact of all writing. The reader, whose linguistic conceptualization of experience answers closely to that of a poet who uses the same language, has his perceptions guided by the poet's performance in language. Imagist theory (which I can do no more than mention here) was an attempt to exalt this fact to a normative rhetoric. Pound championed Fenollosa because he pre-sented written Chinese as a 'language close to *things*': an active, con-crete language in which nouns were derived from verbs and there were no copulas, a language which did not place a barrier between reader and events and objects represented, but enacted them directly.[6] This is, I understand, a questionable view of Chinese, and is certainly an un-happy model of English. (Note also that it implies a literal belief in the existence of 'things' prior to language.) Nevertheless it provided a poetic to be strained for. In fact, English pretty consistently resists the

[6] See Ernest Fenollosa, *The Chinese Written Character as a Medium for Poetry*, San Francisco (no date). The work was discovered by Ezra Pound among Fenollosa's papers after his death in 1908, and hailed by him as 'a study of the fundamentals of all aesthetics'.

Imagists' efforts to make it construct (i.e. induce perception of) concrete symbolic objects. The extension of language in space and time makes it very difficult to assemble complex concepts at one point of time. For example, T. E. Hulme's 'Autumn' is not a moment of unified perception but a procession of cold, night, walking, moon, farmer, not stopping, nodding, stars, faces, and children:

> A touch of cold in the Autumn night—
> I walked abroad,
> And saw the ruddy moon lean over a hedge
> Like a red-faced farmer.
> I did not stop to speak, but nodded,
> And round about were the wistful stars
> With white faces like town children.

The linear organization of syntax disperses the image and creates an expectation of narrative rather than an instantaneous perception.

VI

In a paper of this scale the theory has had to be hurried and the analysis fragmentary. Many major issues have had to be neglected altogether: one that I particularly regret having to ignore is the question of how 'fictional worlds' are created by long-range semantic organization in novels. I hope that the examples at the end have made it clear that I have not been arguing for a practical criticism founded on the technique of linguistics, but for a unified criticism based on a theory of language and a theory of the mutual interpenetration of language, conceptualization and cultural organization. Whereas R. S. Crane, in *The Languages of Criticism and the Structure of Poetry*, suggests that criticism is disparate and literature unified, I would claim that the only criticism capable of treating, at a public and non-idiosyncratic level, the diversity of literature, is a profoundly unified criticism. Literature is diverse linguistically: poems and novels are linguistic universes in which the fictional orderings of experience can be traced in diverse manipulations of language. A subject of such difficulty and complexity demands a very stable empirical theory from which meaningful descriptive terms can be derived; I do not think the anarchy which the Chicago Critics' offer of pluralism entails can satisfy so high a demand.

IX

Criticism as an Individual Activity: The Approach through Reading*

IAN GREGOR

I

IN Christopher Isherwood's novel *A Single Man*, George, an assistant professor of English in San Tomas State College, is conducting a class on Aldous Huxley's novel *After Many a Summer*. He stops and there is a significant pause:

> Before we can go any further, you've got to make up your minds what this novel actually *is* about. . . . At first, as always, there is blank silence. The class sits staring, as it were, at the semantically prodigious word. *About. What* is it about? Well, what does George want them to say it's about? They'll say it's about anything he likes, anything at all. For nearly all of them, despite their academic training, deep deep down still regard this *about* business as a tiresomely sophisticated game. As for the minority, who have cultivated the *about* approach until it has become second nature, who dream of writing an *about* book of their own one day, on Faulkner, James or Conrad, proving definitively that all previous *about* books on that subject are about nothing—they aren't going to say anything yet awhile. They are waiting for the moment when they can come forward like star detectives with the solution to Huxley's crime. Meanwhile, let the little ones flounder. Let the mud be stirred up, first.[1]

It is difficult for anyone engaged in the teaching of literature not to feel a pang of discomfort as he reads that passage and I have quoted it at the beginning of this essay because it describes in an embarrassingly precise way an unease about the practice and precept of much modern

---

* Since my concern here is primarily with the reading of literary texts, I have reserved my few bibliographical comments for a long note at the end of this essay.

[1] *A Single Man* (1964), p. 54.

literary criticism, and, by extension, ways of talking about literature both formally and informally.

There are reason for thinking that after about 1920 literary criticism began to change its character as it was pressed increasingly into serving the interests of teaching this new subject—English literature. It is true that when Dr. Johnson wrote his prefaces to Shakespeare and Coleridge and Hazlitt lectured in London, they were very much aware of communicating their sense of an author to a public—and it was, of course the common reader with whom Johnson rejoiced to concur. But the occasions were casual, the audience select, and the invitation extended because they were already distinguished men of letters. The interest lay in their views, rather than in the nature of the activity they were exemplifying.

If modern literary criticism looks back to the nineteenth century to find its origins, it finds its most congenial ancestor in Matthew Arnold. The title alone of a famous essay written in 1864 is sufficient to record the change of emphasis from Johnson and Coleridge: 'The Function of Criticism at the Present Time'. 'Function' brings with it a new self-consciousness about method, but more importantly criticism of literature is no longer seen as a dominantly literary affair, but as having something distinctive to contribute to 'the present time' and its spiritual well-being. Until the first world war, it is safe to say that it was Arnold's influence, consciously acknowledged or not, which shaped literary preference and prejudice. But it was an influence vulnerable to debasement and the literary tact and social concern which Arnold exemplified all too often evaporated. Saintsbury's *History of Criticism*, for instance, written between 1900 and 1904, is really a history of taste, and any personal engagement on the part of the critic is purely accidental. As Stephen Potter remarked of Saintsbury, he was a man who 'must have read nearly 500 sonnets to Liberty, 600 Odes on the Emancipation of Slaves, and about 7000 different kinds of eloquent condemnation of Church and State. Yet with the most amiable recognition of the literary quality of these pieces, he remained to the end of his life a Tory of the kind that was always expecting, as soon as the right kind of government came along, a repeal of the Reform Bill of 1832.'[2] It was this divorce between literature and life that fuelled the critical revolution that took place, or at least began to gather momentum, in the years between the wars—a revolution that took place on

[2] *The Muse in Chains* (1937), p. 138.

both sides of the Atlantic, and which in England we associate with names such as Eliot, Pound, Richards and Leavis. It was a revolution which, while taking as epigraph Eliot's dictum 'comparison and analysis are the chief tools of the critic', consistently sought to go beyond this and to see in literature, as Arnold had done, the consciousness of the age. Here the critic is drawing on values which transcend the literary. Concern with what we have come to call practical criticism—the close reading of the text—is complemented at every stage by the recognition that literature has a social function to perform, a function seen most noticeably in education.

But as we look back over recent years something seems to have gone wrong. Skills which twenty or thirty years ago had purpose and vitality about them seem to have become 'a sophisticated game'. And though we may feel caricature in Isherwood's description of George's class, it is not difficult to feel a rueful sympathy with the irony under-lying it, an irony directed at the banalities of contemporary criticism. Attempts have been made to do a rescue-operation by calling on other disciplines—history or sociology—but these seem confined to a local need rather than a general one, or else literary criticism emerges as a disguised version of its rescuer.

In the argument that follows I want to suggest that if literary criticism is to shake itself free from the banalities that seem to sap it of purpose, it will only be by trying to become more aware of its own nature, not in some timeless way, but in sensing the needs and pressures of the contemporary intellectual scene, and more intimately, what it actually feels like to read a book.

II

'When you judge poetry it is as poetry you must judge it, not as another thing.' Eliot's austere and judicial warning could serve as a motto for contemporary criticism. It has thrived on purity of purpose, and has sought to disengage itself, sometimes elaborately, always firmly, from the embraces of kindred disciplines, history, philosophy, sociology. Whatever 'entente' has been established, it has been only guardedly 'cordiale'. Literary criticism has been seen to have its own practice, its own aims—which Eliot described crisply as 'the elucida-tion of works of art and the correction of taste'. The firmness of that description is indicative of the language that has been brought into play to maintain this educative and judicial interest. Inevitably, it is a language in which metaphors have been enlisted to give us the sense of *the poem or the novel as object*. It is a language which encouraged persuasive books to find titles like *The Well-Wrought Urn* and *The Verbal Icon*—which uses as a working idiom such terms as 'models' and 'artefacts', and sees in 'the objective-correlative' a useful account of a psychological process, and in 'concreteness' testimony to its success. The whole language of analogy, drawing heavily on terms like 'structure' and 'texture', is so habitual and instinctive with us that it is only by an effort of will that we can recognize it as largely the created idiom of the last forty years. Its creation is the result of a need—a need for us to feel that, in a very important sense, the work of art is 'out there', an embodiment of value in its own right. Analysis is there to demonstrate that value: comparison to relate that value to a hierarchy. The implications of this become clear if we think of our judicial vocabulary of approval—'disinterested', 'detached', 'impersonal'—terms which consistently turn our attention away from the critic to the object of his criticism. Of course, we talk a good deal about response, but this amounts to little more than a series of encouraging murmurs, and the effect of response on our very apprehension of a work of art has found little attention from literary critics.

Faced with such a situation we are tempted to turn back the pages of history, and to recreate what Wordsworth calls 'that serene and blessed mood' before we knew it was an improper question to ask how many children had Lady Macbeth, before Mr. Empson had revealed there were seven types of ambiguity, before we knew in fiction that there was a great tradition, or that, in poetry, paradox was all. But that halcyon mood cannot be ours, partly because this knowledge has been given to us by critics who have enabled us to be much more sharply aware of literature, partly because such criticism is as much part of the literature we know, as the literature it describes.

Our problem can be put in another way. The impulse to turn back the pages of history springs from the feeling that critics of an earlier age were able to find a personal voice more readily than we can. They could speak out. But on the other hand when we look at their criticism we find that on the whole it has little to say to us. They thought too simply of the relationship of the critic to the work; where we look for a personal apprehension they were content to offer us personal taste. And this—the critics of our own time have made abundantly plain—is to sell the work of art short, to trivialize it. What we seem to be in need of is an understanding of criticism which while remaining faithful to the principles of analysis and judgment, will make us more sharply aware of our personal responsiveness.

We want to understand Leavis's phrase 'inner possession' and to see what implications it has, not as an item in our mental autobiography, but as illuminating the work of art. For the remainder of this essay my aim will be to try and suggest ways in which such an understanding might operate in the criticism of one literary form, that of fiction.

III

One of the most suggestive books on the novel has the considerable merit of being one of the shortest. In the tough and professional world of current novel criticism E. M. Forster's *Aspects of the Novel* has a refreshing directness about it. We feel that his comments on character and plot, provoking and speculative as they are, also manage to give us the feeling of what it is actually like to read a novel. That is, we are not in danger of mistaking the genre for a psychoanalytic report, a sociological treatise, or an introduction to the devout life. But for all this, Mr. Forster has lent his considerable authority to permitting a certain neglect in novel criticism, which has done it much damage.

Those seemingly artless chapter headings—Story, Plot, People, Fantasy, Prophecy—in fact outline a veiled argument, which is to indicate a pilgrim's progress along which the postulant should gradually make his ascent from the flats of story to the peaks of prophecy. 'Yes—oh dear yes—the novel tells a story.' The famous regret with which Mr. Forster concludes his first chapter might seem, at first, to be merely the expression of an individual taste, but it is a sentiment to which many a critical bosom would seem to have returned an echo. Mr. Forster's sentiment may find more sophisticated expressions, we may prefer to call the novel a low atavistic form, but it amounts to the same thing in the end.

If we look at critical essays on individual novels, we find a procedure which varies little. In his opening paragraph the critic paraphrases, as economically as possible, the story he is about to discuss, rather in the manner of an acrobat hurriedly unrolling the mat upon which he is about to perform his act. This is a pity because whatever else is engaging our attention in the novel, the element of uncertainty about what is going to happen, crude as this may seem, is not without influence in keeping us turning over the pages, and when we cease to care, a bookmark usually registers the place where interest expired. Most novel readers warm to Wilde's observation, 'This suspense is terrible. I hope it will last'—however oblique, subtle and elegant its communication may be. What I am arguing for is not that the critic should devote more of his time to relating the story, but rather to underline the fact that novel reading is a response to a process, a process which has critical implications insufficiently grasped by those intent on conveying the significance of the completed work. Precisely because it is a process a novel looks and feels different at page 150 from how it looked and felt at page 50. But our methods of criticism often treat a novel as if it were a series of numbered paragraphs simultaneously present in the reader's mind. For all our scrupulous attention to 'words on the page', we seem oddly indifferent to the number on the page. Admittedly, it is easy to be disingenuous here and, obviously, we must look for the relevant passage or passages whenever we try to document impressions, if only to win agreement or submit them to revision. Also we try on the whole to be fair about context. But while freely conceding this, I don't think it puts into dispute that the sequential nature of the novel has had virtually no part to play in shaping our critical accounts.

It might be thought that I am contending for greater attention to story, in the way which, some decades ago, attention was being called to imagery. But I am arguing for more than this. Story is not there in the way that imagery is—an element which can be pointed to and circumscribed; it is inseparable from our very apprehension of the novel, and if we neglect it, our whole critical stance is affected.

I see, for instance, Mr. Forster's 'Yes—oh dear yes—the novel tells a story' together with the veiled argument that follows, creating conditions favourable for a recent critic[3] to commence a study of Mr. Forster's own fiction with the following paragraph:

> Four things may be said about the fiction of E. M. Forster; first that his works are romance rather than novel; second, that symbolism is central to his achievement in the romance form; third, that the principal source of his symbols is ecstatic experience; and fourth, that through the power of ecstatic perception his symbols achieve archetypal significance and mythic wholeness.

[3] George H. Thomson, *The Fiction of E. M. Forster* (Anne Arbor, Mich. 1967), p. 13.

The critic rigidly applies Forster's own categories and finds four things to say—some of which may be true—but there remains a fifth, and that is that no novel could conceivably be read like this, and to think that it could would be to confuse a seed catalogue with a garden.[4]

But what, it may be asked, does 'story' or 'process' look like when it gets into criticism? Seeing that I am trying to describe a process, brevity of illustration becomes more than usually difficult. But the question is in need of an answer and I will attempt to illustrate in outline at least the important consequences of bringing the element of story into play—consequences, I would like to suggest, which go beyond the novel and will take us back to look at literary criticism itself. Since my illustrations have to be sketchy I will take them from situations of consequence. And so I have chosen three places in the English novel where traffic is so heavy that critics are to be found there bumper to bumper.

IV

The most famous sentence in one of the most famous of English novels reads, ' "Justice" was done and the President of the Immortals, in Aeschylean phrase, had ended his sport with Tess.' The fame of the line from Hardy's *Tess of the D'Urbervilles* derives from the impression it seems to have given of summarizing the whole drift and feeling of that novel. It lies behind a view of Hardy as a tragic novelist *par excellence*, the laureate of 'crass causality and dicing time'. Asked to

---

[4] Forster himself of course would never make such a confusion, but the *argument* of *Aspects of the Novel* is vulnerable in this way. The *tone* of that book is quite another matter and is caught in the admirable opening of another study of Forster's work, this time by Lionel Trilling, written in 1944.

> E. M. Forster is for me the only living novelist who can be read again and again and who, after each reading, gives what few writers can give us after our first days of novel-reading, the sensation of having learned something. I have wanted for a long time to write about him and it gives me a special satisfaction to write about him now, for a consideration of Forster's work is, I think, useful in time of war. (*E. M. Forster*, p. 9)

Trilling's study is certainly not immune from criticism, but such an opening encourages us to read on because the critic is writing out of a personal pleasure and conviction and is anxious to relate his discourse to the world of men and to employ the language they commonly use.

restore the line to its context most people would put it as the last
sentence in the novel, certainly the last one of consequence. It comes
then as something of an embarrassment to find that the line was only
pencilled into the manuscript as an afterthought. In fact it is not the
culminating sentence of the novel, but the first sentence of the last
paragraph, a paragraph which reads as follows:

> 'Justice' was done, and the President of the Immortals, in Aeschylean
> phrase, had ended his sport with Tess. And the d'Urberville Knights
> and dames slept on in their tombs unknowing. The two speechless
> gazers bent themselves down to the earth, as if in prayer, and
> remained thus a long time, absolutely motionless: the flag continued
> to wave silently. As soon as they had strength they arose, joined
> hands again, and went on.

And so the novel ends.

I am not suggesting that the affirmative note of the last sentence is to
be preferred to the sardonic note of the first, but simply that it should
be taken along with it. This final paragraph contains that duality of
emphasis, characteristic of Hardy's fiction as a whole. Complementary
to the tragic vision is a self-mockery, a wry humour that gives the
Wessex novels for all their undeniable tragic cast, a resilience of outlook and zest in narrative power, and to which descriptions of Hardy
in terms of his pessimism do a considerable injustice. *Tess* ends in this
way, but how in fact does it begin, what is the reader made to feel as
he turns the pages of the first chapter?

The invariable start of a Hardy novel is on the road, and indeed this
sense of a journey about to be undertaken, with the reader enrolled as a
fellow traveller, is a basic motif in the storyteller's art. It encourages
in the most direct way our sense of movement. If anyone recalls the
first chapter of *Tess* it will probably be as a memory of an antiquarian
clergyman meeting Tess's father, John Durbeyfield, and telling him of
his distinguished ancestry. We are made to sense very strongly the
presence of a story within a story, and the whole chapter is designed to
have the formal and arresting quality of 'once upon a time'. To see
how this is conveyed we can look at it more closely. 'On an evening
in the latter part of May a middle aged man was walking homeward'
—thus the novel opens. The man is rather drunk and, having been
bidden 'Good night, Sir John' by the passing antiquarian, pauses uncer-
tainly, and asks why he has been addressed in this grand manner. The

parson after a momentary hesitation tells him about his distinguished ancestry. Durbeyfield, awestruck, finally asks:

'And where do we raise our smoke, now, parson, if I may make so bold; I mean, where do we D'Urbervilles live?'
'You don't live anywhere. You are extinct—'

The parson leaves Durbeyfield musing on the roadside when a local boy appears:

'Well, Fred, I don't mind telling you that the secret is I'm one of a noble race—it has been just found out by me this present afternoon P.M. . . . There's not a man in the county . . . got grander and nobler skillentons in his family than I'.

And the bewildered boy is ordered to find a horse and carriage to take him home, so that he can break the news in a manner becoming his new status.

While the chapter is not comic, it is genial and wry—however knowingly we may mark phrases like 'our impulses are too strong for our judgments'—and that is the dominant tone which Hardy wants to establish at the beginning of the novel. The consequences are far reaching. The antiquarian's story obviously prompts reflections on 'supposing things had been different . . .' and this casts a shadow before it. But it also reveals the irresistible temptation to tell a story, to recall with relish the quirks of human fortune. This relish is Hardy's also— he came across the family legend in much the same way as Durbeyfield —and in this first chapter we feel the positive pleasure in the writing, the novelist finding his touch straightaway. Gossip is the current coin of fiction, and in this realm we feel the misfortunes of life are possibly even more interesting than the fortunes. A typical germ for a Hardy tale occurs in this entry from his *Life* written about the same time: 'As was the case with Hardy almost always, a strange bizarre effect was noticed by him at the Moulin Rouge—in those days a very popular place of entertainment. As everybody knows, or knew, it was close to the cemetary of Montmartre, being, it seems, only divided therefrom, by a wall . . . as he stood somewhere in the building, looking down at the young women dancing the *can-can* and grimacing at the men, it appears that he could see through some back windows over their heads to the last resting place of so many similar gay Parisiens silent under the moonlight . . .'[5] What seizes Hardy's imagination here is not

[5] *Life of Thomas Hardy* (1962), p. 229.

the transience of life, but its theatrical effects—ideal material for the storyteller. Our interest is aroused by human possibilities rather than by human fortunes or misfortunes, and the first chapter of *Tess* awakens a sense of expectancy which will help to create this world of possibilities, a world inimical to explanation and solution. As Hardy said in the Preface to *Jude*, his fiction was 'an endeavour to give a shape and coherence to a series of seemings'; in the art of storytelling he hoped to find an assurance that this would be so.

The following of a gradually unfolding story has, then, critical consequences, the importance of which may often as in the case of *Tess* be felt most distinctly at the beginning and at the end. This is not, of course, always the case and I want in a second illustration to catch a plot clean in full flow.

I have chosen that celebrated place in *Wuthering Heights* (which seems to have become a compulsory stop in every critical essay on the novel), in which Cathy, questioned by Nelly Dean, describes and distinguishes between her love for Linton and her love for Heathcliff.

> 'My love for Linton is like the foliage in the woods: time will change it, I'm well aware, as winter changes the trees—my love for Heathcliff resembles the eternal rocks beneath, a source of little visible delight, but necessary. Nelly, I *am* Heathcliff . . .' (chapter IX)

These are sentences which have been submitted again and again to analysis. The distinction which Cathy draws has indeed served as a latitude and longitude for discussions about the novel as a whole. But how, we might ask, does this exchange with Nelly occur in the novel? What would a reader, as he comes upon it for the first time, have in his mind as he reads the pages immediately preceding it? This, I would like to insist, is doing something more than recalling a context, which implies something fixed, a circumscribed setting for the passage under immediate view. My stress is on process, so that as we turn the pages over, the passage is approached, read, and then fades in the memory as we proceed. We catch the difference in our attention if we think of ourselves looking at a 'still' from a film, and seeing that scene in the course of the film itself.

If we look at the chapter in which the conversation with Nelly occurs we find it contains a good deal of narrative. It opens at the point where Edgar Linton having declared his love for Cathy, hurriedly leaves 'Wuthering Heights' as Cathy's elder brother, Hindley, is heard approaching in his usual condition of well-oiled wrath. Nelly Dean describes what follows:

> He entered, vociferating oaths dreadful to hear, and caught me in the act of stowing his son away in the kitchen cupboard. Hareton was impressed with a wholesome terror of encountering either his wild beast's fondness or his madman's rage; for in one, he ran a chance of being squeezed and kissed to death, and in the other, of being flung into the fire, or dashed against the wall: and the poor thing remained perfectly quiet wherever I chose to put him.
>
> 'There, I've found it out at last!' cried Hindley, pulling me back by the skin of my neck, like a dog. 'By heaven and hell, you've sworn between you to murder that child! I know how it is now, that he is always out of my way. But, with the help of Satan, I shall make you swallow the carving-knife, Nelly! You needn't laugh, for I've just crammed Kenneth, head-downmost, in the Blackhorse march; and two is the same as one—and I want to kill some of you: I shall have no rest till I do!'
>
> 'But I don't like the carving-knife, Mr. Hindley,' I answered; 'it has been cutting red herrings. I'd rather be shot, if you please.'
>
> 'You'd rather be damned!' he said; 'and so you shall. No law in England can hinder a man from keeping his house decent, and mine's abominable!—open your mouth.'
>
> He held the knife in his hand, and pushed its point between my teeth: but, for my part, I was never much afraid of his vagaries. I spat out, and affirmed it tasted detestably—I would not take it on any account. (chapter IX)

It's an incredible opening to the chapter, teetering on the edge of farce and horror—horror at Hindley's behaviour, but farce at the details—the stowing of Hareton in the cupboard, the local doctor Kenneth 'crammed' head-downmost in the march, the carving knife thrust between Nelly's teeth and the unflinching gentility of her replies. This is uncomfortably close to comedy of the absurd; uncomfortably, because comedy however dark is quite alien to any ordinary reading of the novel. And for reasons which are obvious enough, Emily Brontë has by this stage created an atmosphere in which the intensities and bizarreness of the episode seem wholly appropriate in the world of her novel. As soon as we stop however and we read it aloud we give the scene a deliberation which alters its natural movement. Tempo in reading is certainly something the novelist, quite properly, relies upon to enable him to create his effect; to read in slow motion is to read differently, not as we are sometimes inclined to think, more accurately. What, however, reading aloud does bring out is the extreme unevenness of Emily Brontë's writing, the intimacy between melodrama and tragedy. As soon as Hindley leaves, and Nelly is left alone with Cathy and Hareton, a shift in control takes place, and we find the prose taking on new life. 'I've dreamt in my life,' Cathy says 'dreams that have stayed with me ever after, and changed my ideas; they've gone through and through me like wine through water, and altered the colour of my mind.' When Cathy goes on to tell her dream about how she was thrown out of heaven and woke to find herself on Wuthering Heights 'sobbing for joy'—we feel this is the authentic novel, the place where the critic should pause and comment. But should he? If he does, is it not just as distorting as isolating the paragraphs which begin the chapter?—the effect here being to turn Cathy's replies to Nelly into a prose poem, as of course the intensity of the language encourages us to do. But we have to think of this intensity of feeling as belonging to the same world of feeling as the terrified child and the carving knife, and like that world, it subsides as quickly. By isolating from its context the passage in which Cathy distinguishes between Linton and Heathcliff, we risk seeing it as an opposition between the counterfeit and the true, rather than between the more and less intense. And chapter nine, as we read it, takes us through this kaleidoscope of feelings—Hindley's violence, Nelly's gentility, Cathy's ecstasy and despair—and then—quite suddenly, closes with a laconic account of life over the next three years—Heathcliff's departure, the death of the Lintons, Cathy's marriage. It's in this dramatic oscillation between the commonplace and the profound, the social and the metaphysical, that Emily Brontë finds her theme, so that by the time we come to the last sentence of the novel we have learnt to read it in two quite different ways and both are true. 'I lingered round them, under that benign sky; watching the moths fluttering among the heath and hare bells, listened to the soft wind breathing through the grass, and wondered how anyone could ever imagine unquiet slumbers for the sleepers in that quiet earth.' Is this the calm resolution of 'all passion spent'? Or is it a sardonic exposure of a complacent man still unwilling to believe in the evidence of things not seen? The answer is, surely, both. And we are made to realize this precisely because the story has been told in a certain way; the propulsion of the narrative—and it is, we remember, a narrative largely conveyed by the gossiping Nellie Dean—has coursed through melodrama and tragedy, ecstasy and the commonplace. With *Wuthering Heights* in view we can claim that the unfolding story acts out its meaning.

For my third example of what contribution 'story' can make to an understanding of fiction, I want to look at the situation where the process of reading is actually completed—when, in fact we read again, knowing what is to come. Nowhere is this of more consequence than in the novel of irony, which relies precisely on being re-read for its point to be properly taken. To put the case in specific terms—what is the difference between reading and re-reading Jane Austen's *Emma*?

Reading the novel we are aware of its morally teasing nature. We have, at its centre, someone who is the most attractive and intelligent person in the book and yet, at the same time, someone who is blinkered, selfregarding and patronizing. The moral crisis of the book occurs during the picnic on Box Hill when Mr. Knightley reproves Emma for her thoughtless treatment of Miss Bates. In the course of the picnic, Emma has organized a game in which the players have to say three dull things in succession, and she will undertake to laugh at them all. Miss Bates enters into the spirit of the game and agrees to play: 'Ah! ma'am,' Emma interrupts, 'but there may be a difficulty . . . you will be limited to number, only three at once.' It is this remark which earns her Knightley's rebuke. 'How could you be so unfeeling to Miss Bates? How could you be so insolent in your wit to a woman of her character, age and situation?—Emma, I had not thought it possible.' This criticism is not without justification yet it makes us uneasy be-cause it seems intended by the author to constitute the moral touch-stone in being the moment of Emma's final selfknowledge. Our un-easiness is not abated when Knightley continues, 'This is not pleasant to you, Emma—and it is very far from pleasant to me; but I must, I will,—I will tell you truths while I can, satisfied with proving myself your friend by very faithful counsel and trusting that you will sometime or other do me greater justice than you can do now! . . .' There is a backwash of moral selfregard in these remarks which makes the whole condemnation seem heavy-handed if not priggish. On reading the novel we have no reason to take Knightley's remarks otherwise than at their face value. But on re-reading, how very different that scene looks. Remarks that we thought addressed to one person were in fact addressed to another; the dramatic centre was not, as later events will show, where we thought at all, and Knightley's words are shown to have a very different timbre.

The really wounding remarks at the picnic are not Emma's, but Frank Churchill's to Jane Fairfax. Frank, unknown to the reader, is secretly engaged to Jane. He interprets her consistent discretion in company as indifference, and is determined to provoke her by flirting with Emma. The game is his suggestion, but he encourages Emma to put it forward. Frank's behaviour and remarks are quite clear to Jane Fairfax, but it is only in re-reading the novel that they become clear to us and we see them as cutting, not flirtatious. Knightley, who is in the same position as the reader, is provoked by Frank's behaviour into jealousy and so that when Emma offends Miss Bates, his moral rebuke is charged with the chagrin of an irritated lover. '*I will tell you truths while I can*, satisfied with proving myself *your friend* by very faithful counsel and trusting that you will *sometime or other* do me greater justice than you can do now . . .' (my italics). This remark now sounds rather differently. In re-reading, we see that Emma, so far from managing the scene, and being 'unfeeling and insolent in her wit', is in fact a catalyst for the emotions of others, providing an occasion for Frank to show his irritation with Jane, and Knightley to feel jealous of Frank.

What implications has this for our appreciation of the novel as a whole? Unlike a writer of detective stories, whose aim is to keep us in suspense by hiding the clues, Jane Austen is anxious to make us feel, as a dramatic reality, the truth of her remark made elsewhere in the novel, 'Seldom, very seldom, does complete truth belong to any human disclosure; seldom does it happen that something is not a little disguised or a little mistaken. . . .'

Emma is a novel built on misconceptions; most of these derive from the heroine not from the reader who may be justified in thinking himself simply a genial onlooker. However, he is more involved than he believes and is constantly lured like Emma herself (or, more embarrassingly, like Knightley) into feeling that he is in serene possession of full knowledge. When he re-reads, he experiences the illusion of his possession and can now see that it was Jane Austen's purpose to create that illusion in order that the reading of her story might enact the puzzle she wished to illustrate. Subsequent readings differ from the first, not because we have solved the puzzle, but because we are now in a position to assess our reaction to the experiencing of it. In *Emma*, the story makes us feel our fallibility.

V

I would like to think I have now reached a point where, by way of conclusion, I can bring my two interests, if not together, then at least in to neighbourly contact. Let me recapitulate them briefly.

I began by talking of a crisis of confidence in current literary criticism, a crisis attested to by worries about relevance, by constantly repeated definitions of function. I attributed a large measure of this unease to the way in which modern literary critical practice, in drift and prescription, has emphasized the need to see the work of art as an object and has given hospitality to an idiom generous to that view. If literature was to reveal a hierarchy of value, then it was essential the grounds for such a value be plainly demonstrated. 'Analysis and judgment'—the prescription was a double one, and it undertook at every turn to guard against 'the personal heresy', in which the critic should allow *a priori* beliefs and predilections to influence his response to the work in hand. This was a revolution against the apostles of taste, and its success was decisive. But as in every revolution, yesterday's heterodoxies become today's orthodoxies and the pragmatic spirit, once so challenging and refreshing, has become a manner and not a need. Nevertheless—my argument ran—we are true children of this spirit, and those who try to shake it off we suspect, often rightly, as being 'unreliable', 'modish', or—still a damaging description—'speculative'. What we seem to be in need of is a critical idiom which will do justice to the discipline we have learnt, but one which, for the time being at least, will try to revivify the common pursuit by recovering the personal voice.

My second theme in this paper was offered as a modest illustration of what the recovery of that personal voice might look like in the area of prose fiction. It was an argument which attempted to bring to critical attention, an element, significantly neglected, in current criticism of the novel, namely story. 'Significantly', because story evokes the most instinctive and immediate of our responses, the one which raises personal issues most readily, and therefore which has been looked at with most suspicion. But 'story' takes us into our very apprehension of the novel, and by looking at important moments in three English novels,

I attempted to show the extent and repercussions of this element in our reading of them. The relationship between my two themes is that story sites our response at a highly personal level, it softens our sense of the novel as object and, complementary with this, our selfconfidence as judge. It is asking us to be much more sharply aware of what is happening to us as we read a novel, not as a psychological 'aside', but as an intrinsic element in the work itself. The language of simple preference and prejudice comes from this region, but because we have excluded it too ruthlessly from the language of our criticism, we have created conditions favourable for that 'superior game', which George's class had embarked upon in looking at Huxley's novel.

The clash between what I might call the language of preference and the language of criticism is neatly illustrated by an episode in Virginia Woolf's diary in which she records paying a visit to Hardy in 1926, when he was, of course, the Grand Old Man of English letters. The meeting was an uneasy one, what with the clatter of tea cups, Mrs. Hardy inexorably following one platitude with another, the dog Wessex chewing away at the mat. Repeatedly, Virginia Woolf tried to steer the conversation towards literature, but with little success. Then her account goes on, 'I wanted him to say one word about his writing before we left and could only ask which of his books he would have chosen if, like me, he had had to choose one to read on the train. I had taken *The Mayor of Casterbridge* . . . "And did it hold your interest?" he asked. I stammered that I could not stop reading it, which was true, but sounded wrong.'[6]

Virginia Woolf's stammer is our stammer too—our criticism 'sounds wrong' when suddenly we are confronted with what we tend inevitably to think a banality but recognize as the very justification of our whole critical activity—'and did it hold your interest?' These are the banalities that criticism cannot afford to lose contact with. They tell us about the process of reading and we can all go on to make our own list of these phrases, 'being lost in a book', 'identified with a character', 'seeing a life-like situation'. As D. W. Harding has shown in a fine essay called the 'Psychological Bases of Reading Fiction',[7] we have been content for far too long to make a label—'wish-fulfilment', 'vicarious satisfaction', 'living at the novelist's expense'—do the work of understanding, where understanding implies not simply *self*awareness, but

[6] *A Writer's Diary*, p. 92.
[7] *British Journal of Aesthetics* (1962).

awareness of how the fiction we read actually works. We will find, for instance, fiction is intimately related to gossip, and that there is no difference between the psychological process involved in the reading of trivial and the reading of serious fiction. And Harding goes on to say that a set of values

> may centre round marble bathrooms, mink coats and big cars or they may be embodied in the social ,milieu and *personae* of novels by Jane Austen or Henry James; Cadillacs and their occupants at Las Vegas, or carriages and theirs at Pemberley and Poynton. . . . It seems nearer the truth, therefore, to say that fictions contribute to defining the reader's or spectator's values . . . rather than to suppose that they gratify desire by some mechanism of vicarious experience. In this respect they follow the pattern, not of the dream with its hallucinated experiencing, but of waking supposition and imagination—'Wouldn't it be wonderful if . . .' 'Wouldn't it be sad if . . .' . . . For it has to be remembered that the subtlest and most intense empathic insight into the experience of another person is something far different from having the experience oneself.[8]

Criticism arises from a similar response, involving participation as well as judgment, and in this way it too becomes a kind of story we tell ourselves about what it feels like to read certain books. How much closer it is to story than to report becomes clear if we think of the nature of the conclusions reached. For the criticism we think of as memorable we certainly do not always regard as 'right', and critical arguments we consider 'right' do not always command our greatest interest. The most memorable criticism would seem to occur when the critic has been able to reveal the intensity of his engagement with the work in hand. In writing criticism, he writes himself. This may sound like a re-formulation of the romantic definition of criticism, that it is the confessions of a man's soul among books; but what is forgotten in that definition is the italicizing of 'books', which brings with it its own discipline, and converts the private reflection into public criticism. Nevertheless the romantic definition does recall us to the personal dimension, and it is the absence of this which has made so much of our

[8] *British Journal of Aesthetics*, pp. 144–5. In *Novel* (Fall, 1968) Barbara Hardy has a very suggestive article in which she argues that 'narrative . . . is not to be regarded as an aesthetic invention used by artists to control, manipulate and order experience, but as a primary act of mind transferred to art from life'.

current practice 'the sophisticated game' which the pupils of San Tomas State College knew so well how to play. George's question, what is Mr. Huxley's novel *about*, is all too often the opening gambit in that game, because it transforms the novel from an experience into a riddle. It has neglected,[9] to its cost, the wisdom behind the reproof which Henry James once gave to an exasperated reader of that enigmatic novel *The Golden Bowl*—'Wait, dear lady, wait—and see where I'm coming out.'

O, do not ask 'What is it?'
Let us go and make our visit.
(T. S. Eliot)

[9] It would be disingenuous and unjust to imply that this neglect has been total and this paper would be incomplete if it failed to draw attention to places where issues at least similar in substance, if not in emphasis, to those raised in my paper have been discussed.

Discussions about the relationship between the 'real' and the 'invented' world in fiction have a history as long as fiction itself. It is possible, however, to see that in the last few years the problem has been considered in such a way that we might regard it as taking the shape of a running debate, even though the participants may not have consciously regarded themselves as making interventions of that kind. The impetus was given by the publication in 1961 of Wayne Booth's *Rhetoric of Fiction*, the first book to try and provide something analogous to a *poetics* of the genre. John Bayley published *The Characters of Love* in 1960, and though much more modest in scope and empirical in tone than Booth's work, it has had considerable influence in re-directing attention to the nature and role of 'character' in fiction. Perhaps the book closest to Booth's in mood to be published in England was W. J. Harvey's *Character and the Novel* (1965). Booth's achievement was largely to draw attention to the nature of fiction as a genre, in need of its own critical methods, and this emphasis is strongly present in books as different from Booth's and from each other as David Lodge's *Language of Fiction* (1966) and Frank Kermode's *The Sense of an Ending* (1966).

It is not my purpose in this note to provide a bibliography of recent criticism of fiction, but to point to the existence of a debate about its nature, which is certainly one of the most striking features in the general landscape of contemporary criticism. Though I was not conscious of it at the time, this debate comes closest to the issues which I discussed in my paper, in a critical exchange which took place between Malcolm Bradbury and David Lodge in *Novel* (Fall 1967; Winter 1968). Close enough in fact, to give me an opportunity of stating my position in relation to what might be called 'the words on the page' argument.

Generally speaking, David Lodge re-affirms the position he took in *Language of Fiction* that criticism of fiction must be based on detailed reference to the language a novelist uses, because his medium is language and whatever he does, *qua* novelist, he does in and through language. Malcolm Bradbury, while freely acknowledging the importance of an approach through language, nevertheless feels that this basis is too constricting, and argues that a more flexible and inclusive approach would be through 'structure'. From my paper it will be clear that I am sympathetic to Bradbury's aim, but I think that any attempt to find *inside* the novel, as it were, a term more inclusive than language is foredoomed. Such an argument can always be outflanked, as I think Lodge demonstrates in his reply.

The axiom from which Lodge starts seems to me to be irrefutable, namely, that whatever a novelist does, he does in and through language. That recognition of this axiom, however, automatically dictates a critical *method*—the detailed reference to the language a novelist uses—seems to me to be by no means as selfevident. Sometimes such a method may be fruitful; sometimes not. If that remark, however, is taken to mean that the value of a novelist's work is not dependent upon the quality of his language, then I think Lodge is right to argue, as he does in *Language of Fiction*, that we have not thought the position through. But if the remark is intended to refer to the way in which such an assertion implies a method of procedure, then I think the position is not always what Lodge considers it to be.

It is assumed by him that the kind of attention we engage in when reading, is, or ought to be, of an unvarying kind—and the kind of exercise which we call 'reading-in-slow-motion' is a model of what the ideal reading ought to be. I would contend, however, that reading in slow motion sometimes fulfils this function, but that sometimes it can pervert and distort. At emphatic points in the novel, of which there may be many, such a reading seems wholly justifiable, because the movement of the novel at such moments is towards deliberation and stress. But at other times, which are no less an intrinsic element in our experience of the novel, the tempo changes and language is meant to recede from our attention. Here the rhetoric is working not to create something which is there, but rather towards our anticipation of what *might* be there and, in such an instance, the deceleration implied in deliberate attention, would be fatal to the novelist's purpose. The approach through language neglects the whole question of the *pace* of the novel, the importance of which becomes clear when we consider how very different our experience is in reading a novel, say, without divisions from one written in brief sections. This is to leave aside the fact that when we talk of 'reading' a novel, we are more often than not, talking about a process which is constantly and deliberately interrupted, and may last over several days. We are right in saying that we live *with* a novel and this has implications for literary criticism as well as psychology, implications which are unique to that genre. Unlike poetry and in a different way, drama, the bounding line which separates the reader and the work is finely drawn, and it is precisely the intimacy of the reader's presence that is a shaping factor in the making and understanding of fiction. It is not accidental that the novel has resisted a 'poetics' and when attempts have been made to provide it with one, it seems much more remote from our experience of the genre than a similar undertaking done on behalf of poetry or drama. Of course, there is an indisputable sense in which the novel is a finished work of art, and as such it is as amenable to the same kind of criticism as prevails elsewhere. But there is another sense, and I would say a neglected one, in which the novel is always unfinished—so that 'once upon a time' becomes not simply a fascinating phrase for the critic to ponder; but for the critic who is also a reader it is a summoning sound, an invitation to a mood, a promise of things to come. And to those future tenses, the scrutiny of 'words on the page' fails to do adequate justice, though every child has felt its truth.

Index

[*This index excludes footnotes and the information,
systematically arranged for reference purposes, given
in the notes before each chapter.*]